THE COURT AND THE CROSS

THE COURT

AND

THE CROSS

The Religious Right's Crusade
to Reshape the Supreme Court

Frederick S. Lane

BEACON PRESS

BOSTON

Beacon Press
25 Beacon Street
Boston, Massachusetts 02108–2892
www.beacon.org

Beacon Press books
are published under the auspices of
the Unitarian Universalist Association of Congregations.

11 10 09 08   8 7 6 5 4 3 2 1

This book is printed on acid-free paper that meets the uncoated paper
ANSI/NISO specifications for permanence as revised in 1992.

Text design and composition by Yvonne Tsang
at Wilsted & Taylor Publishing Services

Library of Congress Cataloging-in-Publication Data

Lane, Frederick S.
  The court and the cross : the religious right's crusade to reshape the Supreme Court /
Frederick S. Lane.
    p. cm.
  ISBN 978-0-8070-4424-7
  1. Church and state—United States. 2. Freedom of religion—United States.
  3. Religious right—United States. 4. United States. Supreme Court—Officials
and employees—Selection and appointment. I. Title.

KF4865.L358 2008
342.7308'52—dc22   2007045464

This book is dedicated
to the memory of

THOMAS JEFFERSON
for his devotion to the principles
of freedom of religion and the
separation of church and state,

and to the memory of

ALEXANDER HAMILTON
for his powerful advocacy
on behalf of a strong and
independent federal judiciary.

Contents

"God Wants Me to Be President"

Congress shall make no law respecting
an establishment of religion, or
prohibiting the free exercise thereof . . .
United States Constitution, Amendment I

O N SUNDAY, APRIL 29, 2007, a five-hour prayer service was held in Virginia Beach, not far from where Twentieth Street crosses Atlantic Avenue. The service was the culmination of a four-day event called the Assembly 2007, a gathering of evangelical Christians organized by Rev. John Gimenez, the leader of the nearby Christian evangelical ministry known as Rock Church International. In speech after speech, evangelical leaders ringingly declared that the arrival of the English settlers in 1607 marked the day when America was first claimed for Jesus Christ. The Reverend Joe Barton, executive pastor at Rock Church, told the audience, "We have to educate the American public about the accurate facts about the founding of our nation. America was birthed with a prayer meeting."

The Reverend Pat Robertson, the famed televangelist host of *The 700 Club* and founder of the Christian Broadcasting Network, was even more emphatic:

> Praise God Almighty, this is a great day! We are here at a historic moment. This is the four hundredth anniversary of the founding of the United States of America. And this nation was founded by men and women who planted a cross on this very shore of the Atlantic

Ocean, and they knelt in prayer and they said "we declare that this nation belongs to the Lord Jesus Christ."

And we are here to reclaim again, and to certify again the covenant that was made four hundred years ago by our forefathers, who came to these shores for one purpose—to proclaim the gospel of Jesus Christ to those who didn't know it. What a heritage!

As numerous commentators and historians have pointed out, the English settlers who landed on these shores in 1607 and then in 1620 had many reasons for braving the storm-tossed Atlantic, and evangelizing in the name of Jesus Christ was not particularly high on the list. America was birthed as much by property trespass and vandalism of an East India tea shipment as it was by a prayer meeting. But then, Christian nationalists like Robertson rarely allow a good story to be sullied by grimy historical facts.

In the late 1960s and early 1970s the members of the Religious Right (mostly but not exclusively evangelical Protestants) were horrified by a series of decisions by the United States Supreme Court—on topics like school prayer, evolution, busing, contraception, abortion—that they felt eroded the moral foundation of the nation. During much of that time, the Court was under the leadership of Chief Justice Earl Warren, whose name became an epithet among religious conservatives. Led first by Jerry Falwell and the Moral Majority, and then by Pat Robertson and the Christian Coalition, the Religious Right set out to repudiate the Warren Court and recapture America for Jesus.

Over the last thirty years, the essential give-and-take of the political process has proven frustrating to religious conservatives. Restrictive social legislation has been stymied in Congress, proposals to limit federal court jurisdiction have faltered, and even Ronald Reagan could not persuade the Senate to pass a constitutional amendment in support of school prayer. But Congress was not the Religious Right's only target; the leaders of the movement quickly realized that many of their objectives could be achieved by pushing for the nomination and confirmation of reliably conservative federal judges, particularly on the Supreme Court. While the results of that campaign have also been something of a mixed bag, the nature of the institution and its profound influence on American society continue to make the Court a tempting target for the Religious Right.

The Changing Court:
Fewer Appointments and Fewer Cases

The very ability of the Religious Right to target the Court as a mechanism for social change, of course, lies in the fact that the nomination and confirmation of Supreme Court justices is by design a political process. With clockwork regularity, one or more members of the Senate, and occasionally the president, will bemoan the fact that the ostensibly pure process of selecting judges has been defiled by politics. For example, in 2002 when President George W. Bush was frustrated by successful Democratic efforts to block the nomination of Washington lawyer Miguel Estrada to the D.C. Circuit Court of Appeals, he said: "The Senate should not play politics with this nomination, for [Estrada] will be an outstanding judge. One of the reasons to change the United States Senate is to make sure the good judges I nominate get a fair hearing, a swift vote, and approval." Such protestations bring to mind the smirking observation of Captain Renault, Claude Rains's character in *Casablanca*: "I'm shocked, shocked to find that gambling is going on in here!"

But as Bush's own comment amply illustrates, it should not surprise anyone that both the White House and the Senate "play politics" with judicial appointments—the framers intended it to be a political process. Bush would not have pleaded to his supporters to elect a more compliant and deferential Senate if politics were not an integral part of the process. In fact, even if a president could unilaterally name Supreme Court justices—a disconcerting thought—it would still be a political process. The requirement of consent by the Senate simply makes the role of politics more diverse and, ideally, more reflective of the country as a whole.

More than anything else, this book is the story of how the Religious Right (aka the Christian Right) has powerfully and effectively used the *political* process to push for the nomination and confirmation of federal judges that it believes are more likely to issue legal decisions consistent with its views. When a group successfully uses the tools of politics—political action committees, advertisements, pamphlets, phone calls, fund-raising letters, and the ultimate political tool, access—to influence the selection of judges, then it is disingenuous and hypocritical to suggest that the political beliefs of opponents should not play a part in the process as well.

Institutional changes in the Court make it all the more imperative to balance the undue influence of any particular group. There are few decisions that give U.S. presidents greater opportunity to extend the impact and importance of their administrations than the selection of federal judges. Thanks to the lifetime tenure that the nation's federal judges enjoy under Article III, Section 1 of the U.S. Constitution (unless they deviate from the good behavior requirement), a president's influence can extend for years and even decades past his or her departure from the Oval Office. The current record for postpresidency influence is held by John Adams, whose last appointee—Chief Justice John Marshall—served more than thirty-four years after Adams left office. But there is at least a reasonable chance that either President George H. W. Bush or his son George W. Bush will challenge that record. It is sobering to think, for instance, that if Clarence Thomas serves thirty-four years beyond the end of the first Bush administration, he will be only seventy-eight years old. Similarly remarkable is the fact that if Chief Justice John Roberts serves as long as his predecessor, William Rehnquist, his last day in office will be May 26, 2039.

Prior to the twentieth century, there were relatively few justices who managed to serve thirty years or more. Of the first seventy-five justices appointed to the Court, just eight reached the three-decade mark. But since the middle of the twentieth century, the number of justices serving into their third decade has accelerated rapidly:

- Associate Justice Hugo Black, thirty-four years (Franklin Delano Roosevelt);
- Associate Justice William O. Douglas, thirty-six years (Franklin Delano Roosevelt);
- Associate Justice William J. Brennan, thirty-three years (Dwight D. Eisenhower);

- Associate Justice Byron White, thirty-one years (John F. Kennedy);
- Chief Justice William Rehnquist, thirty-three years (Richard Nixon);
- Associate Justice John Paul Stevens, thirty-two years in 2007 (Gerald Ford).

That is nearly 25 percent of the justices appointed in the last fifty years. And there is a good chance, barring unforeseen developments, that many if not most of the members of the current Court will join that once-exclusive club: Antonin Scalia, Anthony Kennedy, David Souter, Stephen Breyer, and John Roberts will all reach the thirty-year mark in their early to mid-eighties, while Clarence Thomas will celebrate thirty years on the Court just three months after his seventy-third birthday. It is quite possible, if not likely, that in seventeen years or so, Thomas will become the nation's longest-serving Supreme Court justice. Ultimately, as many as a third of the last twenty-five Supreme Court justices either have served or are reasonably likely to serve three decades. It is a dramatic illustration of just how far a modern president's influence can extend beyond his or her administration.

The other significant institutional change that makes Supreme Court nominations increasingly important is the steady decline in the number of cases heard each year by the Court. In the first term of the new Roberts Court (2006–7), the Court issued just sixty-eight decisions, the fewest since 1968. At the start of the Court's second term in October 2007, *Time* magazine ran an article titled "The Incredibly Shrinking Court." Not only is the Court issuing fewer decisions, David Von Drehle wrote, but the cases selected by the justices for review feature increasingly narrow questions of law. As Drehle points out, that may be a result of the fact that the Court is now entirely composed of former federal appeals court judges, but it may also be an indication that the narrowly divided Court is reluctant to take on politically divisive issues in which no clear and convincing decision can be reached. In any case, the slowing turnover on the Court and the decreasing number of cases only heightens the importance of each new confirmation battle.

The Evangelical in the White House

No presidential candidate in the history of the United States has been more directly confronted with the issue of the separation of church and state than was Senator John Fitzgerald Kennedy (D-Mass.). Throughout his campaign for the presidency in 1960, Kennedy's political opponents repeatedly alleged that if he were elected to the White House, he would follow the orders of Pope John XXIII, pontiff of the Roman Catholic Church.

During the primaries, for instance, former U.S. district court judge Albert Levitt, who was running as a Republican for the U.S. Senate in New Hampshire, sent a telegram to the pope and asked for clarification of Kennedy's loyalties as a Roman Catholic. Levitt told the pope that Kennedy's nomination was being opposed on the grounds that he would owe "his primary and complete political allegiance" to the Church and asked Pope John to formally state whether "[an] American citizen who is a Roman Catholic is bound by any political principle of the Roman Catholic Church which is in conflict with any provision of the Constitution and the laws of the United States." According to Judge Levitt's estimate, 140 principles of the Catholic Church were in conflict with the Constitution. There is no indication, however, that the pope bothered to reply.

A more serious example of the intense suspicion faced by Senator Kennedy was the announcement by the Arkansas Baptist State Convention in Little Rock on September 6, 1960, that it planned a statewide campaign against his election. "We cannot turn our government over to a Catholic president," said Rev. Dr. W. O. Vaught, pastor of the Immanuel Baptist Church in Little Rock, "who could be influenced by the pope, and by the power of the Catholic hierarchy." Dr. Vaught's objections may have been more partisan than theological: he was one of three religious leaders to deliver an invocation at the 1960 Republican National Convention that nominated Richard Nixon, a Quaker, for president. Not surprisingly, no one expressed any serious concerns that Nixon would be unduly influenced by a hierarchy of Friends.

A week following the announcement by the Arkansas Baptists, Senator Kennedy gave a televised address to the Greater Houston Ministerial Association, in which he assured the religious leaders, "I do not speak for my church on public matters, and the church does not speak for me." He promised the Protestant ministers that if a situation ever arose in which there was a conflict between his conscience and the national interest (and he could not imagine that happening), he would resign. In his view, Kennedy said, the pope should not tell a president how to act, and Protestant ministers should not tell their parishioners how to vote. In fact, he said, no elected official should take instructions from religious leaders:

> I believe in an America that is officially neither Catholic, Protestant, nor Jewish—where no public official either requests or accepts instructions on public policy from the pope, the National Council of Churches, or any other ecclesiastical source—where no religious body seeks to impose its will directly or indirectly upon the general populace or the public acts of its officials—and where religious liberty is so indivisible that an act against one church is treated as an act against all....
>
> That is the kind of America in which I believe. And it represents the kind of presidency in which I believe—a great office that must neither be humbled by making it the instrument of any one religious group nor tarnished by arbitrarily withholding its occupancy from the members of any one religious group. I believe in a president whose religious views are his own private affair, neither imposed by him upon the nation or imposed by the nation upon him as a condition to holding that office.

In the nearly half-century since Kennedy was elected to the White House, no president has been more closely connected to religious leaders than George W. Bush, the nation's forty-third president. At the age of thirty-nine, struggling with alcohol abuse and in danger of losing his marriage, Bush had a conversation with the Reverend Billy Graham that started him on the path to evangelical Christianity. In his home in Midland, Texas, he joined a Christian Bible-study group. Soon afterward, Bush served as one of his father's most important evangelical liaisons during the 1988 presidential campaign.

Bush's connection with the evangelical community and his ability, through his own experiences, to speak their language, helped him defeat the enormously popular Ann Richards for the Texas governorship in 1994. Four years later, in what was generally a bad midterm election for Republicans at the federal level, Bush handily won reelection to a second term. On the afternoon of his swearing-in in January 1999, Bush told a group of political advisers, "I believe that God wants me to be president." Eighteen months later, running on a platform of "compassionate conservatism" and with the active help of the Religious Right movement, Bush won one of the closest and most controversial presidential elections in the nation's history. Although he received more than a half-million fewer popular votes than Democrat Al Gore, Bush received just one more electoral vote (271) than the minimum needed to win the presidency.

Bush was not the first president to take office despite losing the popular vote, although it had been more than a hundred years since Grover Cleveland outpolled Benjamin Harrison in the popular vote but fell short in the electoral college. But in many ways, the real margin of Bush's victory was 5–4—the unprecedented vote in *Bush v. Gore* (2000), in which the United States Supreme Court ruled that an ongoing Florida recount of the votes for president was unconstitutional and should be stopped. The Court's ruling effectively ratified the decision of Florida secretary of state Katherine Harris that Bush had won the state vote, thereby giving him his razor-thin margin of victory in the electoral college. A consortium of eight newspapers later conducted an exhaustive analysis and concluded that had the recount continued, there is little question that Gore would have won the Florida vote.

Regardless of whether it was God or merely the Supreme Court that wanted Bush to be president, the payoff for the Christian Right was nearly instantaneous: Bush's first executive order, issued less than a month after he took office, established the White House Office of Faith-Based and Community Initiatives (OFBCI). Expanding on the charitable choice program originally championed by Senator John Ashcroft (R-Mo.), Bush used the OFBCI to make it possible for faith-based organizations to win tens of millions of dollars in largely unsupervised federal grants.

Although increased access to the public trough is no doubt gratifying, the Religious Right's most fervent hope is that the Bush administration has finally delivered on the real prize: a much more conservative federal judiciary, one that will help to overturn what Christian conservatives see as decades of religiously hostile decisions. Whether that is the case obviously remains to be seen; one potential irony is that the same conservative judicial temperament that would question the rulings of the Warren Court would also be reluctant to summarily overturn established decisions now thirty or forty years old. But unquestionably, the Religious Right is closer than ever before to realizing its judicial ambitions. This is the story of how it got there and what it has achieved.

THE COURT AND THE CROSS

CHAPTER ONE

Judicial Review

Putting the "Supreme" in Supreme Court

FROM THE EARLIEST DAYS of the Republic, Americans have argued over whether the national Supreme Court and federal judiciary defend or threaten our personal freedom and the autonomy of the states. Despite the passage of more than two hundred years, the individuals who argued for and against the establishment of a Supreme Court in the United States Constitution would find the themes of today's debate over the federal judiciary remarkably familiar.

What many of the founding fathers would have found somewhat puzzling, however, is the intensity of current-day battles over judicial confirmations and the fierceness of the attacks against the Court. It's not that partisan battles were unheard of; far from it. In fact, John Rutledge, the chief justice of the South Carolina Supreme Court and a former associate justice of the U.S. Supreme Court, was rejected as chief justice by the Senate on purely political grounds in 1795, just eight years after the Constitution was adopted. Rutledge was a vocal opponent of a treaty negotiated with England by Chief Justice John Jay. The Federalist Party, which controlled the Senate, strongly supported the treaty and voted along party lines to deny Rutledge his appointment.

Less than a decade later, the shoe was on the other foot. The Federalists lost control of Congress to the Democratic-Republicans, a nascent party led by Thomas Jefferson. Not long after they took power, the Democratic-Republicans in the House of Representatives impeached Associate Justice Samuel Chase for his role in the trial of John Fries, the leader of a Pennsylvania taxpayer revolt. Fries was convicted and sentenced to hang by Chase, although he was later pardoned by President John Adams. Despite the partisan feelings of the time, Chase was acquitted by the Senate and the idea of using impeachment to exact political revenge on the Supreme Court disappeared until conservatives revived it during the Warren Court (1953–1969).

If anything, the founding fathers would be somewhat bemused that anyone today would care that much about the job. At the turn of the eighteenth century, there was little about the position of federal judge or even Supreme Court justice to merit much debate or incite professional ambition. In fact, more than one early president struggled to get nominees to accept the honor, and many Supreme Court justices resigned from the Court after serving just a few years to return to more lucrative law practices, run for political office, or sit on state supreme courts. There were plenty of reasons to leave the Court in those days: there wasn't a lot of work, much of Washington was still a mosquito-infested swamp, the Court did not even have its own building, and the justices were required to spend weeks and even months on horseback, riding circuit to hear appeals from the federal trial courts (which is why the federal appeals courts are still called circuit courts today).

Certainly, however, those early horseback riders and the framers who created their positions would agree that the Supreme Court today is a far more powerful institution than was originally conceived. Applying the well-known judicial doctrine of *res ipsa loquitur* ("the thing speaks for itself"), conservatives of all stripes—legal, social, and religious—argue that the very fact of the Court's increased importance in the country's legal and social controversies is more than adequate proof that it has overreached its constitutional bounds and needs to be restrained.

Attorney Mark Levin, a former chief of staff to U.S. attorney general Ed Meese, offers a typically blunt assessment in his 2005 book *Men in Black*: "Were our forefathers to view the American federal government of the twenty-first century, I believe they'd be appalled." He presents a long list of issues in which "activist judges" have allegedly imposed their personal views, ranging from the expulsion of the Ten Commandments from public spaces to protecting virtual child pornography as free speech, and concludes with the timeworn conservative contention that "the plain language of the Constitution should govern judges when rendering constitutional decisions." Levin clearly believes that the Supreme Court (particularly under the leadership of Chief Justice Earl Warren) stopped reading the Constitution decades ago. Conservative columnist and erstwhile presidential candidate Pat Buchanan is even more strident in his criticism of the Supreme Court. In an article written in May 2004 on the occasion of the fiftieth anniversary of the Warren Court's unanimous decision in *Brown v. Board of Education*, which struck down the concept of "separate but equal" public facilities for blacks and whites, Buchanan stated that the Court "crossed a historic divide" when it reached its decision, but not one that should be celebrated. "It had executed," he wrote, "in the name of the 14th Amendment, a coup d'etat. It had usurped power over state schools that had never been granted to federal courts either in law or the Constitution."

Buchanan went on to argue that the Warren Court effectively launched "a social, cultural and moral revolution" through the arbitrary imposition of its will, particularly with respect to religion. "Under this dictatorship," he thundered, "radically secularist and egalitarian, America's public schools were as de-Christianized as thoroughly as in the Soviet Union."

If the Supreme Court of 1803 or even 1853 had issued some of the decisions that the Court has handed down over the last sixty years, then semihysterical critics like Levin and Buchanan might have a legitimate point. Well into the nineteenth century, the Supreme Court truly was the weakest branch of government, and for a variety of reasons, its role in the constitutional system was much more limited than it is today. But the Court's current importance is not, as Buchanan alleges, the result of a judicial coup d'état; instead, it is the logical consequence of the original language of the Constitution itself and changes that were made to the Constitution just after the Civil War.

Early Political Battles That Helped Shape the Court

In their most private and pleasing dreams, conservative and Christian critics of the Supreme Court envision a nation governed not merely by an unamended Constitution, but instead by its far more impotent predecessor, the Articles of Confederation. The Articles, the first attempt at joining the colonies together following the Revolutionary War, were remarkably brief (consisting of just five handwritten pages), and among other glaring deficiencies, made no provision at all for a national judiciary or a Supreme Court. All legal disputes were the sole province of the various state courts.

When it quickly became clear, however, that the Articles were completely ineffective in guiding the new union and, in particular, regulating commerce among the states, a meeting was held in Annapolis, Maryland, in September 1786 to discuss possible amendments to the Articles. The meeting was chaired by Alexander Hamilton, a New York attorney, former aide-de-camp to General George Washington during the Revolutionary War, and founder of the Bank of New York, today the oldest operating financial institution in the country. With him were just eleven other delegates from five states, a number they collectively decided was too small to reach any meaningful agreement on how the Articles of Confederation should be improved. Instead, the Annapolis Convention recommended that delegates from every state meet in Philadelphia the following May to discuss revisions to the Articles. All but one of the states agreed to participate in the convention (Rhode Island was the lone holdout).

Thanks in no small part to the brilliant, energetic, and fiery Hamilton, who served as one of New York's three delegates to the Philadelphia meeting and who was a passionate advocate for a strong national government, the gathering of state representatives went far beyond the relatively narrow goal of amending and improving the Articles of Confederation. Instead, the fifty-five delegates shut the windows (despite the summer's sweltering heat), posted guards to prevent eavesdroppers, and set about drafting a document that would comprehensively restructure the federal union and its relationship to the states.

At the core of the debate over the new government was one simple but profound concept: the allocation of power. Among the myriad questions facing the delegates were: How much power should the new federal government have? How much should the states retain? What rights would citizens have, and should those rights be enumerated? How best to structure the federal government?

Many if not most of the answers to those questions ultimately were provided by the delegation from Virginia, and in particular James Madison, who submitted to the Philadelphia Convention, now also known as the Constitutional Convention, what became known as the Virginia Plan. After considerable debate and compromise, the convention settled on a structure that would more effectively balance the powers and responsibilities of the three branches of government: a bicameral legislature with a House elected proportionately by population and a Senate with equal representation for each state, a strong chief executive with powers complementary to but independent of the legislature, and a federal judiciary with lifetime appointments. The final wording of the proposed constitution was drafted by the convention's Committee of Style and Arrangement, on which both Madison and Hamilton served, and then signed by thirty-nine members of the convention on September 17, 1787.

Later that same day, when an undoubtedly tired Benjamin Franklin left Independence Hall, a Mrs. Powell reportedly called out to him, "Well, Doctor, what have we got—a Republic or a Monarchy?" Dr. Franklin, then eighty-one years old and nearing the end of his storied life, turned to her and replied, "A Republic, if you can keep it."

Not everyone was convinced that the Constitutional Convention delegates had in fact avoided the establishment of a monarchy. While conceding the obvious flaws of the Articles of Confederation, many also feared that the federal government proposed by the Constitution would weaken or destroy state and individual rights. Ratification of the proposed agreement faced strenuous opposition in every single state, led by powerful political figures like Patrick Henry in Virginia and Governor George Clinton in New York. Collectively, these opponents became known as the Anti-Federalists, and they produced a huge number of speeches, pamphlets, and articles challenging the work of the Philadelphia Convention.

Stung by these criticisms, Hamilton organized the most famous response to the Anti-Federalists. He recruited Madison and John Jay (Governor Clinton's predecessor in New York and soon to be the first chief justice of the Supreme Court) to help him write a series of eighty-five essays defending nearly every clause and sentence of the new constitution and reassuring readers that it would not become, as the Anti-Federalists alleged, the destroyer of personal liberty. Known collectively as *The Federalist Papers*, the essays were published in three New York newspapers between October 1787 and August 1788.

By the time New York held its state convention to consider ratification in July 1788, ten states already had approved the new constitution, which made it a legally binding union under the terms of the Philadelphia agreement. But few people at the time had any illusions that the Constitution (or the new nation) could survive without the support of New York, a large state located in the center of the proposed nation and already of enormous commercial and financial importance. It is impossible to know precisely how influential *The Federalist Papers* were to New York convention delegates. Nonetheless, there is little question that Hamilton, indefatigable in both prose and person, was the main reason that the New York convention voted on July 26, 1788, to approve the Constitution by a narrow margin of just three votes—30 aye, 27 nay.

In the early years of the federal government, it was difficult to imagine the Supreme Court as either the great defender of liberty contemplated by Hamilton or the perilous threat denounced by Patrick Henry; in both organization and operation, it truly was the weakest branch. While Article III of the newly adopted constitution set up the basic structure of the federal judiciary, it did so in just four relatively broad paragraphs, and left most of the devilish details to the new Congress.

For instance, Article III designated only one federal court—the Supreme Court—and gave Congress the power to create "such inferior Courts as [it] may from time to time ordain and establish." Thanks to the Constitution's silence on the specifics, it was apparently also Congress's job to figure out when the Supreme Court should meet and where, and even how many justices there should be. Similarly, while the

Constitution stated that the Supreme Court should have original (or trial) jurisdiction in certain types of cases (those affecting ambassadors, other public ministers and consuls, and those in which a state shall be party), it also gave Congress the authority to establish regulations for and exceptions to the Supreme Court's wide-ranging appellate jurisdiction.

When the First Congress convened in early April 1789, it recognized that one of its highest priorities was to organize the federal courts. Not surprisingly, the political battles between the Federalists and the Anti-Federalists persisted into the new Congress, and they played a significant role in the structure of the new court system. Still wary of a too-strong federal judiciary, some Anti-Federalists argued that no lower courts should be created at all, and that the only federal court should be a narrowly empowered Supreme Court. Other Anti-Federalists conceded that the framers intended the creation of lower federal courts, but argued that their jurisdiction should be limited to admiralty and maritime cases.

The Federalists responded that a strong national court system was necessary to hear a range of cases that could only be fairly resolved by federal judges, including crimes against the United States, cases involving noncitizens, and disputes between the states. They also argued that a system of federal courts, staffed by judges from around the country, would be less susceptible to regional bias than the state courts.

Eventually, after much wrangling and compromise, Congress passed the first Judiciary Act in the early fall of 1789, and President Washington signed it into law on September 24. Congress had decided that the Supreme Court should consist of six members, a chief justice and five associate justices, and Washington sent the names of his nominees to the Senate that same day. Although Washington typically stayed above the political fray (and feared the rise of partisan politics), he selected the notably partisan Hamilton to serve in his cabinet as the country's first secretary of the Treasury. At Hamilton's urging, Washington chose another active Federalist, New York's John Jay, to serve as chief justice, and at least half of the newly appointed associate justices were Federalist supporters as well.

Marbury v. Madison:
Establishing the Principle of Judicial Review

The first step in the growth of the Supreme Court as an institution can be traced to one fairly minor dispute: a lawsuit filed in the United States Supreme Court by William Marbury, a successful Maryland business-man, alleging that the newly elected president, Thomas Jefferson, was wrongfully withholding his commission as a federal justice of the peace in Alexandria, Virginia. Marbury asked the Supreme Court to issue a writ of mandamus, a judicial order instructing Jefferson to deliver Mar-bury's commission to him. Despite the relative insignificance of the office in question, Marbury's lawsuit raised a number of profound questions, chief among which were: could the Supreme Court order the president to do something he did not want to do, and what would happen if the president simply refused?

The controversy arose out of the acrimonious presidential election of 1800. John Adams, a Federalist, was running for reelection against Thomas Jefferson, a Democratic-Republican (the political descendant of the Anti-Federalists), in a rematch of the 1796 race. Although he had prevailed in the first contest, Adams was weakened during the 1800 campaign by criticism from within his own party (chiefly from Hamil-ton and his followers, who felt that Adams was too moderate). On Feb-ruary 11, 1801, Jefferson and his running mate, Aaron Burr, were declared the winners of the general election, but because each of the candidates received the same number of electoral votes, it would take another six days and thirty-six ballots in the House of Representatives before Jef-ferson finally was elected president.

Under the terms of the Constitution at the time, Jefferson was not scheduled to be sworn in until March 4, 1801. On February 13, the Fed-eralist majority in Congress attempted to pack the federal judiciary be-fore Jefferson took office by passing the Judiciary Act of 1801. Among other things, the legislation:

- reduced the size of the Supreme Court from six to five by decree-ing that the Court's next vacancy not be filled;
- doubled the number of circuit courts from three to six, and ap-pointed three judges for each circuit (a change that would have elim-

inated the requirement that the Supreme Court justices ride circuit, which many people conceded would be an improvement);
• increased the number of district courts.

In the nineteen days between the passage of the Judiciary Act and Jefferson's inauguration, President Adams scrambled to fill the new judicial posts. On March 2, Adams submitted the names of sixteen circuit court judges and forty-two justices of the peace (including Marbury) to the Senate for confirmation. The Senate confirmed each of the so-called midnight judges the following day, but in order for the appointments to take effect, a signed commission with the presidential seal had to be delivered to each person. The person responsible for making delivery of the commissions was John Marshall, Adams's secretary of state. Marshall had actually been appointed to replace John Jay as chief justice of the United States Supreme Court three weeks earlier, but had agreed to stay on as secretary of state as well during the last month of Adams's presidency.

Marshall saw to it that most of the commissions were delivered before Jefferson was inaugurated, but a few (including Marbury's) were still on his desk when the Adams presidency ended. When Jefferson discovered the undelivered commissions, he refused to hand them over to the remaining appointees. In a letter written some years later to William Samuel Johnson, a Constitutional Convention delegate from Connecticut and later one of the chief drafters of the Judiciary Act of 1789, Jefferson described the scene and his reasoning in withholding the commissions:

Among the midnight appointments of Mr. Adams, were commissions to some Federal justices of the peace for Alexandria. These were signed and sealed by him, but not delivered. I found them on the table of the Department of State, on my entrance into office, and I forbade their delivery. . . . Whatever is in the Executive offices is certainly deemed to be in the hands of the President; and in this case, was actually in my hands, because, when I countermanded them, there was as yet no Secretary of State.

When it adopted the original Judiciary Act in 1789, Congress gave the United States Supreme Court original jurisdiction over suits seeking a writ of mandamus to "persons holding office under the authority of the United States." Relying on that legislation, Marbury filed his lawsuit directly in the Supreme Court in December 1801, and Marshall issued an order to the new secretary of state, James Madison, to show cause in the June 1802 term of the Court as to why the requested writ should not be issued.

Fearing that the 1801 Judiciary Act would perpetuate Federalism for decades to come—Jefferson famously griped that the Federalists "have retired into the judiciary as a stronghold"—the new Democratic-Republican Congress acted quickly to repeal the law. On April 29, 1802, Congress passed a third Judiciary Act, which largely did away with the judgeships created the year before (so that many of those who actually received their commissions from Adams and Marshall soon found them worthless). But the Democratic-Republicans also were concerned that the Supreme Court, largely composed of Federalists, would use Marbury's lawsuit as an excuse to overturn their repeal of the 1801 law and restore the "midnight judges" to their positions. To delay that possibility, Congress replaced the Supreme Court's two terms per year with a single term beginning in February, effectively abolishing the June 1802 term of the Court. Marbury was forced to wait until the beginning of 1803 for the Supreme Court to hear and decide his case.

In his opinion for the unanimous Court, Chief Justice Marshall identified three issues raised by Marbury's petition:

1st. Has [Marbury] a right to the commission he demands?

2dly. If [Marbury] has a right, and that right has been violated, do the laws of his country afford him a remedy?

3dly. If they do afford [Marbury] a remedy, is it a mandamus issuing from this Court?

After considerable discussion about the mechanics of presidential appointments, Marshall made the following finding: "It is . . . decidedly the opinion of the Court, that when a commission has been signed by the president, the appointment is made; and that the commission is complete when the seal of the United States has been affixed to it by the secretary of state." Since he himself was serving as secretary of state at the time, Marshall could state with some certainty that Marbury's commission was both signed and sealed. Marbury was thus lawfully appointed as justice of the peace under the Judiciary Act of 1801, and it was a violation of his vested right for Jefferson (and later, James Madison) to withhold delivery of his commission. Marshall also concluded that under the laws of the United States, Marbury was entitled to a remedy, i.e., an order directing the secretary of state to deliver his commission.

The only question left for Marshall to resolve was whether the Supreme Court had the authority to issue the requested writ of mandamus. A savvy and experienced politician, Marshall recognized the dilemma the Court faced. If the Court concluded that it inherently did not have the authority to issue a writ of mandamus to the executive branch, it would permanently consign itself to an inferior role in the country's constitutional system. But if the Court ordered Madison to deliver the commission, Marshall knew that there was a very good chance that Jefferson would simply ignore the order, which would set an equally destructive precedent. Moreover, many of the newly elected Republicans in Congress were threatening to impeach Marshall and the other members of the Court if they ruled in Marbury's favor. Adding to the piquancy of the situation was the fact that Jefferson and Marshall were second cousins once removed, and the two distinguished men—complete opposites in both politics and temperament—cordially loathed each other.

Marshall's solution was brilliant. Rather than risk the integrity and authority of the Court on a relatively minor political problem, Marshall used the occasion to establish a broader and much more far-reaching legal principle. In a classic example of constitutional jujitsu, Marshall declared that Congress did not have the authority to expand the powers of the Supreme Court beyond those specified in the Constitution. Marbury, Marshall pointed out, had filed his lawsuit directly in the Supreme Court because Congress, when it passed the original Judiciary Act of 1789, purportedly gave the Court original jurisdiction of petitions for writs of mandamus. But Marshall said that the Supreme

Court's original jurisdiction was both defined and limited by Article III of the U.S. Constitution, which does not mention the issuance of such writs. Thus, the original Judiciary Act and the Constitution were in conflict.

> It is emphatically the province and duty of the judicial department to say what the law is. Those who apply the rule to particular cases, must of necessity expound and interpret that rule. If two laws conflict with each other, the courts must decide on the operation of each.
>
> So if a law be in opposition to the Constitution; if both the law and the Constitution apply to a particular case, so that the court must either decide that case conformably to the law, disregarding the Constitution; or conformably to the Constitution, disregarding the law; the court must determine which of these conflicting rules governs the case. This is of the very essence of judicial duty.

Marshall listed several different reasons, including the language of the supremacy clause of Article VI ("This constitution, and the laws of the United States which shall be made in pursuance thereof...shall be the supreme law of the land"), as to why the provisions of Article III trumped Congress's efforts to expand the Court's original jurisdiction. As a result, Marshall concluded, that portion of the Judiciary Act of 1789 was unconstitutional and void. Since the Court lacked jurisdiction to hear Marbury's lawsuit in the first place, it could not lawfully issue the requested writ.

Although Marbury could have refiled his suit in a lower federal court (and Jefferson later groused that Marshall's opinion all but dictated how the case should come out), there is no indication that he did so. But while Marbury's goal of serving as a justice of the peace went unfulfilled, he unwittingly attached his name to one of the most important legal opinions in the nation's history.

The Civil War Amendments:
Creating a National Definition of Liberty

Not surprisingly, Jefferson was furious over his administration's "victory" in the *Marbury* case. In a letter he wrote to Vermont farmer

William Jarvis in 1820, Jefferson criticized Marshall's conclusion regarding judicial review in Patrick Buchanan–like terms:

> It is a very dangerous doctrine to consider the judges as the ultimate arbiters of all constitutional questions. It is one which would place us under the despotism of an oligarchy.... The Constitution has erected no such single tribunal, knowing that to whatever hands confided, with the corruptions of time and party, its members would become despots. It has wisely made all the departments coequal and cosovereign with themselves.

Alexander Hamilton, not surprisingly, disagreed. An independent judiciary, he famously wrote in *Federalist* No. 78, was in fact an indispensable safeguard for the preservation of freedom:

> The complete independence of the courts of justice is peculiarly essential in a limited Constitution. By a limited Constitution, I understand one which contains certain specified exceptions to the legislative authority; such, for instance, as that it shall pass no bills of attainder, no *ex post facto* laws, and the like. Limitations of this kind can be preserved in practice no other way than through the medium of courts of justice, whose duty it must be to declare all acts contrary to the manifest tenor of the Constitution void. Without this, all the reservations of particular rights or privileges would amount to nothing.

Although it would take nearly a century for the change to be fully realized, the role of the United States Supreme Court envisioned by Hamilton was unequivocally endorsed by the adoption of a series of constitutional amendments following the Civil War. Designated the Thirteenth, Fourteenth, and Fifteenth Amendments, they are known collectively as the Reconstruction or Civil War amendments, and they represented a profound shift in the relationships among the federal government, the various states, and the nation's citizens. "Fairly construed," Associate Justice Noah Swayne wrote in a dissenting opinion a few years after their adoption, "these amendments may be said to rise to the dignity of a new Magna Carta."

In contrast to the first twelve amendments, which were generally intended to enumerate the rights of individuals and limit the powers of the federal government, the Civil War amendments were the first to impose explicit limitations on state authority. Two of the amendments, the Thirteenth and the Fifteenth, are both brief and relatively unambiguous. The Thirteenth, for instance, completed the work of President Abraham Lincoln's Emancipation Proclamation by outlawing slavery throughout the United States, a matter that had previously been left to individual states. The Fifteenth Amendment states that neither the United States nor the state governments may deny or abridge the right of any U.S. citizen to vote "on account of race, color, or previous condition of servitude."

In contrast, the Fourteenth Amendment contains several different sections, but it is the first that over the years has had the greatest impact on American law and society:

All persons born or naturalized in the United States, and subject to the jurisdiction thereof, are citizens of the United States and of the State wherein they reside. No State shall make or enforce any law which shall abridge the privileges or immunities of citizens of the United States; nor shall any State deprive any person of life, liberty, or property, without due process of law; nor deny to any person within its jurisdiction the equal protection of the laws.

Among other things, this clause effectively overruled Chief Justice Roger Taney's infamous opinion a decade earlier in *Dred Scott v. Sandford* (1856), in which the Court ruled by a vote of 7–2 that the term "citizen" as used in the Constitution had never included slaves. The *Dred Scott* case, which historian Gregory J. Wallance described as "the lawsuit that started the Civil War," also declared that Congress had no power under the Constitution to ban slavery (as it recently had done in the Missouri Compromise), because the Constitution prohibited Congress from depriving individuals of their property (i.e., slaves) without due process of law.

In the course of expounding upon and interpreting the language of the Fourteenth Amendment over the years since its adoption, the

Supreme Court has identified and protected two distinct types of due process rights: procedural and substantive. The more obviously intended meaning of the amendment—procedural due process—concerns *how* a state government deprives someone of life, liberty, or property; if the process used by the state violates concepts of essential fairness (for instance, if property interests are taken away without a hearing), it is generally unconstitutional. But over the years, the Court has also concluded that the Fourteenth Amendment protects each citizen's right to substantive due process, i.e., fundamental fairness with respect to *what* is being taken away and *why* the deprivation occurs. Under this doctrine, the federal courts have examined whether a deprivation of life, liberty, or property has occurred, whether the deprivation furthers a valid state goal, and whether there is a reasonable relationship between the state's stated goal and the means used to achieve it.

For historical reasons, the actual phrase "substantive due process" fell out of favor some time ago. Not long after the Fourteenth Amendment was adopted, the due process clause was used to challenge state laws aimed at limiting working hours or improving working conditions. Over the course of nearly half a century, from roughly 1890 through 1937, the Supreme Court routinely struck down state economic legislation on the grounds that it unconstitutionally impinged on an employee's "right to contract," a right that the Court concluded was implicit in the "liberty" and "property" language of the due process clause. The most infamous of the substantive due process cases was *Lochner v. New York* (1905), in which the Court struck down a New York law regulating the hours and working conditions of the state's bakers. "The question whether this act is valid as a labor law, pure and simple, may be dismissed in a few words," Associate Justice Rufus Peckham wrote for the 5–4 majority. "There is no reasonable ground for interfering with the liberty of person or the right of free contract, by determining the hours of labor, in the occupation of a baker."

President Franklin D. Roosevelt, struggling to alleviate the worst effects of the Great Depression and restart the American economy, was deeply frustrated that the Court repeatedly found his legislative proposals unconstitutional. When his first term passed without any appointments (a rare event at the time), Roosevelt proposed a Court reorganization bill in early 1937 that, among other things, would have allowed him to appoint one new justice for each justice over the age of seventy. Due to the advanced age of the justices at the time, Roosevelt would have been able to immediately appoint six new members of the Court.

Although FDR pitched the bill as an effort to relieve the burdens of elderly justices, no one was fooled. Opposition to the idea of tinkering with the Court grew swiftly, and by midsummer even a Democratic-controlled Senate was unwilling to swallow the idea. Just one month later, however, Roosevelt got much of what he wanted anyway when the Court unexpectedly voted 5–4 in *West Coast Hotel Co. v. Parrish* (1937) to uphold the constitutionality of a minimum-wage law passed by the State of Washington, the type of legislation the Court had routinely rejected during the previous forty years. The swing vote was provided by Associate Justice Owen J. Roberts, a move that has traditionally been described as the "switch in time that saved nine" (although some argue that his vote in *West Coast Hotel* had already been cast by the time FDR made his Court-reorganization proposal).

Abandoning its belief in an absolute liberty to contract, the Court said that what is protected by the Fourteenth Amendment is "liberty in a social organization which requires the protection of law against the evils which menace the health, safety, morals, and welfare of the people." The Court found additional support for its reversal in the fact that the Washington statute was designed to provide a minimum wage for women and minors alone.

In a passage for which the only adequate description is paternalistic, the Court made the following finding: "It is manifest that this established principle [the ability of the state to regulate contracts] is peculiarly applicable in relation to the employment of women in whose protection the state has a special interest." Relying on a much earlier case, the Court asserted that "woman's physical structure and the performance of maternal functions place her at a disadvantage in the struggle for subsistence and that her physical well being becomes an object of public interest and care in order to preserve the strength and vigor of the race."

But with the continued press of economic troubles and bloody labor riots in the late 1930s and early 1940s, it did not take long for the Court to uphold labor protections for men as well, and *West Coast Hotel* is generally recognized as the end of the "substantive due process" or *Lochner* era of the Supreme Court. The phrase itself lingered until the early 1960s, when the Court handed down its decision in *Ferguson v. Skrupa* (1963). Writing for a unanimous court, Associate Justice Hugo Black rejected a substantive due process challenge to a Kansas statute that outlawed the practice of "debt adjusting," and purportedly went on to bury substantive due process for good:

> The doctrine that prevailed in *Lochner* [and other similar cases]— that due process authorizes courts to hold laws unconstitutional when they believe the legislature has acted unwisely—has long since been discarded. We have returned to the original constitutional proposition that courts do not substitute their social and economic beliefs for the judgment of legislative bodies, who are elected to pass laws.

The Second Civil War: Incorporation of the Bill of Rights into the Fourteenth Amendment

It is ironic that Justice Black wrote his opinion in *Ferguson* during the height of the Warren Court, the period in Supreme Court history (1953–1969) that social and legal conservatives (including members of the Christian Right) believe was the most outrageous and blatant in its imposition of the justices' personal social beliefs. No conservative or evangelical discussion of the Warren Court or its rulings is complete without some variant of the phrases "judicial activism," "judicial tyranny," or "judicial dictatorship."

Although conservatives have numerous objections to the Warren Court, there are two that are particularly relevant to this discussion: the Court's expansion of individual liberties through the incorporation of various provisions of the Bill of Rights into the due process clause of the Fourteenth Amendment, and its identification and incorporation of fundamental rights not specifically enumerated in the first ten amendments. Taken together, these principles underlie the bulk of the Supreme Court decisions most hated by social, legal, and religious conservatives.

The doctrine of incorporation arises out of the simple and inescapable fact that when Congress adopted the Fourteenth Amendment, it did not attempt to define the general terms used in the amendment, including "privileges or immunities," no deprivation "of life, liberty, or property without due process of law," and "equal protection of the laws." Madison and the members of the First Congress, of course, used similarly broad language in drafting the Bill of Rights—"freedom of speech, or of the press," for instance—with the clear intention that the federal courts would provide the necessary definitions when deciding specific cases. The Fourteenth Amendment was ratified sixty-five years after the Supreme Court decided *Marbury v. Madison*, and the principle of judicial interpretation of the Constitution was certainly well established. It is safe to assume that the Congress that adopted the broadly worded Civil War amendments implicitly agreed with Chief Justice Marshall that "it is emphatically the province and duty of the judicial department to say what the law is," and that the Court could successfully "expound and interpret" the language of the Fourteenth Amendment.

Moreover, the drafters of the first section of the Fourteenth Amendment clearly intended that it would be used by the federal courts to apply the full range of the Bill of Rights to the legislative and administrative acts of the states. The drafters had ample evidence in front of them that in the absence of such a guarantee, the states would restrict the liberties of disfavored groups through the passage of oppressive legislation—a problem that still exists today. During the debate over the final adoption of the Fourteenth Amendment in the House of Representatives, John Bingham (R-Ohio), one of the primary drafters of the proposed amendment, spoke eloquently in its support:

> The necessity for the first section of this amendment to the Constitution, Mr. Speaker, is one of the lessons that have been taught to your committee and to all of the people of this country by the history of the past four years of terrible conflict—that history in which God is, and in which He teaches the profoundest lessons to

men and nations. There was want hitherto, and there remains a want now, in the Constitution of our country, which the proposed amendment will supply. What is that? It is the power of the people, the whole people of the United States, by express authority of the Constitution, to do that by congressional enactment which hitherto they have not had the power to do, and have never even attempted to do; that is, to protect by national law the privileges and immunities of all the citizens of the Republic and the inborn rights of every person within its jurisdiction whenever the same shall be abridged or denied by the unconstitutional acts of any State.

Despite Bingham's stirring words, the intent of the Fourteenth Amendment was not fulfilled until some sixty years after its adoption, and then not necessarily in the manner anticipated by its drafter. Just five years after the amendment's adoption, the Supreme Court heard the *Slaughter-House Cases* (1873), a joint appeal of three cases challenging Louisiana's creation of a city-operated slaughterhouse in New Orleans. The Court used the case as an opportunity to narrowly construe the amendment's privileges and immunities clause. The Court held that the clause merely applied to individuals in their capacity as U.S. citizens and not as state citizens.

"Such a construction," Associate Justice Samuel Freeman Miller wrote, " . . . would constitute this court a perpetual censor upon all legislation of the states, on the civil rights of their own citizens, with authority to nullify such as it did not approve as consistent with those rights, as they existed at the time of the adoption of this amendment." The Court's narrow decision effectively eliminated the use of the privileges and immunities clause as a tool to apply the Bill of Rights to state action.

Eventually, however, the Court began fulfilling the spirit of the Fourteenth Amendment's adoption by undertaking a slow process of incorporating the Bill of Rights into the amendment through the due process clause. Following the Communist Revolution in Russia in 1917, a number of states, and the federal government, passed new antiespionage and antisedition laws aimed at suppressing left-wing radicals who advocated the overthrow of the U.S. government. Shortly thereafter, Communist Party USA founder Benjamin Gitlow was convicted for publishing a "left-wing manifesto" under a New York law that prohibited criminal anarchy. Gitlow challenged his conviction on the grounds that the law deprived him of his free speech rights without due process of law as required by the Fourteenth Amendment.

Although the Court rejected that argument and upheld Gitlow's conviction as constitutional, *Gitlow v. New York* (1925) was the first case in which the Court accepted the due process argument as a legitimate inquiry. "For present purposes," Associate Justice Edward Terry Sanford wrote, "we may and do assume that freedom of speech and of the press—which are protected by the First Amendment from abridgment by Congress—are among the fundamental personal rights and 'liberties' protected by the due process clause of the Fourteenth Amendment from impairment by the states."

Since *Gitlow,* the Court has been engaged in a decades-long process to determine which personal rights and liberties should be incorporated into the Fourteenth Amendment and thus be made applicable to the states. A large number of those cases were decided long before Earl Warren became chief justice of the Court in 1953:

- *Near v. Minnesota* (1931), holding that a statute known as the Minnesota Gag Law violated freedom of the press;
- *Powell v. Alabama* (1932), holding that citizens have a fundamental right to court-appointed counsel in a capital-murder trial;
- *DeJonge v. Oregon* (1937), holding that Oregon's Criminal Syndicalism Law, prohibiting the organization of radical groups, violated the freedom of assembly;
- *Cantwell v. Connecticut* (1940), holding that Connecticut's arrest of Jehovah's Witnesses for alleged breach of the peace violated the right of free exercise of religion;
- *Everson v. Board of Education* (1947), upholding New Jersey reimbursements for transportation costs to religious schools, but incorporating the establishment clause of the First Amendment into the Fourteenth Amendment;
- *McCollum v. Board of Education* (1948), holding that an Illinois pro-

gram of religious instruction in public schools violated the establishment clause under the Fourteenth Amendment;

- *In re Oliver* (1948), holding that Michigan had violated the petitioner's Fourteenth Amendment due process rights by denying him a public trial.

Clearly, then, the Warren Court did not invent the doctrine of incorporation. But the Warren Court still managed to earn the unending antagonism of conservatives in general and the Christian Right in particular for two related but distinct reasons. First, it issued a series of decisions in which it either identified additional fundamental freedoms delineated in the Bill of Rights, or expanded the scope of previously identified freedoms:

- *Brown v. Board of Education of Topeka* (1954), holding that de jure racial segregation in Kansas schools was a violation of the equal protection clause of the Fourteenth Amendment;
- *Mapp v. Ohio* (1961), holding that Ohio state courts violated the petitioner's Fourteenth Amendment due process rights by allowing use of evidence obtained in violation of the Fourth Amendment;
- *Engel v. Vitale* (1962), holding that New York's use of state-sponsored prayer in public schools violated the establishment clause of the First Amendment;
- *Gideon v. Wainwright* (1963), holding that Florida violated an indigent defendant's due process rights under the Fourteenth Amendment when it failed to provide him with state-appointed counsel;
- *Abington Township School District v. Schempp* (1963), holding that Pennsylvania violated the establishment clause of the First Amendment by requiring the reading of Bible verses in public schools;
- *Escobedo v. Illinois* (1964), holding that Illinois violated the Sixth Amendment right to counsel by denying criminal defendants access to an attorney during interrogation;
- *Miranda v. Arizona* (1966), holding that Arizona violated an individual's right against self-incrimination under the Fifth Amendment by failing to inform him of his rights prior to interrogation;

• *Katz v. United States* (1967), holding that California violated the defendant's Fourth Amendment right to be free of warrantless search and seizure by conducting a warrantless wiretap of a phone booth conversation.

Second, the Warren Court peered into the penumbra (or shadows) of the Bill of Rights and identified a new fundamental freedom to incorporate into the Fourteenth Amendment: the right to privacy. As we will see in Chapter 9, the alleged renegades of the Warren Court cannot claim credit (or be blamed) for inventing the right to privacy; the right of individuals to privacy under the federal constitution and the Bill of Rights had been discussed by members of the Court since the start of the twentieth century, in large part because the concept was an increasingly hot topic in law journals and state court opinions.

But for a variety of social and legal reasons, the Warren Court was in fact the first to specifically incorporate the right to privacy into the Fourteenth Amendment, first as an adjunct to the Fourth Amendment in a criminal case involving the use of illegally seized evidence (*Mapp v. Ohio*) and then as a stand-alone right in a challenge to Connecticut's ban on contraceptives (*Griswold v. Connecticut* [1965]). In oft-poetic language, Associate Justice William O. Douglas wrote for the 7–2 majority in *Griswold* that "specific guarantees in the Bill of Rights have penumbras, formed by emanations from those guarantees that help give them life and substance. Various guarantees create zones of privacy. . . . We have had many controversies over these penumbral rights of 'privacy and repose.' These cases bear witness that the right of privacy which presses for recognition here is a legitimate one."

And that is the crux of the debate: legal, social, and religious conservatives emphatically reject Douglas's assertion of legitimacy for the right to privacy and the validity of the decisions that rely upon it (most notably *Roe v. Wade* [1973], which legalized abortion). As a result, for the last three decades Christian conservatives have been working to elect presidents and senators who will appoint justices who at a minimum are hostile to the concept of a penumbral right and, preferably, skeptical about the concept of incorporation as well. There are countervailing forces at work (such as the doctrine of stare decisis, "to stand by things decided"), but two recent appointees to the Supreme Court, Chief Justice John Roberts and Associate Justice Samuel Alito, have demonstrated a surprising willingness to abandon or render irrelevant long-established precedents with which they disagree. The goal of the Christian Right, already closer to realization than most suspect, is not only a Supreme Court markedly more hostile to rights that Americans have taken for granted for more than a generation, but a return to a time when state legislatures and courts could create a patchwork quilt of personal liberties and individual freedoms.

CHAPTER TWO

"In God We Trust"

The Push to Declare America a Christian Nation

T HERE IS ONE FUNDAMENTAL BELIEF that has sustained the Christian Right through long days of campaign speeches, phone banks, leafletting, poll watching, and fund-raising: America has abandoned its historical religious foundations and needs to be restored to its proper status as a Christian nation. A highly profitable industry of Christian Right think tanks, lobbying organizations, law firms, lecturers, historians, writers, and websites has sprung up to defend America's allegedly Christian origins and to push for legislation and policies that would irrevocably save the nation for Jesus Christ.

Conservative author Ann Coulter offered a typically stark statement of the Christian Right's ultimate goals. In an October 2007 interview with Donny Deutsch, host of CNBC's *The Big Idea,* Coulter pointed to the 2004 Republican National Convention as her ideal vision of America:

COULTER: Well, OK, take the Republican National Convention. People were happy. They're Christian. They're tolerant. They defend America, they—

DEUTSCH: Christian—so we should be Christian? It would be better if we were all Christian?

COULTER: Yes.

DEUTSCH: We should all be Christian?

COULTER: Yes. Would you like to come to church with me, Donny?

Admittedly, Ann Coulter is to civil discourse what Cruella de Vil is to Dalmation puppies, and she certainly doesn't speak for all Christians or even all evangelical Christians. But her belief that America would be better off if it were predominantly and avowedly Christian is not an isolated view.

One of the leading websites for the Christian Right is the Conservative Voice, a news and commentary site founded by Nathan Tabor, who holds a master's degree in public policy from Pat Robertson's Regent University. As the site proudly proclaims, Tabor was once described by the late Jerry Falwell as a "young Jesse Helms." Tabor entered the Republican primary for Congress in North Carolina's Fifth Congressional District, but despite support from some of the Christian Right's most influential leaders—Robertson, Bob Jones III, Representative Jim Ryun (R-Kans.), Beverly and Tim LaHaye, Michael Farris, and others—Tabor finished a distant fifth out of eight candidates.

Tabor's Conservative Voice website, however, has been a much more successful endeavor. Committed to promoting "Faith, Family, Freedom," Tabor's site features over one hundred columnists, including a number of conservative icons: Pat Buchanan, William F. Buckley, Robert D. Novak, Phyllis Schlafly, Paul M. Weyrich, to name just a few. One of the more strident "conservative voices" is Bill Gray, a former computer industry worker who runs an online Christian ministry called the Bill & Dory Gray Christian Ministries. In an editorial published in 2007 on the Conservative Voice website, Gray emphatically summarized the fundamental fears of the Christian Right movement:

America is in a fight for its very life—from the inside! Our American society, our American culture, is on the brink of implosion.

This may sound very dramatic; but, it is true. America is like a huge keg of dynamite, and the fuse—is the fallacy of "Separation of Church and State" perpetrated by Secular Humanism, comprised of the ACLU, the NEA, Liberal Politicians, Gay/Lesbian Activist groups, and other atheistic organizations.

After recounting numerous references to God and the Creator in the history of the American colonies and the early days of the Republic, Gray concluded his essay with an unequivocal call to Glory:

> We must protect our nation, founded UNDER GOD and for the GLORY OF GOD.
>
> The next time you hear some fanatic screaming "First Amendment Rights" or "Separation of Church and State"—tell him to go lock himself in a padded room and scream to himself. For we no longer want to hear it.
>
> We are Americans, living in a Christian nation which was founded by Christian believers. You have a right to read your Qur'an, your Torah, or any other sacred book you have; you have a right to worship rocks, stars, the sun, and the moon, or plaster statues, if you like. You have the right to live as you like, in any lifestyle you chose. Just do not try to force that lifestyle upon me, or upon my children or grandchildren.

Gray also took the time to defend on the Conservative Voice site the comments that Coulter made on CNBC, although Coulter may wish that he had chosen a more felicitous metaphor. "What is my opinion of Ann Coulter?" Gray asked rhetorically. "Ann is like a beacon light—a lot of pigeons will leave their droppings on it—but, it raises awareness and guides people. Ann, like Jerry Falwell, often says things that, to some, are outrageous. But, you have to admit, it does make you think." Gray asserted that even though it might not have been expressed well, Coulter's fundamental argument was correct:

> Will Jews who do not acknowledge Jesus Christ as their long awaited Messiah be saved? No. Neither will Germans, Africans, British, Polish, Latin Americans, Mexicans, etc.,—no one, regardless of your nationality or ethnic culture, will be saved except

through Jesus Christ. He makes this very clear in John 3:3, "Truly, truly, I say to you, unless one is born again, HE CANNOT SEE THE KINGDOM OF GOD." . . .

So, when you think of Ann Coulter; do not think of her as a loudmouth—but, instead think of her as a beacon light covered with pigeon poop—but, still making her case for Conservative Christianity. God bless Ann Coulter!

The claim by Christian conservatives like Gray and Coulter that America is a Christian nation is disturbing enough when preached from the pulpit or proclaimed on national television. It assaults the fundamental premise of this country, that it is a pluralistic society that draws its strength in large part from the varied contributions of numerous cultures and traditions. Moreover, the insistence that the United States is a Christian nation, a claim heard at increasingly high levels of government, unnecessarily antagonizes non-Christian nations and makes it more difficult for this country to play an effective role on the increasingly crowded and diverse global stage.

There may be one or two salutary aspects to the strident insistence that America is a Christian nation: the debate over what the Constitution's framers intended is generally healthy for democracy, and the dredging of historical documents for quotes allegedly affirming America's Christian foundation provides much-needed work for liberal arts majors. But the insistence on a Christian identity for the nation is far more dangerous and divisive when the claim is made by state and federal legislators, and downright destructive when laws, public policies, and judicial decisions are explicitly based on that premise. In those circumstances, the assertion that America is a Christian nation threatens to erect a wall between the federal government and those of its citizens who are not devotees of Ann Coulter, Bill Gray, and other Christian Right demagogues.

Attempts to codify God in the nation's laws have occurred throughout American history, with varying degrees of success. But over the last three decades, politicians at both the state and federal levels have been increasingly aggressive in their efforts and increasingly narrow in their definition of God. In 2004, for instance, the platform for the Republican Party in Texas flatly stated that "the United States of America is a Christian nation," and in 2006, expanded on that theme to urge the teaching of "school subjects with emphasis on the Judeo-Christian principles upon which America was founded and which form the basis of America's legal and its political and economic systems."

In Missouri, state representative David Sater proposed a resolution in the spring of 2006 that would have declared the United States a Christian nation and also recognized Christianity as the state's "majority religion." The resolution went on to state that the founding fathers "recognized a Christian God and used the principles afforded to us by Him as the founding principles of our nation." The resolution caused a stir when it was sent to the full House for a vote, but it was ultimately dropped from the House calendar in late March.

At the federal level, various legislators—most notably Representative Roscoe Bartlett (R-Md.)—have given speeches on the floor of Congress declaring that the United States is a Christian nation, and have even sponsored legislation to codify that belief in various ways in the nation's laws. The Christian Right lost two of its most fervent advocates—Representative Tom DeLay (R-Tex.) and Senator Rick Santorum (R-Pa.)—in 2006, but a number of others remain. In the heady days following the success of conservative politicians in 2004, Santorum was mentioned as a possible presidential candidate, but that prospect faded with his loss to former Pennsylvania governor Bob Casey. In Santorum's absence, each of the remaining 2008 Republican presidential candidates trumpeted his religious values and slavish devotion to the Christian Right's core issues—but the possibility that Rudy Giuliani, the thrice-married, semi-pro-choice, occasionally cross-dressing former Mayor of Sodom (New York), would win the nomination had evangelicals threatening a general-election boycott.

"My position remains the same," the Family Research Council's Tony Perkins told the *Los Angeles Times*, "as I think it does for a number of pro-life conservatives—that we draw a line that we will not cross in supporting a pro-abortion-rights candidate."

While the push to formally codify America as a Christian nation may play well on the political stage in some parts of the country, even the more moderate of the proposals would destroy the religious and social pluralism that has been at the core of this nation's success for more than two hundred years. The most extreme proposals, made by individuals surprisingly and disturbingly influential in contemporary conservative political circles, would literally impose Old Testament law for criminal behavior, strip the voting rolls of all but the godly, and turn civil government into little more than a beadle for evangelical Christian churches.

The Secular Constitution and
the National Reform Association

The Constitution that was drafted in Philadelphia is radical in numerous respects but especially because it was the first to propose the formation of a civil government without invocation of or obeisance to a deity. As Susan Jacoby pointed out in her well-received history of America's secular origins, *Freethinkers*, the Constitution's predecessor, the Articles of Confederation, included the assertion that "it hath pleased the Great Governor of the World" to persuade the various state legislatures to ratify the Articles. But the framers of the Constitution recognized, as many today do not, the perils of a government with a cross in one hand and a sword in the other.

Not surprisingly, the omission of God from the text of the Constitution troubled many religious leaders of the time. According to Jacoby, the Reverend Mr. John M. Mason, a noted leader of the American Presbyterian Church in New York at the time, preached that "the absence of God in the Constitution [is] an omission which no pretext whatever can palliate." Equally troubling to many Protestant leaders was the language of Article VI of the Constitution, which stated in part that "no religious test shall ever be required as a qualification to any office or public trust under the United States." Some even went so far as to warn that without an appropriate religious test, a Roman Catholic or a Jew might someday be president.

During the contentious ratification debate in 1787 and 1788, various state legislatures proposed amendments to the U.S. Constitution that would have acknowledged God and/or Jesus Christ as the source of all governmental power. But in the end, support for the concept of religious freedom and excitement over the economic possibilities inherent in the new union trumped religious concerns, and the various Christian amendments all were defeated.

The debate over the omission of God from the Constitution was resurrected during the Civil War. In January 1864, at a meeting in Allegheny, Pennsylvania, a group of concerned Protestants formed the National Association to Secure the Religious Amendment to the Constitution (which in 1875 was renamed to its more familiar title, the National Reform Association [NRA]).

As its first act, the NRA drafted a petition to Congress asking that the Preamble to the Constitution be amended by adding the following text (in italics):

> We, the People of the United States, *humbly acknowledging Almighty God as the source of all authority and power in civil government, the Lord Jesus Christ as the Ruler among the nations, his revealed will as the supreme law of the land,* in order to form a more perfect union, establish justice, insure domestic tranquility, provide for the common defence, promote the general welfare, and secure the blessings of liberty to ourselves and our posterity, do ordain and establish this Constitution for the United States of America.

The NRA's petition was presented to Congress by the great abolitionist senator from Massachusetts, Charles Sumner, on February 17, 1864, along with a similar request from the committee of the synod of the Reformed Presbyterian Church; Sumner submitted five other petitions later that spring. But Congress, not surprisingly, was otherwise occupied, first with the end of the Civil War and then the assassination of President Abraham Lincoln in April 1865. Moreover, opposition to the proposed amendment had arisen in some non-Christian religious groups; in early February 1865, for instance, Sumner also presented the Senate with a petition from "the executive committee of the American Israelites" in which they protested the idea of a Christian amendment to the Constitution.

A short time later, Senator Lyman Trumbull, the slim, bespectacled chairman of the Senate Committee on the Judiciary, asked that his committee be discharged of its responsibility of considering the various requests for a "Christian amendment," and the Senate agreed. His request caused some stir in the daily papers, which reported that the Committee on the Judiciary was against recognizing God in the Constitution. In a brief speech in the Senate on March 2, 1865, Trumbull sternly denied that assertion, saying, "The committee considered that such an amendment of the Constitution as was prayed for by those memorialists was unnecessary; and it is for that reason the committee ask to be discharged from the further consideration of this memorial."

Trumbull's comments slowed the push for a Christian amendment, but did not stop it altogether. In 1866 William Strong, a Presbyterian elder and member of the Pennsylvania Supreme Court, was elected president of the NRA, and the group renewed its efforts to organize local chapters. Under Strong's leadership, the NRA began publishing *The Christian Statesman* in September 1867.

"The design of this sheet, as its name suggests," the editors affirmed, "is the discussion of the principles of government in the light of Christianity." In addition to advocating for a Christian amendment to the Constitution, the editors promised to promote efforts to limit divorce and protect marriage, to honor the Sabbath (and support the legislation needed to enforce it), to promote temperance, to restrict the voting franchise to "godly" persons, to apply the standards of Scripture to criminal trials and punishments, and in general to subsume civil government to the Word of God.

Not long after it was founded, *The Christian Statesman* helped organize one of the first widespread citizen-lobbying efforts in the nation's history. In 1868 the journal advised its readers that they could submit citizen petitions asking both the House and Senate to pass a Christian amendment, and urged them to do so before Congress adjourned. The call for action was echoed in local meetings of the NRA and in congregations across the country. By the end of March 1869, senators introduced nearly 150 Christian-amendment petitions, containing the signatures of thousands of constituents. But despite the best efforts of the NRA and the *Statesman*, the petitions languished in the Judiciary Committee, and legislation to adopt a Christian amendment never received a vote in either the House or the Senate.

President Ulysses S. Grant nominated Strong to the U.S. Supreme

Court in 1870; following his confirmation, Strong remained the head of the NRA and continued to work on the group's religious agenda. On January 18, 1871, for instance, he organized a convention in Philadelphia to promote "the recognition of the Almighty in the Constitution," despite the fact that any challenge to the constitutionality of a Christian amendment would almost certainly have come before the Supreme Court. Two years later, when rising New York moralist Anthony Comstock came to Washington to lobby for stronger federal legislation prohibiting the mailing of obscene and indecent materials, Justice Strong helped Comstock draft the restrictive law that was ultimately and famously adopted by Congress.

Despite Strong's high profile and repeated calls for conventions to consider proposals to amend the Constitution to "suitably acknowledge Almighty God as the Author of the Nation's existence and the ultimate source of its authority," the issue received little political support. The objections to the proposed amendment were best summarized by an editorial in the *Ohio Democrat* in February 1873:

> This will be tantamount to a union of Church and State, which it would be well for thoughtful people to consider.—The call for the Convention is signed by William Strong, a Judge of the U.S. Supreme Court, at Washington, who is President of the Association seeking to bring about this radical change in the organic law of free America—thus undoing the labors of the fathers of the Republic. Let the press speak out upon the subject. For ourselves, we say, let well enough alone.

Clearly, the vast majority of the country agreed. The NRA slowly slipped into historical obscurity, although the organization still exists in a diminished form and remains committed to the belief that "the civil government of our nation, its laws, institutions, and practices must therefore be conformed to the principles of Biblical law as revealed in the Old and New Testaments."

The specific idea of acknowledging God and Jesus Christ in the Preamble to the Constitution has reappeared at odd intervals since: there was a brief flurry of interest following World War I, and again in the late 1950s and early 1960s. One of the more recent proponents was Representative John B. Anderson (R-Ill.), who in 1961, 1963, and 1965 sponsored legislation "to recognize the authority of Jesus Christ, Savior and Ruler of nations, through whom are bestowed the blessings of Almighty God." The proposal never made it out of committee, but it became something of a political albatross when Anderson, a lapsed Republican, later ran for president as an Independent in 1980. Shortly after announcing his long-shot bid for the presidency that spring, Anderson told the *New York Times* that the "Christian amendment" has "[hung] over my head as an embarrassment 15 years after it was disavowed, and I have had to deliver many public mea culpas."

Numismatists and Philatelists Take on the Communists

Although the NRA was unsuccessful in its attempts to promote the adoption of a Christian amendment, it played a role in the one formal recognition of God by the United States to emerge from the Civil War era: the inscription of "In God We Trust" on the nation's coinage.

Even before the NRA was formed, a Pennsylvania pastor named Mark Watkinson wrote to Salmon P. Chase, the secretary of the Treasury, in November 1861 and suggested an inscription acknowledging God:

> One fact touching our currency has hitherto been seriously overlooked. I mean the recognition of the Almighty God in some form in our coins.
>
> You are probably a Christian. What if our Republic were now shattered beyond reconstruction? Would not the antiquaries of succeeding centuries rightly reason from our past that we were a heathen nation?

If his suggestion were adopted, Watkinson argued, "This would relieve us from the ignominy of heathenism. This would place us openly under the divine protection we have personally claimed. From my heart I have felt our national shame in disowning God as not the least of our present national disasters." Chase apparently agreed, and a week later sent a note to James Pollock, the director of the U.S. Mint, ordering him to commission a design expressing the nation's trust in God in the "fewest and tersest words possible."

Pollock was a former governor of Pennsylvania and a member of the newly formed National Reform Association, and he took up Chase's charge with enthusiasm. He had models of new coins created with several possible mottoes, including "Our God and Our Country," "God and Our Country," and his personal favorite, "God, Our Trust" (a phrase taken from the fourth stanza of "The Star-Spangled Banner"). When Chase was slow in responding to his various ideas, Pollock included a gentle chastisement in the 1863 annual report for the Mint:

> I would respectfully and earnestly ask the attention of the Department to the proposition in my former report, to introduce a motto upon our coins expressive of a National reliance on Divine protection, and a distinct and unequivocal National recognition of the Divine Sovereignty. We claim to be a Christian Nation—why should we not vindicate our character by honoring the God of Nations in the exercise of our political Sovereignty as a Nation?
>
> Our national coinage should do this.

A few months later, Chase finally focused his attention on the issue and approved Pollock's recommendation with one change: he altered the motto to read "In God We Trust," which he felt looked better in the coin's design. Congressional action, however, was required before the new motto could be minted, since an existing law specified what should appear on American coins. Chase drafted the necessary language, and on April 22, 1864, Congress adopted "An Act Relating to Foreign Coins and the Coinage of Cents at the Mint of the United States," which gave Chase and Pollack the authority to fix "the shape, mottoes, and devices of said coins." A year later, Congress adopted a new coinage act that formally instructed the Treasury to inscribe the motto "In God We Trust" on all subsequent coins "as shall admit of such legend thereon."

The loophole created by that last phrase resulted in one last motto controversy involving the nation's pocket change. Enamored of the stunning statue of General William Tecumseh Sherman that stands at the southeast entrance to New York's Central Park, President Theodore

Roosevelt hired its sculptor, Augustus Saint-Gaudens, to design new ten- and twenty-dollar gold pieces for the U.S. Treasury. During the course of his work, Saint-Gaudens concluded that the motto "In God We Trust" detracted from the appearance of the coin. Believing that the use of the motto was discretionary, Saint-Gaudens decided not to include it in his design.

The omission came to the public's attention in early November 1907, when the first of the ten-dollar gold pieces were shipped from the Philadelphia mint to the Treasury Department in Washington. Saint-Gaudens unfortunately having died some three months earlier, President Roosevelt was left to bear the brunt of the public uproar that ensued. Treasury officials piously told the *Washington Post* at the time that they were not involved in the design of the coin and had merely carried out the president's instructions.

Roosevelt (who ironically was one of the country's more personally devout presidents) was denounced in sermons and editorials alike, and the White House was all but snowed under with letters from angry and disappointed citizens. Never one to shirk from a good fight, however, Roosevelt staunchly defended his decision in a letter to one correspondent and released his reply for publication. He agreed that the motto should be inscribed on the nation's great public buildings, where it might serve as an inspiration, but that it did not serve such purpose on coins.

> My own feeling in the matter is due to my very firm conviction that to put such a motto on coins, or to use it in any kindred manner, not only does no good, but does positive harm, and is in effect irreverence, which comes dangerously close to sacrilege. A beautiful and solemn sentence, such as the one in question, should be treated and uttered only with that fine reverence which necessarily implies a certain exaltation of spirit. Any use which tends to cheapen it, and above all, any use which tends to secure it being treated in a spirit of levity, is from every standpoint to be profoundly regretted.

This was not a battle, however, that Roosevelt would win on either artistic or reverential grounds. Responding to the public outcry, Congress passed a brief piece of legislation on May 13, 1908, ordering the restoration of the motto to all denominations on which it previously appeared, and Roosevelt signed it into law five days later.

For the next half century, the debate over mottoes and amendments largely languished. In the early 1950s, however, when America was in the throes of the Cold War with the so-called godless Communists, three separate initiatives brought "In God We Trust" to the forefront of public debate once more.

First, a letter-writing campaign was directed at the United States Postal Service, urging it to incorporate the motto "In God We Trust" on the nation's stamps. Postmaster General Arthur Summerfield was initially resistant to the idea, in large part because the service's engravers and the nation's numerous philatelists were concerned that the motto would take up too much space and would not blend in well with many stamp designs (imagine, for instance, trying to artfully incorporate the phrase into the recently released series honoring George Lucas's *Star Wars* films). On February 25, 1954, however, Summerfield announced the planned release of a single new stamp design incorporating the motto. The purple eight-cent stamp, intended for international use, featured the Statue of Liberty with the phrase "In God We Trust" forming an arch over the statue.

The stamp was formally unveiled during a nationally televised broadcast on April 8, 1954, in a ceremony that was remarkably well-attended: the guest list included President Dwight D. Eisenhower; Secretary of State John Foster Dulles; Postmaster General Summerfield; Dr. Roy G. Ross, general secretary of the National Council of Churches; Francis Cardinal Spellman, the Roman Catholic archbishop of New York; and Dr. Norman Salit, president of the Synagogue Council of America.

In his remarks, President Eisenhower unequivocally endorsed the religious message of the stamp and its motto. "Throughout its history," the president said, "America's greatness has been based on a spiritual quality that is best symbolized by the stamp issued today. The flame of liberty symbolizes our determination always to remain free, a haven for the oppressed. It is an acknowledgment that all men are dependent on the Almighty." By affixing the stamp to an international letter, he added, a citizen can feel that he or she has done something "definite and constructive" to promote American values.

The following spring, Representative Charles E. Bennett, a Democrat from Jacksonville, Florida, introduced legislation to require the inclusion of "In God We Trust" on all of the nation's coins and paper currency (at the time, the motto was omitted from some coins and all bills). The idea for the legislation originated with Matthew Rothert, an Arkansas businessman and, more significantly, the president of the Arkansas Numismatic Society. On November 11, 1953, Rothert gave a speech to his fellow Arkansas coin collectors in which he proposed that "In God We Trust" be printed on the nation's paper currency so that when it circulated around the world, it would broadcast America's belief in a higher power. Encouraged by the enthusiastic reception he received, Rothert lobbied Congress to carry out his suggestion. In the House, Bennett agreed to sponsor a bill, as did Lyndon Johnson in the Senate.

The timing of the proposal was propitious, since the Bureau of Printing and Engraving was just then preparing new dies for engraving currency and installing new, faster printing presses, which meant that the motto could be added to currency designs with relatively little disruption. The bill quickly passed Congress and was signed into law by President Eisenhower on July 11, 1955.

No doubt inspired by the rapid passage of his currency legislation, Bennett introduced another brief bill in 1956, to make "In God We Trust" the national motto. The bill passed Congress and was signed into law with relatively little fanfare by President Eisenhower on July 30, 1956. In 2006, on the fiftieth anniversary of the law, the United States Senate adopted a resolution reaffirming the national motto and declaring that "the success of civil government relies firmly on the protection of divine Providence."

Francis Schaeffer and the Fight
against Secular Humanism

For the more reactionary members of the Christian Right, acknowledging a belief or faith in divine Providence on coins and stamps is laughably insufficient. What is needed to save America, they assert, is not the tepid baptism of the United States as a Christian nation, but instead the application of biblical or Old Testament law to contemporary society so as to better promote the kingdom of God on earth. This small but increasingly influential movement, known generally as Christian Reconstructionism, is in large part a response to what most Christians perceive as the long and inexorable rise of a competing religion: secular humanism, the Enlightenment-inspired belief in reason and critical thinking as the primary tools for understanding the world and structuring society.

To avoid the alleged ills brought on by secular humanism, the proponents of Reconstructionism, to varying degrees, believe that the literal language of the Bible should govern all areas of life. Society should be reorganized or "reconstructed" so that governance is divided into three spheres: family, church, and civil government. Within the family, wife and children would be subservient to the husband, who in turn would submit to the authority of Jesus Christ and the Scriptures of the Old Testament. The authority of civil government would be sharply limited and would be primarily devoted to aiding ecclesiastical government in enforcing biblical law.

The origins of the movement can be traced most directly to former missionary Rousas John (R. J.) Rushdoony, who was an adherent of the views of American theologian Cornelius Van Til. In the early 1960s Rushdoony began popularizing Van Til's ideas as Christian Reconstructionism, and in 1965 he founded the Chalcedon Foundation, a Reconstructionist think tank committed to the restoration of a Christian civilization first in America and then around the world. "We propose an explicitly Biblical system of thought and action as the exclusive basis for civilization," the foundation's website proclaims today. "Only by restoring the Christian Faith and Biblical law as the standard of all of life can Christians hope to re-establish Christian civilizations."

A central source of Rushdoony's argument for the reconstruction of a Christian civilization and the imposition of biblical law is the so-called cultural or dominion mandate contained in Genesis 1:28 of the Bible: "And God blessed them, and God said unto them, Be fruitful, and multiply, and replenish the earth, and subdue it: and have dominion over the fish of the sea, and over the fowl of the air, and over every living thing that moveth upon the earth." As a result, the term "do-minionism" is often used interchangeably with "Christian Recon-structionism," although the former is mostly used by those who are critical of the movement. The efforts of the National Reform Associ-ation to amend the Preamble of the Constitution to declare the United States a Christian nation, or to emblazon its currency with "In God We Trust," are the types of initiatives typically described as soft domin-ionism, while the campaign by Rushdoony and his adherents to im-pose the precepts of the Old Testament on contemporary society is more commonly referred to as hard dominionism.

In a three-volume treatise titled *Institutes of Biblical Law* published in 1973, Rushdoony gave some indication of just how hard such domin-ion might be (at least for those on the receiving end). Based on his reading of the Old Testament, Rushdoony advocated a return to cap-ital punishment for a wide range of offenses, including homosexuality, adultery, incest, bestiality, idolatry or apostasy, public blasphemy, kid-napping, rape, and more. Despite its provocative suggestions, the book did not receive widespread attention when it was published, in part be-cause of its antediluvian views on criminal law and in part because Rushdoony also used the work to deny the Holocaust, defend segre-gation and slavery, and condemn interracial, intercultural, and interre-ligious marriages.

Rushdoony's work might have vanished into historical obscurity but for the efforts of the Reverend Francis Schaeffer, a minister in the fun-damentalist Bible Presbyterian Church. Assigned by the church to Eu-rope as long-term missionaries in 1948, Schaeffer and his wife, Edith, moved to the small Alpine village of Huémoz, Switzerland, where they spent years hosting people interested in discussing and debating the application of Christian truth to contemporary society. As the popu-larity of the Schaeffers steadily grew, their chalet home expanded into an institute they called L'Abri (the shelter), which *Time* magazine de-scribed in a 1960 article as a "mission for intellectuals."

Schaeffer himself told *Time* that L'Abri's chief draw was the failure of Protestantism to remain relevant to an increasingly materialistic society. "These people are not reached by Protestantism today," he said. "Protestantism has become bourgeois. It reaches middle-class people, but not the workers or the intellectuals. What we need is a presentation of the Bible's historical truth in such a way that it is acceptable to today's intellectuals. Now as before, the Bible can be acted upon, even in the intellectual morass of the 20th century."

Schaeffer was an active reader of Reconstructionist literature (including Van Til and, somewhat later, Rushdoony), but his numerous publications avoided the more inflammatory positions that marginalized Rushdoony's *Institutes of Biblical Law.* In particular, Schaeffer rejected the idea of applying Old Testament law to modern society, a position that over the years has earned him occasionally harsh criticism from some of the more aggressively dominionist proponents of Christian Reconstructionism.

Without Schaeffer's tireless efforts and keen sense of political and cultural timing, it is unlikely that evangelical Christians would have approached anything close to the electoral success that they have enjoyed. In the mid-1960s, Schaeffer decided to come to America to give a lecture tour in the Boston area; his presentations were very well received and formed the basis of his 1968 book, *Escape from Reason.* By the mid-1970s, Schaeffer had published seventeen more books and given hundreds of lectures and talks around the country. He was well on his way to establishing himself as one of the most prominent intellectuals in the Religious Right, and a leading champion against the forces of moral relativism and secular humanism.

Schaeffer believed that his dire predictions about the decline of American culture were fulfilled when the United States Supreme Court handed down its 1973 ruling in *Roe v. Wade* (coincidentally, the same year that Rushdoony's *Institutes of Biblical Law* was published). That decision, in which the Court ruled that a woman's right to privacy trumped the state's right to prohibit abortion during the first trimester, and under specific circumstances in the second trimester as well, outraged Schaeffer and provided him with a powerful platform from which to encourage evangelical political activity. "If evangelicals will not take a stand on this issue," Schaeffer said at the time, "I doubt if they will take a stand on anything."

Conservative Republican politicians, sensing untapped and potentially powerful political resources, welcomed Schaeffer's call for evangelical activism and befriended the theologian. Michael Ford, the oldest son of then vice president Gerald Ford, was a student of Schaeffer's at L'Abri and invited the Schaeffers to have dinner with his father at the White House. On Capitol Hill, Schaeffer spent time advising Representative Jack Kemp (R-N.Y.) and Senator Jesse Helms (R-N.C.), who along with other congressional conservatives were looking for ways to exploit the evangelical outrage following *Roe v. Wade.*

Although Schaeffer was becoming increasingly well known in conservative and evangelical circles during the 1970s, few in the mainstream were aware of him and his ardent push for evangelical opposition to abortion. That changed quickly in 1979 when Schaeffer produced a five-hour film titled *Whatever Happened to the Human Race?* The movie, which cost $1 million to produce, was a scathing look at abortion in America, a practice that Schaeffer compared to slavery and which he said would eventually lead to legalized euthanasia, among other things. Schaeffer's son, Frank A. Schaeffer, assisted his father in the production the movie but later repudiated his work, and in a dramatic book of his own, *Crazy for God,* expressed regret for his role in helping to make evangelical Christians a political force in America.

Throughout 1980, Schaeffer conducted seminars and presented his film in twenty cities around the country with fellow Christian fundamentalist Dr. C. Everett Koop, a noted pediatric surgeon, who also appeared onscreen in a segment on the relationship between abortion and euthanasia. Three years later, Koop was nominated by President Ronald Reagan to serve as surgeon general of the United States, and he credited his appearance in *Whatever Happened to the Human Race?* as the first step toward being nominated by Reagan (although the film caused some antagonistic questioning during his confirmation proceedings).

Schaeffer's most famous and influential book, *A Christian Manifesto,* was published in 1981; the title is a deliberate reference to the Humanist Manifesto (1933) and Humanist Manifesto II (1973), two declarations by prominent intellectuals of the day, each of which called for the replacement of existing religions with "humanism," a central tenet of which is the belief that "no deity will save us; we must save ourselves." Ironically, Schaeffer espoused a variation on that theme, that "God helps those who help themselves." He declared abortion to be the single most critical issue for America and urged Christians to engage in civil disobedience to oppose it. He even suggested that, if necessary, outright defiance of the government by force would be appropriate: "There does come a time, when force, even physical force, is appropriate. The Christian is not to take the law into his hands and become a law unto himself. But when all avenues to flight and protest have closed, force in the defensive posture is appropriate." Contemporary Christians, Schaeffer argued, are in the same position as the American colonists who used force to defend themselves from the oppression of Great Britain. "If there is no final place for civil disobedience, then the government has been made autonomous," Schaeffer said, "and as such, it has been put in place of the Living God."

The book received widespread coverage in both evangelical and mainstream circles, and cemented Schaeffer's position as the intellectual guru for the Religious Right. During a final speaking tour in 1982 to promote the book (Schaeffer died of cancer eighteen months later), he told an enthusiastic gathering at the annual convention of the National Association of Religious Broadcasters, "When a government negates the law of God, it abrogates its authority."

Jerry Falwell and the Moral Majority:
From the Pulpit to Politics

Even before the uncompromising language of Schaeffer's *A Christian Manifesto* helped crystallize evangelical commitment to political activism, his speeches and personal advocacy triggered a profound change in American politics. In many ways, Schaeffer's most visible success was the late Jerry Falwell, whom he advised throughout the early 1970s to put aside the traditional evangelical reservations about political involvement that stemmed, in part, from the derisive treatment of fundamentalists and biblical literalists during the so-called Scopes Monkey Trial in 1925. Before meeting Schaeffer, Falwell clearly disdained politics: in 1965 he preached, "Nowhere are we commissioned to reform the externals. I feel that we need to get off the streets and back into the pulpits and into our prayer rooms." However, Schaeffer believed that the steadily growing popularity of Falwell's *Old Time Gospel Hour* broadcasts put the Virginia Baptist preacher in a powerful position to call evangelical Christians to political activism, particularly on the issue of abortion.

Whatever reluctance Falwell may once have had about Christian political activism, he warmed rapidly to Schaeffer's ideas. In 1976, during America's Bicentennial, he organized a series of "I Love America" rallies in state capitals across the country that were heavily tinged with politics. During a July 4 sermon, he told the audience, "This idea of 'religion and politics don't mix' was invented by the devil to keep Christians from running their own country." Later that same year, Falwell generated controversy by criticizing Democratic presidential nominee Jimmy Carter on his television program for Carter's remarks on sex and religion in the November 1976 issue of *Playboy*. Falwell said that Carter's agreement to do the interview was a "real moral breakdown" and described the language used by the born-again Christian from Georgia as "vulgarity, profanity, obscenity."

"This is a moral issue," Falwell remarked three weeks before the election. "Let us insist our candidates go God's way—the Bible way. If they do not, then let's get them out. Let us forget party affiliation and put Jesus first."

The following summer, Falwell traveled to Miami to support the singer turned activist Anita Bryant in her successful campaign to overturn a gay rights ordinance passed by Dade County. Inspired by those experiences and buoyed by his reported viewership of 18 million people per week, Falwell clearly had no difficulty envisioning a more openly political role for evangelism in general and himself in particular.

At a meeting of conservative leaders in Falwell's office at Liberty University in June 1979, conservative activist Paul Weyrich told Falwell, "There is in America a moral majority that agrees about the basic issues [like abortion and homosexuality]. But they aren't organized." Falwell seized on the phrase "moral majority," which echoed Schaeffer's long-standing belief in cobelligerence, the idea that Christians and non-Christians could collaborate to fight for change on social issues. Like Schaeffer, Falwell initially envisioned a big-tent organization that would also include Protestants from nonfundamentalist denominations, Catholics, Jews, and even atheists. In practice, however, the focus of the Moral Majority, the political action group that resulted from this

meeting, was clearly on the recruitment of evangelical Christian supporters, the promotion of conservative Christian policies, and the election of theologically acceptable candidates (notwithstanding the
Constitution's prohibition of a religious test): "If a man stands by this
book," Falwell would say at rallies, holding up a Bible, "vote for him.
If he doesn't, don't."

The tremendous popularity of the Moral Majority, which signed
up 4 million members in its first eighteen months alone, and its role in
the election of the conservative candidate Ronald Reagan in 1980, appeared to ratify the central point of Schaeffer's *Christian Manifesto*, that
Christians should engage more fully in the political process. Even more
compelling was the impact of newly politicized evangelicals on the various U.S. Senate races around the country: a storm warning was heard
in 1978, when the abortion issue played a role in the defeat of Iowa's
Dick Clark and New Hampshire's Thomas J. McIntyre. During the so-
called Reagan Revolution of 1980, several of the Senate's more liberal
members also lost their seats, including Frank Church (D-Idaho), Birch
E. Bayh II (D-Ind.), John Culver (D-Iowa), George S. McGovern
(D-S. Dak.), Warren Magnuson (D-Wash.), and Gaylord Nelson
(D-Wis.). In most cases, the outgoing senators were replaced by
markedly more conservative candidates.

But the very success of the Moral Majority and the overtly biblical
language often used by Reverend Falwell scared nearly as many voters
as it attracted, which made Falwell something of a mixed blessing for
the more mainstream candidates he supported. Over time, his influence
waned even as his political instincts remained solid: in early 1988 he
was one of the few evangelical leaders to support the candidacy of
George H. W. Bush over the Religious Right's preferred candidate, Pat
Robertson, the law student turned televangelist best known for his
show *The 700 Club*.

But Falwell's attention to the 1988 campaign was distracted by his
ongoing efforts to run his own evangelical empire in Tennessee and, at
the same time, clean up the myriad scandals created by Jim and Tammy
Faye Bakker in their PTL ("Praise the Lord") ministry, which Falwell
took over in 1987. Obviously worn down by the challenge of running
two multimillion-dollar ministering and media empires, Falwell de-

cided to declare victory and dissolve the Moral Majority in early 1989. At the time, he told reporters that the organization had achieved its objective of galvanizing Christians and promoting political involvement. "The religious conservatives in America," Falwell proudly said, "are now in for the duration."

Evangelical and Christian Right groups that followed in Falwell's footsteps learned not only what to do but what not to do. Although Pat Robertson's 1988 campaign for president faltered in the early primaries, it led to the founding of the Christian Coalition, staffed by a new generation of evangelicals educated in the basic skills of retail politics and the power of using nonthreatening language to convey biblical objectives. Led by its oleaginous director, Ralph Reed, the Coalition quickly perfected the so-called San Diego strategy, in which Religious Right candidates for local offices were instructed to hide their real views until after the election. The strategy got its name from the 1990 local elections in San Diego, in which Christian Coalition–backed candidates quietly won sixty out of ninety races. Two years later, in a speech to Coalition members, Reed announced, "The first strategy, and in many ways the most important strategy, for evangelicals is secrecy."

But even the occasionally bombastic Falwell had his quiet, long-range-planning side. Largely overlooked in the media coverage surrounding his death in May 2007 was the pending graduation of the first fifty students from the Liberty University School of Law, a graduate school affiliated with the thirty-six-year-old Liberty University. Falwell created the law school with the goal of "training a new generation of lawyers, judges, educators, policymakers, and world leaders in law from the perspective of an explicitly Christian worldview." To help his law students prepare for careers at the highest levels of government, Falwell had carpenters re-create the bench on which the United States Supreme Court sits, as well as the tables and lectern used by attorneys appearing before the Court. It reportedly cost Falwell $1 million to build his down-to-the-inch replica.

In an interview with the *Chicago Tribune* just a few days before he died of a heart attack, he explained his version of the evangelical "stealth strategy":

The 10 Commandments cannot be posted in public places. Children cannot say grace over their meals in public schools. No prayers at football games and on the list goes, virtually driving God from the public square. And then, of course, *Roe vs. Wade* in the middle of all that, legalizing abortion on demand. Now, the redefining of the family or the attempt to. So all of this reinforced our belief that we needed to produce a generation of Christian attorneys who could, in fact, infiltrate the legal profession with a strong commitment to the Judeo-Christian ethic.

Although Falwell himself is no longer leading the charge, the idea of a biblical fifth column has proven enormously enticing to the Religious Right, and in particular to its Reconstructionist wing. By blending the formidable fund-raising capabilities of evangelism with startling levels of political access, a new generation of Reconstructionist-inspired educators is working to make Falwell's vision a reality.

CHAPTER THREE

God's Farm Team

The Growing Evangelical Education System

R ELIGION HAS PLAYED A significant and frequently controversial role in the long history of public education in the American colonies and the United States. The first statute making a "proper" education compulsory was passed by the Massachusetts Bay Colony in 1642, just twenty-two years after the Pilgrims first landed on Plymouth's rocky shore. The law was goal-oriented rather than procedural: it specified that the colony's children should have sufficient education to understand religious principles and the colony's laws, but it did not specify how such education should be provided. Five years later, when colony leaders concluded that parents were not doing an adequate job educating their children, it updated the law to require towns to either hire a teacher or establish a grammar school, depending on their size. Similar laws were soon passed in other colonies, and by the mid-seventeenth century, elementary education was generally compulsory up and down the East Coast. In structure and operation, the schools were closer to contemporary private schools, since they were supported by funds from the parents of the children who attended the school, rather than by the entire community through generally levied taxation.

The most well known early proposal for true public education, not surprisingly, came from the estimable Thomas Jefferson. While serving in the Virginia legislature, he proposed a "Bill for the More General Diffusion of Knowledge," which laid out a three-level system of public education, from elementary through high school to college. The preamble to the legislation is a classic blend of Jefferson's innate egalitarianism with a farmer's practicality. Even the best governments, Jefferson argued, tend toward tyranny, and the best safeguard is to sufficiently educate the citizenry so that they can recognize such ambitions and take action against them:

> Whence it becomes expedient for promoting the publick happiness that those persons, whom nature hath endowed with genius and virtue, should be rendered by liberal education worthy to receive, and able to guard the sacred deposit of the rights and liberties of their fellow citizens, and that they should be called to that charge without regard to wealth, birth or other accidental condition or circumstance.

A key component of Jefferson's plan was dividing each county of Virginia into a hundred parts, so that all children within each "hundred" could readily attend a school near them. The concept of local control of publicly funded elementary schools was consistent with Jefferson's strongly Anti-Federalist belief in decentralized government, and it remains a powerful concept in public education to this day.

Jefferson's education bill, however, did not pass the Virginia legislature, and despite Jefferson's ongoing advocacy for public education, elementary and secondary education remained largely a private endeavor until the mid-1800s. Then in 1837, education reformer Horace Mann was appointed by Governor Edward Everett to lead a new Board of Education in Massachusetts. With the governor's active support, Mann set about creating a statewide system of common schools, an initiative that was driven by Mann's belief that "education . . . beyond all other devices of human origin, is the great equalizer of the condition of men,—the balance wheel of social machinery." Fifteen years later, Massachusetts became the first state to pass a compulsory-attendance law, and over the next half century, virtually every other state followed suit.

But the idea of common education and compulsory attendance for all children was not warmly received by everyone. In his annual report of 1848, Mann described the controversy in terms that will be familiar to observers of our contemporary school debates:

> It is known, too, that our noble system of free schools for the whole populous is strenuously opposed by a few persons in our own State, and by no inconsiderable numbers in some of the other states of this Union; and that a rival system of "parochial" or "sectarian schools" is now urged upon the public by a numerous, a powerful, and a well-organized body of men. It has pleased the advocates of this rival system, in various public addresses, in reports, and through periodicals devoted to their cause, to denounce our system as irreligious and anti-Christian. They do not trouble themselves to describe what our system is, but adopt a more summary way to forestall public opinion against it by using general epithets of reproach, and signals of alarm.

The compulsory-attendance requirement was particularly objectionable to the nation's immigrants, the majority of whom at the time were Roman Catholic. Resistant to the assimilative forces and the overwhelmingly Protestant bent of the religious expression in the schools, they established their own private elementary schools and sent their children to them instead.

The rise of parochial schools, however, exacerbated already growing nativist sentiments in various areas of the country. In Oregon, for instance, the 1922 gubernatorial election was roiled by a ballot referendum on a bill titled "Compulsory Education," which stated that every Oregon child between eight and sixteen (with limited exceptions) must attend a public school. Supporters issued a statement arguing that the law was necessary because public primary schools are "the only sure foundation for the perpetuation and preservation of our free institutions":

> The assimilation and education of our foreign-born citizens in the principles of our Government, the hopes and inspiration of our people, are best secured by and through attendance of all children

in our public schools. We must now halt those coming to our country from forming groups, establishing schools and thereby bringing up their children in an environment often antagonistic to the principles of our Government.

Not surprisingly, the bill was strenuously opposed by a variety of religious groups, including Catholics, Lutherans, Episcopalians, Presbyterians, Seventh-Day Adventists, and the operators of nondenominational private schools. But on Election Day, voters not only approved the law but replaced Governor Ben W. Olcott with his Democratic opponent, Walter M. Pierce, in large part because Olcott had opposed the education bill. A dark undercurrent to the election was the fact that the state's Ku Klux Klan enthusiastically supported the compulsory-education bill and campaigned on behalf of Pierce in the general election.

The compulsory-education bill was challenged in federal court, and eventually made its way to the United States Supreme Court, which struck down the statute in a brief but highly significant opinion in *Pierce v. Society of Sisters of the Holy Names of Jesus and Mary* (1925). The legislation, Associate Justice James McReynolds affirmed, "interferes with the liberty of parents and guardians to direct the upbringing and education of children under their control. . . . The fundamental theory of liberty upon which all governments in this Union repose excludes any general power of the state to standardize its children by forcing them to accept instruction from public teachers only."

In reaching the decision in *Pierce*, McReynolds explicitly relied on the Court's decision two years earlier in *Meyer v. Nebraska* (1923), which he also wrote, in which the Court struck down a state law that forbade the teaching of any modern language in school to any child who had not graduated from the eighth grade. The question presented in *Meyer*, McReynolds said, was "whether the statute as construed and applied unreasonably infringes the liberty guaranteed to the plaintiff in error by the Fourteenth Amendment."

In a ruling that presaged later readings of the Fourteenth Amendment (including those of the much-criticized Warren Court), Mc-

Reynolds concluded that the statute was in fact an unconstitutional infringement on individual liberty:

> While this Court has not attempted to define with exactness the liberty thus guaranteed, the term has received much consideration and some of the included things have been definitely stated. Without doubt, it denotes not merely freedom from bodily restraint but also the right of the individual to contract, to engage in any of the common occupations of life, to acquire useful knowledge, to marry, establish a home and bring up children, to worship God according to the dictates of his own conscience, and generally to enjoy those privileges long recognized at common law as essential to the orderly pursuit of happiness by free men.

With the spirit of Chief Justice John Marshall smiling behind him, McReynolds made it clear that "determination by the [state] legislature of what constitutes proper exercise of police power is not final or conclusive but is subject to supervision by the courts."

Division and Dominion: The Religious Right and the Homeschooling Movement

Michael Farris did not invent the concept of homeschooling, but many people think he did, and he has not taken enormous pains to disabuse anyone—particularly those in Congress—of the notion. Certainly, no other person has been more prominently or enthusiastically associated with the movement over the last two decades. Farris, an ordained Baptist minister and constitutional lawyer, is himself the father of ten homeschooled children and an outspoken opponent of public education; during his unsuccessful 1993 campaign for lieutenant governor in Virginia, he described the public schools as a "godless monstrosity" and a "multibillion-dollar indoctrination machine," although, as his national profile has risen, he has found more moderate ways to phrase those sentiments.

Farris began his public career in the early 1980s as the president of the Washington state chapter of the Moral Majority, where among other things, he filed a public records request with the Washington State Library for the names of any public schools or public school employees who borrowed the film *Achieving Sexual Maturity* for use in public schools. The Moral Majority later filed a lawsuit against the library, but dropped it after the library said that no schools were on the list of borrowers. Citing privacy concerns, the library refused to release the names of individual borrowers. However, the library added that the Moral Majority's lawsuit sparked so· much interest in the film that it had a six-month waiting list for its three copies.

With California lawyer Michael Smith, Farris founded the Home School Legal Defense Association (HSLDA) in 1983, and together the two undertook an aggressive campaign to promote homeschooling through legislation and court cases around the country. At the end of the first year, HSLDA had about two hundred members; three years later, roughly thirty-six hundred families had joined at a cost of one hundred dollars per year.

In part because of the HSLDA's initially slow growth, Farris moved from Washington to Virginia to take a job as a staff attorney for Concerned Women for America (CWA), a conservative advocacy group founded by Beverly LaHaye in 1979. LaHaye, the wife of Dr. Timothy LaHaye (best known for his phenomenally popular Left Behind series of religious fiction, but also an adherent of Francis Schaeffer and a longtime proponent of Christian dominionism), founded CWA to serve as a political counterweight to the National Organization for Women (NOW); by 1984 the conservative group outnumbered NOW by nearly two to one, and Farris was hired to head a seven-person office in Washington charged with handling CWA's lobbying efforts, education, and, most importantly, its litigation.

One of his first cases at CWA not only garnered Farris national attention but spurred interest in HSLDA as well. In Hawkins County, Tennessee, a group of Christian fundamentalist parents sued the local school district in 1983, arguing that the Holt, Rinehart and Winston reading series selected by the district (which contained passages from titles like *The Wizard of Oz* and *The Diary of Anne Frank*) unconstitutionally infringed on their religious beliefs. Although the formal title of the litigation was *Mozert v. Hawkins County Public Schools,* the media quickly dubbed the case Scopes II, after the famous 1925 trial of Tennessee teacher John Scopes, who was charged with violating a state law prohibiting the teaching of evolution.

Farris made headlines by winning the case at the trial level; according to the finding of chief district court judge Thomas G. Hull (a recent appointment by President Ronald Reagan), "The plaintiffs believe that, after reading the entire Holt series, a child might adopt the views of a feminist, a humanist, a pacifist, an anti-Christian, a vegetarian, or an advocate of a 'one-world government.' . . . This is their religious belief. They have drawn a line, and it is not for us to say that the line [they] drew was an unreasonable one." Judge Hull ruled that the state could not require the children of the plaintiffs to read the Holt series, and ordered that the children be allowed to opt out, provided that the parents agreed to provide homeschool reading instruction as provided by Tennessee law.

A year later, however, the Sixth Circuit Court of Appeals reversed the district court by a 2–1 vote (interestingly, one of the judges voting to overrule the district court was Judge Cornelia Kennedy, who had been mentioned as a possible candidate for the slot taken by Sandra Day O'Connor on the Supreme Court). The appellate judges concluded that Chief Judge Hull had erred by equating mere exposure to different ideas with interference with the free exercise clause of the First Amendment. Their description of the plaintiffs' objections is a good primer to the approach that many religious conservatives take to politics in general:

It is clear that to the plaintiffs there is but one acceptable view— the biblical view, as they interpret the Bible. Furthermore, the plaintiffs view every human situation and decision, whether related to personal belief and conduct or to public policy and programs, from a theological or religious perspective. [One plaintiff] testified that many political issues have theological roots and that there would be "no way" certain themes could be presented without violating her religious beliefs. She identified such themes as evolution, false supernaturalism, feminism, telepathy, and magic as matters that could not be presented in any way without offending her beliefs.

The only way to avoid conflict with the plaintiffs' beliefs in these sensitive areas would be to eliminate all references to the subjects so identified. However, the Supreme Court has clearly held that it violates the establishment clause to tailor a public school's curriculum to satisfy the principles or prohibitions of any religion.

At risk, the Sixth Circuit said, is the central mission of the public schools: "Teaching fundamental values essential to a democratic society. These values include tolerance of divergent political and religious views while taking into account consideration of the sensibilities of others." The court dissolved Chief Judge Hull's injunction against the Holt reading program and reversed his award of damages.

Although Farris ultimately lost the *Mozert* case, the notoriety surrounding the litigation provided a burst of publicity for HSLDA, which Farris used to help make the organization one of the leading national voices on the issue of homeschooling. The rapid rise of the Christian homeschool advocacy group, however, caused a sizable rift in homeschooling circles. Homeschooling has a long history, and adherents range across the political spectrum; in fact, much of the early impetus for homeschooling came from disaffected liberals in the 1960s and early 1970s. For decades, homeschoolers had quietly defied compulsory-attendance laws with relatively limited interference from state and local education officials. Among many homeschoolers there was deep concern that HSLDA's focus on high-profile litigation and legislation would result in increased state and federal regulation of homeschooling in general.

Of much greater concern is the way in which Christian Reconstructionist homeschoolers (for whom HSLDA is a leading voice) have tried to assert dominion over the homeschooling movement as a whole; in many ways, it is an illustrative example of what Christian Reconstructionists hope to accomplish in the broader society.

The co-opting of the homeschooling movement was led by a group that dubbed themselves "the four pillars of homeschooling": Farris and the HSLDA, which concentrated on legal and legislative issues; Gregg Harris, an early proponent of Christian homeschooling, who organized conferences and workshops; Brian Ray, head of the National Home Education Research Institute (a subsidiary of the HSLDA), who provided research support; and Sue Welch, editor of *The Teaching Home*, billed as "a Christian magazine for home educators," who handled communications. Together, the four pillars created a loose network of Christian Home School Associations (CHSAs) in various states.

What sets these groups apart from existing homeschool organizations is their strongly hierarchical nature and their exclusivity; most CHSAs require homeschoolers to sign a "statement of faith" before they can serve as officers or, in some cases, even join at all. Employing a modus operandi popular with the Religious Right, however, those requirements are not always disclosed up front. In an article written in 1991 for *Home Education Magazine*, a homeschooling educational resource, editors Mark and Helen Hegener reported that "many new exclusive groups are being encouraged to 'hide' their exclusivity, with the goal of appearing to have a much broader base of support." In some cases, they added, national leaders of Christian homeschooling advise the CHSAs not to work with or, in extreme cases, not to speak with unapproved homeschooling groups.

The precise wording of the statement of faith varies from state to state, but at a minimum, an acknowledgment of the Bible as the authoritative and inerrant word of God generally is required. In some cases, however, the statements of faith contain very precise policy statements; the Utah Christian Home School Association, for instance, requires affirmation of the following "tenet of Christian theology": "We reject the anti-Christian tenets of secular humanism, including the general theory of evolution, one world government, government mandated sex education, government mandated parenting classes, modern feminist ideology and abortion." In their *Home Education Magazine* article, the Hegeners warned that the actions of "the four pillars" were damaging the homeschooling movement. In particular, they noted that Farris's strenuous efforts to cast himself as the spokesperson for the homeschooling movement "foster[ed] society's view that the majority of homeschooling families are 'religious fanatics.'" As the couple astutely observed:

The rationale that urges an exclusive hierarchy is the rationale for religious domination, which serves to encourage a climate of religious intolerance within the hierarchy itself. It is often advantageous to skirt the issue of religious domination, those who draw their political power from exclusive hierarchies demonstrate that there can be very tangible rewards in fanning the flames of religious intolerance. Neither domination nor intolerance will lead in any way to a greater degree of freedom for any of us.

Patrick Henry College: "The Tip of the Spear"

The logical extension of Farris's homeschooling advocacy was the founding of a college that caters specifically to homeschooled students. Farris has said in various interviews that he got the idea for the school when homeschooling parents asked him for the name of a college of good "Christian character," and members of Congress approached him for the names of homeschooled students who could work on Capitol Hill as interns. After successfully raising $11 million to fund the new facility, Farris began construction of Patrick Henry College (PHC) in the fall of 1999 and opened it for classes the following fall.

In selecting a name for his new school, Farris chose to honor the great American patriot and Virginian Patrick Henry, primarily in recognition of Henry's 1784 proposal as a colonial legislator of "A Bill Establishing a Provision for Teachers of the Christian Religion." The bill nearly became law but opponents succeeded in postponing a final vote until the 1785 legislative session, in part by kicking Henry upstairs to the governorship. By the time the bill came back up for consideration, Henry's fellow Virginian James Madison had successfully rallied opposition to it, and the proposal was firmly defeated. A few months later, Madison and Thomas Jefferson effectively ended government-supported religion in Virginia by adopting Jefferson's "Act for Establishing Religious Freedom," which boldly declares as a natural right

that no man shall be compelled to frequent or support any religious worship, place, or ministry whatsoever, nor shall be enforced, restrained, molested, or burthened in his body or goods, nor shall otherwise suffer on account of his religious opinions or belief; but that all men shall be free to profess, and by argument to maintain, their opinion in matters of religion, and that the same shall in no wise diminish, enlarge, or affect their civil capacities.

Without expressly saying so, it is clear that much of the focus of Patrick Henry College is aimed at reversing both its namesake's legislative defeat and the course of American history over the succeeding two-hundred-plus years.

In the years since Farris broke ground on the college, the institution has grown slowly but steadily. Its initial graduating class in 2002 had just fourteen students, all of whom already had started their college careers with two years at another school. In May 2007 the school graduated fifty-nine students in a variety of different disciplines, including government, journalism, history, literature, and classical liberal arts, and reported a student body of over three hundred. Its physical growth has been somewhat more rapid. Less than a year after it opened, the college doubled its property holdings by paying nearly $1 million in privately raised cash for sixty-six acres of adjoining farmland, and in the fall of 2006 began construction on a $27 million, 106,000-square-foot student life center with a gymnasium, new dining hall, indoor track, and other facilities.

The campus of PHC stands on rolling countryside just east of the downtown of Purcellville, Virginia, roughly fifty miles northwest across the Potomac River from the nation's capital. For founder Farris, the college's proximity to Washington, D.C., is a physical manifestation of his goal to educate a "generation of Patrick Henrys" who will, according to the school's stated mission, "lead our nation and shape our culture with timeless biblical values and fidelity to the spirit of the American founding." The college's motto—*Pro Christo et Libertate*—aptly characterizes the school's priorities: "For Christ and Liberty."

To further that goal, a significant portion of the school's culture and curriculum is organized around preparing students for success in the public sphere. Participation in debate is mandatory, and PHC has one of the best undergraduate moot court teams in the country. (Moot court is a mock trial competition that typically occurs in law school, but is growing more popular at the college level. PHC won the national undergraduate competition in both 2005 and 2006.) In the evenings, the school frequently holds town-hall style meetings on different topics, and students are required to earn some of their credits through work experience.

Thanks to Ferris's extensive political contacts, PHC has been remarkably successful, despite its small size, in placing its students in desirable and highly competitive Washington internships. In the spring of 2004 *New York Times* reporter David Kirkpatrick caused a stir by noting that seven of the nearly one hundred interns working for the Bush White House were students at PHC, an eighth intern was volunteering in the Bush reelection campaign, and a PHC graduate (and former D.C. intern) was on the staff of presidential adviser Karl Rove. In addition, Kirkpatrick said, twenty-two members of Congress, all conservative Republicans, have hired PHC students to work as interns in their offices or on their reelection campaigns.

Farris is not bashful about his ambitions for the school's students. "We are not homeschooling our kids just so they can read," Farris told Kirkpatrick in 2004. "The most common thing I hear is parents telling me they want their kids to be on the Supreme Court." In other interviews, Farris has mused happily about the day when a Patrick Henry College graduate is elected president of the United States.

One of PHC's most significant challenges so far has been finding an organization that will give it accreditation as an institute of higher learning. Not long after it started classes in 2000, the college applied for certification with the American Academy for Liberal Education (AALE), but the application was denied. In a letter announcing the organization's decision, AALE president Jeffrey D. Wallin told PHC that its "Statement of Biblical Worldview"—to which each trustee, college administrator, and faculty member must ascribe—conflicted with the AALE's criteria that "liberty of thought and freedom of speech are supported and protected, bound only by such rules of civility and order as to facilitate intellectual inquiry and the search for truth."

Chief among the AALE's objections is the fact that in a document discussing specific applications of its biblical worldview, PHC begins with the requirement that "any biology, Bible, or other courses at PHC dealing with creation will teach creation from the understanding of Scripture that God's creative work, as described in Genesis 1:1–31, was completed in six twenty-four-hour days. All faculty for such courses will be chosen on the basis of their personal adherence to this view." Although the college expects its faculty to provide "a full exposition" of other theories, including "Darwinian evolution," the academic outcome is preordained: its biology faculty, PHC says, will "teach creation as both biblically true and as the best fit to observed data."

The college appealed the denial by the AALE, and while the appeal was pending, received preaccreditation status in 2002. However, when the AALE announced that it was planning a site visit to the college to review various issues, the college withdrew its accreditation application altogether. An application for accreditation by the Southern Association of Colleges and Schools was also dropped shortly thereafter. In early 2007, however, PHC received accreditation from the Transnational Association of Christian Colleges and Schools (TRACS), an organization recognized by the U.S. Department of Education as a national accrediting body for forty-four Christian educational institutions around the country (including Falwell's Liberty University and Bob Jones University).

Despite the college's accreditation struggles, it has been remarkably successful at its primary goals: placing its students and graduates as interns and employees at the highest levels of American government, and inculcating a mission to apply a Christian worldview to public service. During the college's first graduation in May 2002, for instance, senior Rebecca Durnell told a reporter with the *Washington Post* that she was heading to Indiana University law school in the fall. Her goal, she said, was to become a judge and make rulings based on biblical standards of right and wrong.

Generation Joshua and Tyndale's Ploughmen

Much like Falwell before him, Farris is a passionate believer in Francis Schaeffer's message that Christians must engage the world around them and actively work to change society to reflect Christian principles. But thanks in large part to his long association with Timothy and Beverly LaHaye, Farris's ultimate objective is the full Reconstructionism advocated by Rushdoony, rather than the mere activism, however forceful, of Schaeffer. The best way to bring about Reconstruction, Farris believes, is to raise children with a dedicated biblical worldview and give them the tools to change the secular worlds of law and politics from within.

Farris's goal of establishing a Patrick Henry law school for students like Rebecca Durnell remains a distant dream, but thanks to his extensive political contacts among congressional Republicans, he has successfully launched two different programs that are giving Christian homeschoolers and PHC students remarkable political experience.

In 2003 Farris started Generation Joshua, a public-service program designed to promote the involvement of Christian youth, ages eleven to nineteen, "in the civic and political arenas." The program's glossy twelve-page brochure sets forth the objective of Generation Joshua in no uncertain terms: "Our goal is to ignite a vision in young people to help America return to her Judeo-Christian foundation. We provide students with hands-on opportunities to implement that vision." The "GenJ" program's offerings include the following:

- An online civics curriculum consisting of a range of politically oriented classes such as Founding Fathers; Intro to Constitutional Law; Campaign School; Declaration of Independence; Revolutionary War Era Sermons; Federalist Papers; and GenJ Book Club.
- Voter registration training, with an emphasis on signing up new Christian voters: "Voting is a vital part of every Christian's civic responsibility. Christians have a duty to rebuild the walls of American politics that were originally constructed on the foundation of biblical values and self-government."
- The Benjamin Rush Awards, given to GenJ students who "complete the online civics curriculum, write letters to the editor in which they cite original sources, register voters, write to public officials, volunteer in local campaigns, and sign up new members for Generation Joshua." Winners receive scholarships to Patrick Henry College and all-expenses-paid trips to Washington, D.C. The award is named after a Pennsylvania physician who was one of the signers of the Declaration of Independence and a strong proponent of Christianity in both public life and in the schools. He is also known as

the father of American psychiatry and was an early voice against slavery (although he considered dark skin color to be a hereditary disease and opposed interracial marriage to prevent its spread).

- Student Action Teams, groups of high school and college-aged students who provide campaign support for conservative candidates. The teams are fully funded by the political action committee of the HSLDA, and perform a variety of campaign-related tasks, including phone calls, literature drops, and voter registration. In 2002 seven teams were deployed and six conservative candidates won; in 2004, the number of teams doubled to fourteen, and eight out of nine candidates supported by GenJ were elected. The HSLDA website says that over one thousand teens and parents worked on campaigns in 2006, helping to elect four pro-homeschooling candidates to Congress: Marilyn Musgrave (R-Colo.), Geoff Davis (R-Ky.), Peter Roskam (R-Ill.), and Michele Bachmann (R-Minn.).

At Patrick Henry College, the school's effective internship program gives all students a variety of opportunities to participate in the Washington political process. At the end of 2006, however, Farris announced that he was creating a new program, called Tyndale's Ploughmen, to give select PHC students an even more intimate look at national politics.

"My goal for Tyndale's Ploughmen," Farris wrote in a fund-raising letter, "is to provide personal mentoring to our students who believe that God may someday call them to serve in elected office." Roughly thirty students participate in the program, which includes shadowing Farris during political meetings in Washington, D.C., and occasional dinners during the year with national political leaders.

Farris named the program after William Tyndale, a sixteenth-century English Protestant best known for translating the Bible from Latin into Early Modern English, the vernacular of his day. Tyndale's work was opposed by the Catholic Church, which was uncomfortable with the idea that laypeople might try to interpret the word of God without the intercession of priests or the pope, an attitude that essentially lingered until the Second Vatican Council discontinued the Latin Mass in 1962. When a local clergyman challenged Tyndale's work, he allegedly replied: "I defy the pope and all his laws; and if God spares my life, I will cause the boy that drives the plow in England to know more of the Scriptures than the pope himself!"

Tyndale did live long enough to translate the full Bible into English, although his last ten years were spent in hiding in Europe. He was eventually betrayed and transported back to England in 1536, where he was convicted as a heretic, strangled to death, and his body burned at the stake. As is often the case, however, the efforts of the Church to suppress Tyndale's work ultimately were unsuccessful. Although just one complete version of his translation survives today, much of his elegant language (including phrases like "let there be light," "the salt of the earth," and "gave up the ghost") found a place in the King James Bible eighty years later.

Farris describes his modern-day ploughmen as God's farm team, and promises potential donors that the students in the group will make headlines. "Someday," he wrote, "some of these people are going to be in the major leagues. We may not know which ones, but I am completely confident that some will become national leaders at the highest levels."

Farris's pitch on behalf of the Tyndale's Ploughmen program is best summarized by the phrase "as ye sow, so shall ye reap." A good portion of Farris's fund-raising solicitation is spent reassuring donors that the funds given to PHC's Fund for Excellence have already produced results and will continue to do so. He pointed to the fact that PHC graduates "are now working in places of influence such as the White House, on Capitol Hill, the FBI, media organizations, and political campaigns." Others, he proudly said, are enrolled in various graduate schools around the country.

Farris's fund-raising letter closes by pointing out that the cost of a single congressional race exceeds the amount of PHC's entire annual budget. "While I believe in giving to campaigns," Farris said, "think of how much more cost effective it is to invest in a program like Tyndale's Ploughmen where thirty young leaders are being mentored for future elected office. I want to urge you to invest in the future of a godly and free America by partnering with Patrick Henry College to train the leaders of tomorrow."

The Rise of Conservative Christian
Law Schools and Law Firms

Although the Tyndale's Ploughmen program is unique in its level of political access, it is merely one of the efforts to reshape American law in God's image. The first law school founded on avowedly Christian principles was the O. W. Coburn School of Law, established in 1979 by televangelist and charismatic faith healer Oral Roberts. The money to found the law school came from a $3.5 million donation by Oklahoma businessman O. W. Coburn, the father of Oklahoma's junior U.S. senator, Tom Coburn. Elected in 2004 during a strong Republican showing in the Senate elections, the younger Coburn is one of the chamber's most conservative members: a licensed obstetrician, Coburn has endorsed the use of the death penalty for abortion providers (a popular dominionist proposal) and among other restrictive contraceptive initiatives, has pushed for warning labels on condoms on the grounds that they are "ineffective" in preventing the spread of sexually transmitted diseases like HIV.

The Centers for Disease Control and Prevention, a subdivision of the federal government's Department of Health and Human Services, has a different view: according to its website, "Latex condoms, when used consistently and correctly, are highly effective in preventing heterosexual sexual transmission of HIV, the virus that causes AIDS." Nonetheless, Coburn's views on birth control earned him an appointment as cochair of President George W. Bush's Presidential Advisory Council on HIV/AIDS in January 2002.

Along with the equally conservative Senator Sam Brownback (R-Kans.), Coburn was appointed by the Republican leadership to the powerful Senate Judiciary Committee, where his evaluation of judicial nominees is informed by his commitment, as he states on his website, "to confirming federal judges who will respect the Constitution and the original intent of our Founding Fathers," and his belief that "Congress has a constitutional obligation to limit the jurisdiction of activist judges who abuse their judicial power."

After the law school's opening in 1979, the Coburn name did not remain on it for long. Due to steadily declining revenues in the early 1980s (at one point, Oral Roberts pleaded—successfully, as it turned out—

with his followers to contribute $8 million or God would "call him home"), Roberts shut down several of the graduate schools associated with Oral Roberts University, including the law school. In the spring of 1986 he transferred the physical assets of the law school (and many of its students) to CBN University, the Virginia Beach–based institution founded in 1977 by televangelist Pat Robertson. Ironically, Robertson himself is a 1955 graduate of Yale Law School, but when he failed the New York bar examination, he entered the New York Theological Seminary and earned a divinity degree.

Although its existence was brief, the Coburn School of Law achieved one very important objective: accreditation by the American Bar Association. The ABA initially refused to accredit the school, arguing that a requirement that every student and faculty member adhere to "charismatic Christian tenets" was discriminatory. Without ABA accreditation, the school faced hurdles in attracting qualified instructors, and its students were barred from taking the bar exam in most states. After an impassioned debate in the ABA's House of Delegates (and under the threat of a federal court ruling that might have stripped the group of its law school accreditation authority altogether), the ABA amended its standards "to allow religion-affiliated schools to adopt policies of admission and employment that directly relate to its religious purpose so long as all job and student applicants are notified in advance of the policies."

When Roberts gave the Coburn School of Law to Pat Robertson's CBN University, however, the ABA ruled that the accreditation did not transfer with it, so Robertson had to seek his own ABA approval. As with the Coburn School of Law, the ABA was reluctant to grant accreditation to a school whose express mission "is to bring to bear the will of our Creator, Almighty God, upon legal education and the legal profession." The law school's entire first graduating class sued the ABA in 1989 over the accreditation issue; although they lost their case, the school did receive provisional accreditation, which was enough to allow its graduates to take the bar examination. Seven years later, the law school—now named Regent University School of Law—resolved the last of the ABA's objections, and the House of Delegates unanimously awarded the school full accreditation in August 1996. When Pat Robertson announced the news to a cheering gathering of law students and faculty, he said that it was the first time that a law school "founded on the truth of the gospel of Jesus Christ" had been accredited by the ABA.

Other law schools recently have been founded on strict religious principles, and thanks to Regent's leadership have generally found it easier to get ABA accreditation. Three are affiliated with Catholic institutions: Barry University–Dwayne O. Andreas School of Law (1999); University of St. Thomas School of Law (2001); and Ave Maria School of Law (2003), founded by conservative Catholic and antiabortion activist Thomas Monaghan, the multimillionaire founder of Domino's Pizza. Falwell's Liberty University School of Law (2004) incorporates fundamentalist Baptist views, and the as-yet-unbuilt Judge Paul Pressler School of Law at Louisiana College, scheduled to open in 2009, plans "to train and equip young men and women to view the practice of law through a biblical worldview" based on Southern Baptist doctrine.

So just how much of an impact will lawyers with a dedicated biblical worldview have on American institutions? It is of course difficult to say precisely, since most of the schools have only recently begun to graduate students. However, there are a host of Christian law firms and organizations looking for new associates, and collectively they are playing an increasingly important role in religious-oriented litigation around the country. Among the most notable are:

- The American Center for Law and Justice (ACLJ), founded by Pat Robertson and housed at Regent University. Under the leadership of its director, Jay Alan Sekulow, the ACLJ has developed into a powerful opponent of the American Civil Liberties Union (ACLU). Sekulow himself was dubbed one of the "25 Most Influential Evangelicals" by *Time* in 2005.
- The Rutherford Institute, founded by John Whitehead, a leading figure in the Christian Reconstructionist movement. The institute provided key financial and logistical support for the Paula Jones lawsuit against President Bill Clinton, and Whitehead served as Jones's cocounsel;
- The Thomas More Law Center (TMLC), established by Ave Maria

School of Law founder Thomas Monaghan. Named after Henry VIII's lord chancellor (and the Catholic patron saint of lawyers), the TMLC is particularly active in litigation opposing same-sex marriage, abortion rights, and pornography. To the dismay of some in the Religious Right, the center has been particularly aggressive in pushing for the teaching of intelligent design.

- The Alliance Defense Fund (the ADF), a pro-religion, anti–gay rights organization that is well funded by a coalition of more than thirty evangelical ministries headed by the Christian leader Dr. James Dobson's Focus on the Family. The ADF is particularly active in promoting public prayer and the display of religious symbols on public property.

Over time, some graduates of the Coburn School of Law and Regent University School of Law have begun to achieve prominence in the fields of law and politics. For instance, Virginia's attorney general, Bob McDonnell, elected in 2005, has both a master's degree and a law degree from Regent University. According to Regent's 2007 spring/summer alumni newsletter, Judge Ronald J. Pahl ('89) reached his tenth year as a member of the Oregon State Circuit Court. The alumni news notes (which advertised an Executive Leadership Series Luncheon with presidential candidate Rudy Giuliani) contained the usual smattering of announcements about new law firms, corporate legal department promotions, and growing families. It also included a brief sentence reporting that Michele Bachmann ('86) "was recently elected to the House seat for Minnesota's Sixth Congressional District."

Bachmann, who actually graduated from Regent's predecessor, Coburn School of Law, was one of the candidates aided by Michael Farris's Generation Joshua program in the 2006 elections. While serving in the Minnesota Senate prior to her election to Congress, she was active on antiabortion issues and was the chief author of a proposed amendment to the state constitution to define marriage as "the union between a man and a woman."

Long ignored by most media outlets, Regent hit the headlines in the spring of 2007, when one of its graduates generated the type of notoriety few law schools seek: a subpoena from the U.S. Congress to testify under oath, and the grant of limited immunity to overcome her announced intention to plead the Fifth. Monica Goodling ('99) was first hired to work in the press office of the U.S. Department of Justice following the election of George W. Bush in 2000. She quickly became deputy director of the department's executive office, which oversees hiring and personnel management, and then was promoted to the position of counsel to the attorney general, where she served as liaison to the White House. In the spring of 2006, Attorney General Alberto Gonzales issued an unsigned order giving Goodling and his chief of staff, Kyle Sampson, the power to hire or fire any political appointee in the Justice Department, apart from U.S. Attorneys (who serve at the pleasure of the president of the United States).

In early December 2006, the Department of Justice abruptly dismissed seven U.S. Attorneys. Their firings cleared the way for interim appointments under controversial provisions of the 2005 Patriot Act. Outraged over the dismissals, Congress opened hearings on the controversy and, during the course of the investigation, learned that Goodling was deeply involved in planning the ousters. She had been scheduled to appear before the House Judiciary Committee on March 26, 2007, but declined to do so, citing the Fifth Amendment. After the Judiciary Committee authorized a limited grant of immunity, Goodling testified before the committee on May 23. During her opening statement she admitted: "I may have gone too far in asking political questions of applicants for career positions and I may have taken inappropriate political considerations into account on some occasions, and I regret those mistakes."

Among the "mistakes" to which Goodling alluded were questions both personal and political: she reportedly asked one jobseeker if "he had ever cheated on his wife," and rejected another as a "liberal Democrat" because he attended Howard University and worked for the Environmental Protection Agency. She also allegedly prepared a spreadsheet detailing each U.S. Attorney's participation (or lack thereof) in conservative political organizations and noted whether they were mem\bers of the Federalist Society, the highly conservative and influential legal fraternity. At the height of the controversy over her hiring practices, the *National Journal* also questioned her interior decorating choices: she was rumored to be the person responsible for committing "statuary drape" in 2002, spending eight thousand dollars on floor-to-ceiling blue drapes to hide the naked aluminum breast of the art deco statue *Spirit of Justice* in the Great Hall of the Department of Justice.

Her rapid rise to a position in which she could ask those questions (and buy those drapes), just eight years after graduating from law school, almost certainly resulted from the close relationship that Bush's first attorney general, John Ashcroft, had with Regent's founder, Pat Robertson. In the spring of 1998, when he was considering his own run for the presidency, Ashcroft gave the commencement address at Regent University, and Robertson said approvingly, "If the Republican Party would give its nomination to John Ashcroft, he'd win the presidency." Earlier in the spring, Robertson had shown his enthusiasm for a possible Ashcroft candidacy by writing a ten-thousand-dollar check to Ashcroft's political action committee. In turn, Ashcroft was an "Inner Circle Sponsor" for the Pat Robertson Seventieth Birthday Celebration in 2000 (although he did not attend the party itself).

Following Bush's election later that fall, he named Ashcroft as attorney general, a move that thrilled his Religious Right supporters. Even more thrilling were the number of Regent-affiliated hires made by the administration. Kay Cole Dean, the former dean of Regent University, was selected to run the Office of Personnel Management (OPM), a position she held for more than four years. During her tenure, over 150 alumni of Regent University and its law school (including Goodling) went to work for the federal government. Attorney Jay Sekulow, the head of Robertson's American Center for Law and Justice, smugly told the *Boston Globe*, "We've had great placement. We've had a lot of people in key positions."

Not surprisingly, the relationship between Regent and the federal government worked both ways. After resigning as attorney general, Ashcroft was given a sinecure at Regent to teach two weeks every semester as a Distinguished Professor of Law and Government. Joining him at Regent was another Bush alumnus, Jim Davids, who currently serves as the assistant dean for administration in the Robertson School of Government. Davids worked in the Bush administration as the deputy director and counsel of the U.S. Department of Justice's Task

Force for the Faith-Based & Community Initiative. According to his biography on the Regent website:

> As Deputy Director, Jim provided guidance on constitutional issues to the White House and the other departmental Offices of Faith-Based & Community Initiatives. In addition, he audited the Department of Justice to determine the barriers faith-based and community organizations faced in participating in DOJ-funded programs, and he monitored cases which impacted the Faith-Based & Community Initiative.

The willingness of Bush appointees like Dean and Goodling to put religious belief before professional competence and objectivity when hiring is first and foremost an indictment of Bush's administration and governance. But as the number of graduates from religiously oriented (particularly evangelical Christian-based) law schools continues to grow, the experiences of the Bush administration offer a warning of just how easily the tools of government can be bent to serve not merely an ideology but a creed, to the detriment of all.

CHAPTER FOUR

Advice and Consent

The Cross-Examination of Supreme Court Nominees

T O PARAPHRASE FORMER SECRETARY OF DEFENSE Donald Rumsfeld, the federal courts decide cases on the basis of the jurisdiction they have, not the jurisdiction the Religious Right wants them to have. And as thirty years of legislative frustration have demonstrated, it is difficult to trim the jurisdiction of the federal courts. A parallel and somewhat easier solution, then, is to change the roster of federal judges exercising that jurisdiction. Recognizing this central fact, the Christian Right has made the appointment of more conservative and sympathetic federal judges a central priority since the founding of the Moral Majority in 1979.

The Religious Right has been remarkably successful in extending its influence from the pulpit to the voting booth, and in gaining access to the highest levels of the Republican Party, both in the White House and in the Senate. But despite those successes, the Christian Right has been frustrated in many of its most precious policy goals: *Roe v. Wade* has not been overturned, prayer has not returned to the public schools, evolution remains the dominant theory for the origins of the human species, and the display of the Ten Commandments in public places is sharply limited. Most significantly, the Right's efforts to reshape the federal judiciary (and especially the Supreme Court) have been largely stymied by the inherent give-and-take of the American political process.

The Constitution is an exquisite system of checks and balances, a governmental structure that rarely delegates power without creating a corresponding brake on its exercise. Fearing potential abuse by a president with unbridled appointment powers, the framers divided the responsibility for appointing justices to the United States Supreme Court between two branches of the new government, the executive and the legislature. Article II, Section 2, Clause 2 of the U.S. Constitution provides that the president "shall nominate, and *by and with the advice and consent of the senate* . . . appoint . . . judges of the supreme court" (emphasis added). But the framers left it to the two branches to sort out the specifics of the confirmation process.

While the framers were unquestionably optimistic and even idealistic in their creation of a new government, no one can fairly describe them as naive. In the summer of 1787, Philadelphia's Independence Hall was filled with seasoned politicians who were sanguine about the motivations of elected officials, and not one person in that sweltering room expected that future presidential appointments in fact would be free of either politics or ideology. By vesting consent in the Senate, the framers anticipated that the president would be forced to balance his personal desires against the diverse concerns of the numerous senators.

Not surprisingly, given the often impressive egos and political ambitions at both ends of Pennsylvania Avenue, it has proven over the years to be an uneasy partnership. Presidents often resent the compromises required to actually get the consent of the Senate, while senators in turn have struggled to strike a balance among various competing concerns, including the demands of their own constituencies, due deference to the president's choice, respect for the Supreme Court as an institution, and their responsibility to function as a coequal branch of government.

But that political tension is precisely what the framers sought. As Alexander Hamilton wrote in *Federalist* No. 76:

To what purpose then require the co-operation of the Senate? I answer, that the necessity of their concurrence would have a powerful, though, in general, a silent operation. It would be an excellent check upon a spirit of favoritism in the President, and would tend greatly to prevent the appointment of unfit characters from State prejudice, from family connection, from personal attachment, or from a view to popularity.

The Senate, at a time when nearly one-third of its members had served in the Constitutional Convention, quickly demonstrated its willingness to reject a Supreme Court nominee on largely political grounds. In the summer of 1795, just six years after the Court was formed, the first chief justice, John Jay, announced that he was retiring from the Court to serve as governor of New York. When the news reached South Carolina, John Rutledge, then chief justice of the South Carolina Supreme Court, wrote to President George Washington and offered his services as Jay's replacement. Washington agreed and gave him a recess appointment, which required confirmation by Congress when it reconvened in December 1795. It was Rutledge's second tour of duty on the Court, a unique honor in American history; he had served as the Supreme Court's first senior associate justice under Jay from 1789 to 1791 before resigning to take the position of South Carolina chief justice.

The burning political issue of 1795 concerned a treaty that Chief Justice Jay had negotiated the year before with England. At the suggestion of Treasury Secretary Alexander Hamilton, Jay's friend and fellow Federalist, President Washington had sent Jay to strike a deal that would ease rising economic tensions between the two nations. Although the so-called Jay Treaty achieved that goal, it largely did so on terms favorable to Federalist interests.

The Anti-Federalists, who had quickly coalesced into a Democratic-Republican Party led by Thomas Jefferson and James Madison, were furious with the agreement, which they felt favored the monarchical Britain over the newly republican France and shortchanged American landowners in favor of the young country's mercantile class. In August 1795, after a bitter yearlong national debate, the Senate barely ratified the treaty by a vote of 20–10—exactly the two-thirds specified in the Constitution. Jay later ruefully remarked that he could have traveled from one end of the country to the other by the light of his burning effigies.

Rutledge arrived in Washington, D.C., to accept his commission as chief justice at the start of the Court's August term, at the height of the debate over the Jay Treaty. The son of South Carolina plantation owners, Rutledge was a conservative politician who strongly defended the practice of slavery, and he was sharply critical of the Jay Treaty's failure to arrange recompense from the British for slaves lost during the Revolutionary War. Before leaving home, Rutledge had denounced the Jay Treaty in a lengthy and impassioned speech at Charleston, South Carolina, on July 16, 1795. Reports of the speech were printed in various Federalist newspapers and Rutledge himself was harshly criticized for his intemperate remarks.

Shortly after the Fourth Congress convened on December 7, 1795, for its first session, Washington formally submitted Rutledge's name for confirmation as chief justice. Given his position on the South Carolina Supreme Court and past U.S. Supreme Court experience, there was no question concerning his legal abilities. But Hamilton, reportedly appalled that his friend and mentor, President Washington, had appointed the Anti-Federalist Rutledge as chief justice, opposed the nomination and helped spread rumors that Rutledge was mentally unsound. Even though the Jay Treaty had been ratified four months earlier, the partisan resentments against Rutledge still ran deep and his nomination was rejected on December 15 by a largely party-line vote of 10–14. Hamilton, it subsequently turned out, was correct: throughout December 1795, Rutledge's mental health had steadily deteriorated, so much so that he tried to drown himself in a pond the day after Christmas. He was rescued, and two days later resigned as chief justice and departed from public life.

While Rutledge's confirmation process is perhaps unique for its poignant end, he is hardly the only Supreme Court nominee that the Senate has rejected for largely political or ideological reasons. In a report prepared for Congress in March 2005, Henry B. Hogue of the Congressional Research Service listed thirty-four Supreme Court nominations that did not receive confirmation by the Senate, beginning with John Rutledge and ending with Robert Bork (two more nominations were withdrawn prior to Senate action in 2005). Of that total, Hogue said, thirteen Supreme Court nominees were not confirmed either entirely or partly due to Senate objections to the nominee's politics or judicial philosophy.

From the Silent Majority to the Moral Majority

The Warren Court, arguably the most politically engaged Court in the nation's history, officially came to an end on June 23, 1969, when Warren Earl Burger replaced Earl Warren as chief justice. Burger was the first appointment by President Richard Nixon, who had won the 1968 presidential election in part by promising to nominate "strict constructionists" to the Supreme Court. It was unusually clear during the election that the winner would have a chance to nominate someone to the Court: Chief Justice Warren had announced his retirement in June 1968, but President Johnson was unable to fill the seat. When Johnson nominated the relatively liberal associate justice Abe Fortas to replace Warren, Senate Republicans and the increasingly conservative Southern Democrats filibustered his nomination. On October 2, 1968, a cloture motion (a call to close debate) failed to get the two-thirds vote required, and Fortas asked Johnson to withdraw his nomination. With just one month until the 1968 election, Johnson did not have time to nominate someone else as chief justice.

Sensitive to concerns about the Warren Court—particularly in the South, where resistance remained strong to the Court's civil rights rulings—Nixon made it clear during the campaign that he intended to appoint someone "who recognizes that it is the role of the Court to interpret the law and to leave to Congress that of writing the law—that's the kind of man I want." Although there was widespread speculation that Nixon planned to promote Associate Justice Potter Stewart, he instead nominated Judge Burger, a member of the Court of Appeals for the District of Columbia. Burger had frequently been critical of the Warren Court's increasingly liberal decisions, particularly in the area of defendant rights, and was widely viewed as precisely the type of strict constructionist Nixon had promised.

After Burger's appointment, Nixon tried to repay his political debt to Southern Democrats by nominating first Clement Haynsworth (a member of the Fourth Circuit Court of Appeals) and then G. Harrold Carswell (a member of the Fifth Circuit). Both were conservative southern judges who were strenuously opposed for their long-standing views on labor and race relations, and both were rejected by the Senate. Stymied, Nixon turned to a childhood friend of Burger's, Harry Blackmun, who was easily confirmed. In 1972 Nixon finally succeeded in appointing a southerner to the Court, Virginian Lewis Powell, who was confirmed at the same time as Arizonan William Rehnquist.

Were it not for Watergate, President Nixon would have had an opportunity to appoint at least one more member of the Court. On December 31, 1974, just four months after Nixon resigned the presidency, Associate Justice William O. Douglas, the nation's longest-serving justice, suffered a stroke while on vacation, and underwent treatment at New York University's Institute for Rehabilitation Medicine. Although questions were quickly raised about Douglas's judgment and ability to handle the Court's workload, Douglas told reporters as late as mid-July, "There's no chance I'll retire. I'll be there in October, positively."

As one of the liberal stalwarts of the Warren Court, Douglas undoubtedly was reluctant to give President Gerald Ford, Nixon's replacement, the opportunity to appoint another conservative justice; as a result of Nixon's four appointments, the Court was appreciably more conservative than it had been under Chief Justice Warren. And Douglas was particularly disinclined to give that opportunity to Ford, who as House minority leader in 1970 had launched an ill-advised and much-ridiculed effort to impeach Douglas for his liberal opinions and other alleged offenses, including authoring an article on folk music that Ford complained "praises the lusty, lurid, and risqué along with the social protest of left-wing folk singers."

It quickly became apparent during the first month of the Court's 1975 term, however, that Douglas would not be able to continue serving, and in a poignant letter to President Ford, he resigned on November 13. "It was my hope when I returned to Washington in September," Douglas said, "that I would be able to continue to participate in the work of the Supreme Court. I have learned, however, after these last two months, that it would be inadvisable for me to attempt to carry on the duties required of a member of the Court. I have been bothered with incessant and demanding pain which depletes my energy to the extent that I have been unable to shoulder my full share of the burden." Despite their previous disagreements, President Ford accepted Douglas's resignation with "profound personal sympathy," and graciously praised his long service on the Court.

Ford sought advice on potential nominees from three members of his administration: Attorney General Edward Levi (who some considered a leading possibility himself); White House counsel Philip Buchen; and White House chief of staff Richard Cheney (he wasn't widely known as "Dick" then), who had taken over from his predecessor, Donald Rumsfeld, on November 5, just one week prior to Douglas's resignation. Although Ford was an accidental president, it was still his responsibility under Article II of the Constitution to nominate Douglas's replacement. His chief problem, as his advisers recognized, was that he did not have a lot of political maneuvering room. Ford's position, of course, was inherently tenuous, but within just weeks of his inauguration, it had become far more fraught. Tapping into voter disgust over the Watergate scandal and Ford's complete pardon of Nixon just two months before the 1974 midterm elections, Democrats picked up forty-nine seats from the Republicans in the House and three seats in the Senate. When the dust had settled, Democrats held a more than two-thirds majority in the House (291–144) and a filibuster-proof margin in the Senate (61–39). Not surprisingly, Ford had more vetoes overridden than any president since the much-beleaguered Andrew Johnson.

Ford's advisers reportedly gave serious consideration to J. Clifford Wallace, a member of the U.S. Court of Appeals for the Ninth Circuit. But in all likelihood, nominating Wallace would have caused a stiff confirmation fight: a devout Mormon, Wallace was well known for his skepticism about the doctrine of the separation of church and state. Some conservative Republicans urged Ford to nominate his solicitor general, Robert Bork, but the consensus was that Bork's notorious role in the so-called October 1973 Saturday Night Massacre—carrying out Nixon's order to fire Watergate prosecutor Archibald Cox after Attorney General Elliot Richardson and Deputy Attorney General William Ruckelshaus resigned in protest—would make confirmation difficult, if not impossible. Instead, Levi, Buchen, and Cheney recommended that Ford nominate John Paul Stevens, a fifty-five-year-old member of the U.S. Court of Appeals for the Seventh Circuit with extensive experience as an antitrust litigator.

If the goal was to minimize the likelihood of a difficult confirmation fight, then the selection of Stevens was canny. His nomination was greeted warmly by members of both parties, and Senator Edward M. Kennedy (D-Mass.), one of the Senate's most liberal members, expressed a common sentiment when he described the nomination as "a really quality appointment the president has made." Ironically, given Justice Stevens's near-record-setting tenure on the Court since, the main concern raised by the Senate Judiciary Committee was his health; a few years prior to his nomination, Stevens had had open-heart surgery, but he assured the committee that he had made a complete recovery.

Remarkably, despite the fact that the landmark *Roe v. Wade* decision had been handed down just eighteen months earlier, the abortion issue received no attention at all from the Senate Judiciary Committee. Over the course of three days of confirmation hearings held in early December 1975, not one single senator asked Judge Stevens about his views on either abortion or *Roe v. Wade*. In fact, the word "abortion" only came up once, in testimony by Margaret Drachsler of the National Organization for Women (NOW). Drachsler told the committee that NOW was strongly opposed to Stevens's confirmation and believed that his published decisions reflected a "record of antagonism to women's rights." As happens so often with nominees of the Court, however, it is unlikely that NOW would raise similar concerns about Stevens today. Similarly, it is hard to imagine that Vice President Dick Cheney looks back on the selection of Stevens as one of his more successful official acts.

Insufficient Payoff: The Reagan Nominees

Six years later, when Justice Potter Stewart unexpectedly announced that he was retiring (he was just sixty-six at the time and in good health), the political and cultural landscape had changed considerably. Thanks in part to the efforts of the Moral Majority (exactly how much so was a subject of some debate), his replacement would be selected by Ronald Reagan, a much more conservative Republican president than

Gerald Ford. Even more importantly, Reagan would be asking the advice and consent of a Republican Senate. Of course, the last time that had happened, in the fall of 1953, President Eisenhower sent to the Republican Senate the name of California governor Earl Warren.

But this was not the same type of Republican Senate. The change in the Senate power structure was most notable in the influential Senate Judiciary Committee. The Democratic chair who presided over the decorous Stevens hearings, Missouri's James Eastland, had retired in 1978, and when the Republicans took over in 1981, Senator Strom Thurmond of South Carolina was chosen as chair. The committee also featured several new Republican members, including three very conservative senators who were part of the Reagan–Moral Majority tidal wave in 1980: John P. East of North Carolina, Charles E. Grassley of Iowa, and Jeremiah Denton of Alabama. All three had taken strong pro-life, anti-*Roe* positions during their campaigns, and had received substantial support from state Moral Majority chapters. While understanding that the new appointee would not be able to single-handedly overturn *Roe* (since the departing Stewart was just one of seven votes in the majority of that case), the Religious Right eagerly anticipated that Reagan's nomination would be the first step toward the promised land.

But the Moral Majority and its supporters were about to discover that their champion had other concerns besides keeping his most ardent and demanding constituents happy. During the course of the campaign, Reagan had essentially promised that he would rectify a long-standing omission by appointing the first woman to serve on the Supreme Court, and it was clear that he intended to keep that promise. Although a number of prominent women were mentioned as possible candidates, few predicted the actual nominee: Sandra Day O'Connor, a member of the Arizona Court of Appeals.

Reagan and O'Connor shared some superficial similarities—both loved the West and were probably happier on horseback than in a motorcade—but those qualities alone would hardly have brought her to the Supreme Court without the active support of Arizona's senior senator, Barry Goldwater. The weight of Goldwater's opinion can be seen in the fact that O'Connor was the only person Reagan interviewed, and he made up his mind after talking to her for just one hour.

Reagan's Christian Right supporters were, to put it mildly, irate. Conservative direct-mail expert Richard Viguerie told the *New York Times* that the White House rushed O'Connor's nomination to quell rising opposition over her allegedly pro-abortion stance, and others accused Reagan of betraying the 1980 Republican Party platform, which called for the appointment of judges who "respect ... the sanctity of innocent human life." Moral Majority leader Jerry Falwell said that the White House was either uninformed about O'Connor's legislative record or willfully ignorant. He also said that every good Christian should be concerned about the nomination, which prompted the increasingly crusty Senator Goldwater to suggest that "every good Christian ought to kick Falwell in the ass."

"I am probably one of the most conservative members of Congress," Goldwater said to a *Washington Post* reporter, "and I don't like to get kicked around by people who call themselves conservatives on a non-conservative matter. It is a question of who is best for the court. If it is going to be a fight in the Senate, you are going to find Old Goldy fighting like hell."

Thanks to the seismic shift that had occurred in American politics, O'Connor had the dubious privilege of being the first Supreme Court nominee to be extensively grilled on her attitudes regarding abortion. By far the most aggressive questioner was the freshman senator from Alabama, Jeremiah Denton. By agreement, each senator was supposed to have two fifteen-minute sessions to question O'Connor, but Denton requested and was granted an additional half hour to press O'Connor on her voting record on abortion-related legislation, her personal views on the subject, and her attitude toward the Supreme Court's decision in *Roe v. Wade.*

Denton focused much of his questioning of O'Connor on a memorandum written by Kenneth Starr, whose investigation of President Bill Clinton and White House intern Monica Lewinsky would make him a household name in later years, but at the time was working in the Justice Department as counselor for Attorney General William French Smith. As part of the administration's background investigation into O'Connor, Starr had called her in early July to discuss various abortion-related issues and had summarized his conversations in the memorandum. Of particular concern to the Religious Right, as Denton pointed out, was the fact that the Starr memo made no mention of a vote O'Connor took in April 1974 opposing the passage of a bill in the Arizona legislature that would have petitioned Congress to pass a human life amendment to outlaw abortion in all cases except when the mother's life was in danger.

Similarly, antiabortion activists took grave exception to the closing line of the Starr memo, which stated, "[O'Connor] knows well the Arizona leader of the right-to-life movement, a prominent female physician in Phoenix, and has never had any disputes or controversies with her." The physician in question, Dr. Carolyn F. Gerster, who lived in the same community as O'Connor in the Scottsdale–Paradise Valley area of Arizona, later testified before the Judiciary Committee and strongly opposed her confirmation.

O'Connor made it clear that she was not trying to suggest to Starr that she necessarily agreed with Dr. Gerster: "What I am trying to reflect is that because I may have voted differently than Dr. Gerster would have, had she been a legislator, does not mean that we were adversaries." Her response left Denton unsatisfied: "It has been represented or perceived by many that that memorandum, which many understand to have been the principal input to the president regarding your record, you might say is a bit optimistic from the standpoint of those who are pro-life in its characterization of your record. That is why I brought it forward." But Chairman Thurmond admonished Senator Denton for his persistence on the issue, saying, "We, the members of this committee, will determine her fitness for this position and not the method by which the president went about making his selection. That was his business, not ours."

In the end, there was little that Denton could do to elicit more specific answers from O'Connor on how she might handle cases involving abortion. At the end of his questioning, Denton expressed his frustration: "My only problem," he told O'Connor, "is that I do not feel I have made any progress personally in determining where you stand on the issue of abortion."

It is highly ironic that O'Connor's refusal to answer questions about how she would rule on specific topics, which so frustrated the conservative Denton, was suggested to her by another future Supreme Court nominee, who would later use the tactic himself to frustrate senators on the other end of the political spectrum. On the eve of her confirmation hearings, a young Justice Department lawyer named John Roberts—then a senior aide to Attorney General Smith—advised O'Connor that answering any such questions would create "an appearance of impropriety." Roberts and another Justice Department colleague, Carolyn Kuhl, also assisted O'Connor in politely rejecting a demand by Senator Jesse Helms for a statement of her views on *Roe v. Wade.*

The "appearance of impropriety" strategy that Roberts recommended worked perfectly; regardless of whatever lingering reservations that Denton or Helms might have had, O'Connor was confirmed by the Senate on September 21, 1981, by a vote of 99–0. When his memorandum to O'Connor surfaced during his own confirmation hearings twenty-four years later, Roberts was acknowledged as the architect of a policy that has substantially, if not totally, reduced the Senate's ability to effectively advise and consent.

Members of the Religious Right who were upset by the appointment of Justice O'Connor were somewhat mollified in 1986, when President Reagan successfully nominated Justice William Rehnquist to replace Chief Justice Warren Burger, and then nominated Antonin Scalia to take Rehnquist's slot. Having fulfilled his campaign pledge to appoint a female justice, Reagan was ready and even eager to reward his disappointed supporters. These were precisely the types of appointments the Christian Right expected Reagan to make: Rehnquist was an established conservative commodity on the Court, and Scalia is one of the nation's leading proponents of originalism, a judicial doctrine that is used to interpret legislation (including the Constitution) according to the "ordinary meaning" of words in use at the time the legislation was adopted. In particular, originalists reject the concept of a "living Constitution" or the identification of new rights (most notably, the right to privacy) that are not specifically spelled out in the Constitution.

Despite some loudly expressed liberal objections, both nominees were confirmed for their respective positions in late September 1986:

Scalia received the unanimous support of the Senate, while Rehnquist was confirmed by a comfortable if somewhat more skeptical margin, 65–33. In both instances, Reagan was greatly aided by the obvious intellectual capabilities of the two candidates and the fact that Republicans still controlled the Senate and therefore the confirmation process.

The timing of their appointments was not happenstance, and perfectly illustrates the fact that Supreme Court justices occasionally act out of political considerations themselves. In the spring of 1986, Chief Justice Burger announced his intention to step down on June 17; the primary reason for Burger's retirement was his plan to work full-time as chair of the upcoming bicentennial celebration for the United States Constitution in 1987. But as the *Washington Post*'s David Broder later pointed out, the timing of Burger's decision made it possible for confirmation proceedings for his replacement to take place while the Republicans still controlled the Senate, something that opinion polls strongly suggested would not be true after the 1986 midterm elections.

And in fact, that's precisely what happened. The Democrats picked up a remarkable eight Senate seats in the election, including the seat held by Alabama's Jeremiah Denton, and emerged with a 55–45 majority. When Justice Lewis Powell, widely regarded as one of the moderate members of the Court (and part of the *Roe* majority), announced that he was retiring in the summer of 1987, President Reagan found himself in a much more difficult political situation than he had been the year before. Nonetheless, he pressed ahead with long-standing plans to nominate Judge Robert H. Bork, whom he had earlier appointed to serve on the influential U.S. Court of Appeals for the D.C. Circuit. According to conservative columnists Rowland Evans and Robert Novak, Reagan's advisers had been divided between Scalia and Bork as a replacement for Rehnquist's associate justice slot in 1986, but ultimately gave the nod to Scalia due to his age (nearly a decade younger than Bork) and the public relations benefit of nominating the first Italian American to the Court.

It is certainly possible, if not likely, that if the order of their nominations had been reversed, both Bork and Scalia would be on the Court today. With his decades of teaching and academic writing, numerous and highly conservative judicial opinions, and outspoken opposition to both *Roe v. Wade* and the fundamental right to privacy on which it is based, Bork would have fared far better with a Republican-controlled Senate. Instead, he appeared before a Senate Judiciary Committee led by Senator Joe Biden (D-Del.) and controlled by some of the chamber's most liberal Democrats: Ted Kennedy, Robert Byrd of West Virginia, Howard Metzenbaum of Ohio, Patrick Leahy of Vermont, and Paul Simon of Illinois. There was no question how the liberal wing of the Democratic Party viewed the sixty-year-old Judge Bork. Within an hour of his introduction as President Reagan's next nominee, Senator Kennedy gave a speech on the Senate floor that denounced the appointment, in language that is disturbingly prescient of where the Court is slowly drifting even without Bork's presence on the Court for the last twenty years:

> Robert Bork's America is a land in which women would be forced into back-alley abortions, blacks would sit at segregated lunch counters, rogue police could break down citizens' doors in midnight raids, schoolchildren could not be taught about evolution, writers and artists could be censored at the whim of government.

Kennedy's speech was merely the opening salvo in what can only be described as an epic confirmation battle. The Senate Judiciary Committee heard fifteen days (and some nights) of testimony from dozens of witnesses and Judge Bork himself testified over five grueling days.

Leading the charge against Bork outside of the Senate was People for the American Way (PFAW), a relatively new liberal advocacy group founded by Hollywood producer Norman Lear, best known for his television shows *All in the Family* and *Maude*. Originally founded to defend against efforts to ban books and censor textbooks, PFAW was inspired to focus on the judicial nomination process when President Reagan floated the possibility in early 1985 of appointing Herbert Ellingwood as assistant attorney general and giving him primary responsibility for selecting judicial nominees.

Consideration of Ellingwood was one of the more blatant attempts by Reagan to reward his supporters in the Religious Right. At the time,

Ellingwood was serving as chair of the Merit Systems Protection Board (the civil service's top review panel), and reports quickly emerged that he was actively collaborating with the American Coalition for Traditional Values (ACTV) and its president, Timothy LaHaye (author of the Left Behind series), to "flood the bureaucracy with Christians." Curtis Maynard, ACTV's executive director, told reporters that when Ellingwood learned of vacancies, he provided the information to ACTV, and then helped guide reliably Christian applicants to the front of the line. ACTV was enthusiastic about the possibility that Ellingwood could do for the judiciary what he was doing for the civil service.

Following PFAW's publicity campaign and an investigation into civil service hiring practices by Representative Patricia Schroeder (D-Colo.), Ellingwood's nomination was withdrawn. The following year, the group was also successful in helping to defeat the nomination of Jeff Sessions, a conservative Alabama lawyer, to the U.S. District Court. In Sessions's case, the victory was only temporary: in 1995, he was elected to the U.S. Senate, replacing Howard Heflin, the Democrat who cast the deciding vote against him in the Senate Judiciary Committee. Sessions later became a member of the Judiciary Committee, making him the first person to join that body after being questioned by it.

PFAW devoted enormous resources to the campaign against Bork, including a controversial ad campaign on television and in the newspapers. Thanks to Lear's Hollywood connections, various actors volunteered to appear in PFAW ads. The one that generated the most controversy opened with a shot of a young white family on the steps of the United States Supreme Court, and featured the narration of actor Gregory Peck, most famous for his depiction of the principled lawyer Atticus Finch in the film version of Harper Lee's *To Kill a Mockingbird*:

Robert Bork wants to be a Supreme Court justice. But the record shows he has a strange idea of what justice is. He defended poll taxes and literacy tests, which kept many Americans from voting. He opposed the civil rights law that ended "whites only" signs at lunch

counters. He doesn't believe the Constitution protects your privacy.
. . . Please urge your senators to vote against the Bork nomination.
Because, if Robert Bork wins a seat on the Supreme Court, it will
be for life. His life . . . and yours.

White House spokesman Marlin Fitzwater strenuously denied that
Bork's confirmation would cost Americans their freedoms and added,
"Gregory Peck ought to be ashamed." Reagan, a former actor himself,
suggested that Peck had been "miscast." Bork reportedly asked Reagan
administration officials to help coordinate a supportive advertising
campaign in response, but eventually changed his mind, concluding that
the whole idea was unseemly.

In any case, neither the White House nor its Religious Right supporters were in a position to be much help. After naming Bork as his
nominee in early July 1987, President Reagan took an extended vacation
on his ranch in Santa Barbara, undermining any sense of urgency about
Bork's nomination to the point that one anonymous White House official said the Bork nomination "was lost on the beaches of California."
Although some Christian Right groups were active in their support for
Bork, such as Tim LaHaye's ACTV and Beverly LaHaye's Concerned
Women for America, the credibility of the movement as a whole had
been badly damaged by the recent fraud and sex scandals of Jim Bakker
and Jimmy Swaggart. The Christian Right's most visible leader at the
time, Jerry Falwell, was consumed with trying to run the Bakker's PTL
empire and his own sprawling enterprise, and was just a few months
away from stepping down as the leader of the Moral Majority. And
above all, there were the reams of Bork writings that expressed profound skepticism for many of the Supreme Court's most significant
rulings over the last half century. Despite Bork's repeated disavowals of
his most outrageous positions, which Senator Leahy derisively dismissed as a "confirmation conversion," the collective weight of his own
words was simply too great to overcome.

From the Religious Right's perspective, the failure to effectively rally
behind Bork was costly. Following the judge's rejection, Reagan famously growled that he would nominate someone "they'll object to as
much as they did to this one." His pick, Douglas Ginsburg, met that cri-

teria: at forty-one years old, he was a startlingly young member of the U.S. Court of Appeals for the D.C. Circuit, and he was described by Senator Kennedy as an "ideological clone" of Judge Bork. But Ginsburg's nomination to the high court lasted just a week, foundering on reports that while a professor at Harvard Law School, he smoked marijuana with some of his students.

Rapidly running out of time to successfully nominate anyone to the vacancy on the Court, Reagan then selected Anthony Kennedy, a relatively moderate member of the infamously liberal Court of Appeals for the Ninth Circuit. Although Senator Jesse Helms reportedly said "No way, Jose" when Kennedy's name was first raised, he reportedly changed his mind after meeting the judge. At Kennedy's confirmation hearing, Senate Judiciary chair Joe Biden asked Judge Kennedy to clarify comments published by the conservative syndicated columnist Cal Thomas, who was a vice president in the Moral Majority from 1980 to 1985. Hoping to offer assurances of Judge Kennedy's reliability, Thomas described Senator Helms's summary of a conversation that the senator allegedly had with the judge prior to the confirmation hearings:

> I am as certain as I can be, without having heard him say I shall vote to reverse *Roe v. Wade*—which of course he wasn't going to say— on what he called this "privacy garbage"—recent Supreme Court decisions involving not only abortion but civil rights, protection for homosexuals—Mr. Helms indicated a certain collegiality with what he believes to be Judge Kennedy's views.

Judge Kennedy told Senator Biden, "It would be highly improper for a judge to allow his, or her, own personal or religious views to enter into a decision respecting a constitutional matter," and said that in his view, Thomas's account of his conversation with Senator Helms was incorrect.

Kennedy's smooth handling of that minor flap was an accurate preview of his deft handling of three days of testimony, all of which was far less hostile than what Judge Bork faced. Even though much of the Religious Right was unenthusiastic about Reagan's nomination, there was little they could do to prevent his confirmation, as Kennedy gathered support from across the spectrum and was confirmed unanimously in February 1988.

A "Stealth Candidate" and a "High-Tech Lynching"

Reagan had barely been reelected in 1984 when Republican activists began looking toward the next election. In particular, the Religious Right was eager to build on its political gains over the past five years. Although the movement had not gotten everything it hoped from President Reagan, the future seemed bright (the Bork/Ginsburg/Kennedy debacle still lay in the future). Some activists boldly predicted that the GOP's 1988 nominee actually would be chosen by the Religious Right; at the very least, evangelicals said that they would be able to deny the nomination to three possibilities: "George, Bob, and Howard," or Vice President Bush, Senate majority leader Dole, and former Senate majority leader Baker.

The Christian Right's antagonism to George H. W. Bush was particularly long-standing. His brand of tweedy New England Republicanism had never played well among evangelicals, and most had strenuously opposed his selection as vice president; the fact that Reagan offered the lower half of the ticket to him anyway was the movement's first sign that the Reagan administration might be both more mainstream and less tractable than it had expected. Reagan himself did not help matters by dispatching Bush to Houston the week after the election to issue a polite but firm message to Christian conservatives, who were already agitating for a hard line on abortion and school prayer. Bush perhaps did his job too well: "I take violent exception to certain individuals in some of these groups, some of their positions, and have stated it publicly and am not intimidated by those who suggest I better hew the line. Hell with them."

When the time came to replace Associate Justice William Brennan in the summer of 1990, with Bush in office, the Religious Right found that it lacked the level of access to the White House that had made it such a force during the Reagan administration. Although they were cheered by Brennan's departure—conservative columnist Patrick

Buchanan described it as a sad day for "all pornographers, go-go dancers, flag burners, and criminals looking for a hook to escape justice"—there was widespread concern about whether Bush's nominee, Judge David Souter of the First Circuit Court of Appeals, would be sufficiently reliable on the issue of abortion. It was clear, at least to Buchanan, that Souter (dubbed the "stealth justice") was selected in large part because "he had left no 'paper trail' to follow, no body of writing or list or opinions liberals could use to indict him as pro-life." Although Buchanan, ever the pitchfork waver, hungered for a Bork-like confirmation battle, Bush clearly did not, and with his reelection campaign still two years away, he obviously felt that it was more important to avoid a divisive confirmation battle than to cater to the demands of the conservative wing of his party.

Still, in the weeks following Souter's selection, Bush tried to reassure the Religious Right about Souter's views. In late July 1990, Pat McGuigan, the legal affairs analyst for Coalitions for America, an umbrella organization of conservative action groups founded by longtime activist Paul Weyrich, complained to Bush's chief of staff, John Sununu, that the appointment of Souter was a "blooper single which has barely cleared the mitt of the first baseman." Sununu, the often-gruff New Hampshire governor who had appointed Souter to the state supreme court and recommended him as Brennan's replacement, told McGuigan not to worry and that for conservatives, the nomination of Souter was a "home run, and the ball is still ascending." McGuigan wrote a confidential memo about his exchange with Sununu, which not surprisingly was leaked to the press prior to the confirmation hearings.

Much like Justice Kennedy, Souter was questioned about whether he had made any promises of specific votes to President Bush or his aides, and he took pains to reassure the Judiciary Committee that he had not done so. In particular, he reassured the committee that he was open-minded on the subject of abortion, something that gave little comfort to nervous conservatives. Additional conservative hackles were raised when Souter avoided repeated opportunities to criticize the Warren Court and its rulings, and praised the retiring Justice Brennan as "one of the most fearlessly principled guardians of the American Constitution that it has ever had and ever will have." It is expected that a nominee will say polite things about the justice he or she is replacing, but most conservatives, particularly those of the Christian Right, found Souter's words disturbingly fulsome.

The political situation was entirely different the following year, when the near-legendary associate justice Thurgood Marshall announced his retirement in June 1991. With the start of the primary season just six months away, Bush could not afford to ignore his already skeptical conservative base. And according to columnists Rowland Evans and Robert Novak, the Bush White House felt that its success in "slipping Souter onto the Court without being forced by Democrats to give his views on abortion" meant that the president could take the political risk of nominating someone more openly antiabortion. After considering conservative favorite Judge Edith Jones of the Fifth Circuit Court of Appeals for the second time (she was runner-up to Justice Souter the year before) and several Hispanic judges, President Bush finally settled on forty-three-year-old Clarence Thomas, whom Bush had nominated to serve on the Court of Appeals for the D.C. Circuit just the year before. While introducing Thomas to reporters in Kennebunkport, Maine, at the Bush family's famous home, the president said that Thomas was "the best person at the right time."

For the Religious Right and conservatives in general, that was arguably true. There was little question that Bush, by replacing Marshall with Thomas, was substantially shifting the ideological balance of the Court to the right. Thomas was particularly well known for his opposition to affirmative action programs, specifically those with race-based quotas or other minority preferences. His views on the controversial subjects of abortion and a right to privacy were less clear, however, although he repeatedly told the Senate Judiciary Committee during his confirmation hearings that he had not formulated any opinion as to the correctness of *Roe v. Wade* or the deference it should be shown under the principle of stare decisis. Many senators were openly skeptical of Thomas's answers on that point, particularly in light of reports that he had once given a speech in which he praised the idea that all fetuses have an "inalienable right to life." Thomas frustrated some conservative supporters by distancing himself from his earlier positions during the hearings, but the tactic made it more difficult for many senators, and in particular Southern Democrats, to vote against him.

On September 27, 1991, the Senate Judiciary Committee refused to endorse his nomination by a vote of 7–7, but sent his nomination to the full Senate for a vote, which most observers believed he would win by a slim margin. Just before the Senate was scheduled to vote, however, National Public Radio's Nina Totenberg broke the news of Professor Anita Hill's sexual harassment charges against Thomas, who was Hill's supervisor at the Equal Employment Opportunity Commission. In the uproar following Totenberg's report, the Senate sent Thomas's nomination back to the Judiciary Committee for additional hearings, made famous in part by Thomas's description of the process as a "high-tech lynching." In the end, the allegations did not change the outcome significantly: Thomas was confirmed on October 15 by a vote of 52–48, the narrowest margin in more than a century.

The Anita Hill–Clarence Thomas controversy was obviously an enormously significant historical moment in its own right; it served to highlight the ineffectiveness of the Senate and the increasingly empty puffery of its confirmation role, as well as deeply challenging issues of gender and sexual harassment in the workplace. But it also is significant for the tremendous spur that it gave to conservative groups. Among the most important was the *American Spectator*, a highly conservative magazine funded in large part by multimillionaire Richard Mellon Scaife, who for the last forty years has been one of the leading contributors to some of the nation's most conservative organizations, including the Heritage Foundation and the Federalist Society. Freelance writer David Brock (who would later found the website Media Matters) wrote a highly critical article of Anita Hill for the magazine, and then published a very successful, albeit extremely mean-spirited book in the spring of 1992 called *The Real Anita Hill* (which he later recanted).

During the first term of President Bill Clinton, Scaife donated more than $2 million to the *American Spectator* to support research by Brock and others into Clinton's alleged affairs and other misdeeds in Arkansas. It was Brock's subsequent article, "Troopergate," that contained the first reference to Paula Jones, a reference that led her to file the sexual harassment lawsuit against Clinton that ultimately led to his impeachment in December 1998. After Jones's first two attorneys withdrew from the case, she was represented in part by John Whitehead, the founder of the Rutherford Institute, a law firm and advocacy group with strong ties to the Christian Reconstruction movement.

The Sins of the Father: "No More Souters"

For the Religious Right, the issue of judicial nominations during the 2000 presidential election boiled down to one simple slogan: "No More Souters." The muted but fervent rallying cry—only a small handful of mainstream media stories mentioned it during the campaign—stemmed from the deep disappointment and even sense of betrayal that legal conservatives and the Christian Right felt in Associate Justice David Souter's increasingly solid identification with the liberal wing of the Court. As conservative columnist Robert Novak put it: "It is impossible to measure the impact of the Souter fiasco on the Republican Party. Far more than his capitulation on taxes, the presidency of George Bush is damned by the lifetime tenure of one of the Supreme Court's most liberal justices ever shaping the nation's history."

For a period of time during the 2000 election campaign, Governor George W. Bush, son of the former President Bush, attempted to finesse the issue of judicial nominations, simply saying that he planned to appoint judges who would be "strict constructionists." That phrase had been standard stump speech boilerplate for Republican nominees ever since Richard Nixon, who was the first to make judicial activism a campaign theme. But rote promises to nominate strict constructionists were insufficiently reassuring for Religious Right activists, who demanded more concrete examples of the type of people Bush planned to nominate to the Court.

In a brief July 1999 article in the *Weekly Standard*, the conservative journal founded by Fred Barnes and William Kristol (Vice President Dan Quayle's former chief of staff), Barnes said that Bush had cited Justice Antonin Scalia as the type of judge he would like to appoint. "I have great respect for Justice Scalia," Bush told Barnes, "for the strength of his mind, the consistency of his convictions, and the judicial philosophy he defends." The specific reference to Scalia helped calm the fears of Christian conservatives and reassured them that Bush (and his advisers) understood the importance of the issue.

Not long after Bush's controversial election, he held a White House ceremony to introduce his first group of appeals court nominees. It was a startlingly divisive list for a president recently elected by just 537 votes in Florida, and single votes in both the electoral college and the Supreme Court. Ralph Neas of People for the American Way said that nine of the nominees could be relied on "to move the courts solidly to the right," while Clint Bolick, the head of the conservative Institute for Justice, called them "the most distinguished group of nominees ever put forward at one time." Included in President Bush's East Room introductions were a number of names that would become familiar to Americans over the next few years:

- John G. Roberts, a Washington-area attorney who had previously worked in the Justice Department and as deputy solicitor general under Kenneth Starr, nominated to the D.C. Circuit;
- U.S. District Court Judge Terrence Boyle, a former aide to conservative senator Jesse Helms, nominated to the Fourth Circuit;
- Miguel Estrada, a partner in the law firm that represented President Bush in the Supreme Court over the contested Florida recount, nominated to the D.C. Circuit;
- U.S. District Court Judge Edith Brown Clement, nominated to the Fifth Circuit;
- Texas Supreme Court Justice Priscilla Richman Owen, also nominated to the Fifth Circuit;
- University of Utah law professor Michael McConnell, nominated to the Tenth Circuit.

When Bush introduced his first group of nominees, the Republicans held a tenuous majority in the Senate; the chamber was evenly split, 50–50, but Vice President Cheney gave the GOP the deciding vote. Just two weeks later, liberal Republican Jim Jeffords of Vermont announced that he was leaving the party to become an Independent; in exchange for chairmanship of the Senate Environment and Public Works

Committee, he agreed to vote with the Democrats on procedural matters, giving the Democrats effective control of the Senate. Chairmanship of the Senate Judiciary Committee changed from Orrin Hatch
(R-Utah) to Patrick Leahy (D-Vt.), and although the vast majority of
President Bush's nominees were confirmed, the committee declined to
hold hearings on or rejected a handful of the most conservative nominees, including Miguel Estrada, Carolyn Kuhl, Janice Rogers Brown,
Charles Pickering, and William Pryor.

Just eighteen months later, however, Republicans retook control of
the Senate in the 2002 midterm elections and began moving Bush's de-
layed nominations once again through the Judiciary Committee, now
back under the control of Senator Hatch. Lacking any other mechanism to delay or stop the nominations, Democrats resorted to the filibuster, a threat of unlimited debate, to prevent votes on the nominees
by the full Senate. In February 2003 Estrada became the first appeals
court nominee to be filibustered, and was quickly followed by Pryor,
Pickering, and Owen.

The move outraged Republicans, so much so that they gave serious
consideration to a proposal by Senator Ted Stevens (R-Alaska) to or-
chestrate a complicated vote under the Senate rules to declare the use
of filibusters unconstitutional by a simple majority, rather than the 60
percent required to formally end a filibuster (also known as a cloture
vote). Stevens made the suggestion shortly after the filibuster of Estrada
began, and in a nod to the radioactive green figure on the senator's
tie that day, Republican staffers gave the proposal a code name: "the
Hulk." Some weeks later, Senator Trent Lott (R.-Mo.) raised the stakes
by describing the parliamentary maneuver to declare the practice of
filibusters unconstitutional as "the nuclear option." Ever image conscious, some Republicans later tried to change Lott's slogan to "the
constitutional option," but the more provocative name has stuck.

During the Estrada filibuster, the new Senator majority leader,
Bill Frist (R-Tenn.), told conservatives at a luncheon hosted by Paul
Weyrich that he did not have the votes to invoke the nuclear option, but
promised to do so if the 2004 election went well for Republicans. In
the meantime, Frist scheduled an all-night session of the Senate in November 2003 in an effort to break the Democratic filibuster of the ju-

dicial nominees, and dramatically rolled cots into the Capitol so that Republicans could catch a few winks in the wee hours. But at the end of the long session, the cloture vote to end the various judicial filibusters failed to garner the three-fifths, or sixty, votes required.

The Republicans did do well in the 2004 election, winning six previously Democratic seats (five of which were in the Deep South) and losing just two Republican seats, which gave them a 55–44–1 edge in the 109th Congress. Something else had changed as well: one week before the election, Chief Justice William Rehnquist announced that he had cancer, raising the very real possibility that a vacancy would occur shortly on the Supreme Court. The White House began pushing Republicans in the Senate, and in particular, Majority Leader Frist, to do whatever was necessary to bring the Democratic filibusters to an end.

In December 2004, as a goad to Frist and the other Senate Republicans, President Bush renominated a number of people previously blocked by the Democrats, including Terrence Boyle, Patricia Richman Owen, William Pryor, and Janice Rogers Brown. No longer on the list were Miguel Estrada, who withdrew his nomination in 2003, and Charles Pickering, who announced that he would retire in December after receiving a temporary recess appointment by Bush the previous January. Nonetheless, Democrats were outraged by Bush's stubbornness: "The Bush administration is ending the year as they began it," Senator Leahy said in a statement, "choosing confrontation over compromise, ideology over moderation, and defiance over cooperation."

Angered by the refusal of state and federal courts to intervene to block the state court order allowing Michael Schiavo to disconnect the feeding tube for his brain-injured wife, Terri, the Religious Right was also putting tremendous pressure on Frist to end the filibusters. Frist had already announced that he was exploring a run for president in 2008, and religious activists made it clear that their enthusiasm for his candidacy would be linked in large part to his success in getting President Bush's nominees onto the bench. At the height of the filibuster controversy in April 2005, Senator Frist appeared by videotape at Justice Sunday, a religious conference organized by James Dobson's Focus on the Family (FOF), and FOF's advocacy group, the Family Research Council, led by Tony Perkins. Although Frist's remarks were studiously secular, he was still widely criticized for participating, even remotely, in a religious-based attack on the Supreme Court and the federal judiciary.

Less than a month later, matters came to a head in the Senate. A cloture vote was scheduled for Tuesday, May 24, 2005, on the nomination of Judge Priscilla Richman Owen to serve on the Fifth Circuit. It was widely anticipated that the cloture vote would fail, and that the Senate Republicans would then take the steps to declare filibusters unconstitutional. On the eve of the vote, however, fourteen senators (seven from each party) formed the "Gang of 14" and struck an agreement to avoid the deployment of the nuclear option. Under the terms of the agreement, the Gang of 14 agreed to support a cloture vote for Janice Rogers Brown (D.C. Circuit), William Pryor (Eleventh Circuit), and Priscilla Owen (Fifth Circuit), all of whom were subsequently confirmed by narrow margins. The senators also agreed that they would only support filibusters of future nominees under "extraordinary circumstances," and would oppose the implementation of the nuclear option. The agreement by the Gang of 14 was harshly criticized by partisans on both sides of the aisle, but it did succeed in at least temporarily defusing the judicial nomination controversy in the Senate.

The lingering question, of course, was whether the agreement by the Gang of 14 would survive the crucible of a Supreme Court nomination. The answer came quickly: Associate Justice Sandra Day O'Connor announced her retirement just one month later, giving President Bush his first opportunity to nominate someone to the Supreme Court. For the Religious Right, appellate judgeships were important, but this was the test of their patient support of "their" president, the man who once told the conservative *Washington Times* that he could not imagine anyone serving in the Oval Office "without a relationship with the Lord." As James Dobson told *Time* magazine in February 2005: "At the very top of the list is the judiciary, which we feel is out of control and threatening to religious liberty and to the institution of the family. That would be the most important thing to us because every other issue that we care about is linked, one way or another, to the courts."

There were widespread reports that Bush was thinking seriously about nominating Attorney General Alberto Gonzales, which would make him the first Hispanic on the Court if confirmed. While various groups in the Religious Right were split on who should be nominated, they were united in one belief: that Gonzales should not be chosen. "The only nomination that would cause the people that I really associate with consternation would be Gonzales," Michael Farris, president of Patrick Henry College, told the *Washington Post.* "I don't think many people in the socially conservative movement would openly oppose him, but the enthusiasm would be sufficiently dampened to the point that many would not participate."

Among the potential nominees most commonly cited by Christian Right groups like Focus on the Family and the Christian Legal Society were Samuel Alito and Janice Rogers Brown, both of the D.C. Circuit; Edith Brown Clement and Edith Hollan Jones, both of the Fifth Circuit; J. Michael Luttig, of the Fourth Circuit; and Michael McConnell, of the Tenth Circuit. Each had extensive right-leaning credentials and a long list of reliably conservative decisions on the bench that could be cited to reassure the faithful that he or she was not another closet Souter.

Ultimately, Bush settled on Judge John Roberts of the D.C. Circuit. Roberts had been mentioned by some conservative groups, but with some muted enthusiasm, since his philosophical positions were not well known. The subsequent release of fifteen thousand documents from his work as a government lawyer, however, helped to calm conservative fears; to build further support among the Christian Right, the Bush White House recruited Jay Sekulow, head of Pat Robertson's American Center for Law and Justice, to make the rounds. Robertson himself told viewers of *The 700 Club,* his long-running televangelist show, that Roberts had been in the "top 20" of the list of judges compiled by Sekulow and the ACLJ. Tony Perkins said that he was ecstatic with Bush's choice. "The president promised us a judge along the lines of [Antonin] Scalia and [Clarence] Thomas, and he kept his promise," Perkins said to *USA Today.* "There will be a philosophical shift in the Court back to where it operates within its proper boundaries and respects the proper role of legislatures."

As the Senate was gearing up to conduct confirmation hearings on Judge Roberts, Chief Justice William Rehnquist's thyroid cancer suddenly worsened, and he died on September 3, 2005—making him, in-cidentally, the first justice in half a century to die in office. President Bush withdrew Roberts's nomination to replace Justice O'Connor, and nominated him instead to serve as chief justice. After brief and un-eventful confirmation hearings, Roberts was confirmed on September 29 by a vote of 78–22 by the full Senate, and was sworn in that after-noon by the senior associate justice, John Paul Stevens.

Bush now had the pleasant dilemma of selecting another nominee to replace Justice O'Connor. His supporters in the Religious Right ea-gerly looked forward to the White House announcement, anticipating that Bush would pick a strong conservative who would finally provide the elusive fifth vote to overturn *Roe v. Wade*. But his decision to nomi-nate White House counsel (and his former personal counsel) Harriet Miers dumbfounded and infuriated many of his supporters. Prior to joining the Bush White House, Miers had a successful career as a busi-ness lawyer in Dallas, and also served as the first female president of the State Bar of Texas, but she had little or no constitutional law experience and had never served as a judge. Others also expressed con-cern about the closeness of her ties to Bush, which they felt raised separation-of-powers concerns. In fact, she once famously described the president to reporter David Frum as "the most brilliant man she had ever met."

More than anything else, leaders of the Christian Right protested her lack of clear conservative credentials; with a fifty-five-member ma-jority in the Senate, and the threat of filibuster largely defanged by the Gang of 14, conservative leaders refused to support someone that they viewed as a potential Souter. Gary Bauer, former Republican presiden-tial candidate and president of American Values, said that "the future of the Supreme Court is too important to leave to chance." Weighing in from the far, far right was Troy Newman, president of Operation Rescue, the antiabortion group founded by Randall Terry: "We must reject the nomination of Harriet Miers to the Supreme Court. Miers is no Thomas or Scalia."

What little support Miers received from the Religious Right did more harm than good. Although Bush had repeatedly said that it was inappropriate for senators to grill Judge Roberts on his beliefs and how they might affect his rulings on the Court, the White House began trumpeting Miers's faith to overcome conservative objections. Jay Sekulow appeared on *The 700 Club* to reassure viewers that the nomination of Miers is "a big opportunity for those of us who have a conviction, that share an evangelical faith in Christianity, to see someone with our positions put on the Court." Similarly, James Dobson declared, "I know the church that she goes to and I know the people who go to church with her," and "I know the individual who led her to the Lord." However, when he added, "Some of what I know I am not at liberty to talk about," members of the Senate began asking what type of inside information the White House might have given to the evangelical leader, and whether that same information would be shared with the Senate.

Despite Bush's intense loyalty to his friends and his profound reluctance to change course, it quickly became evident that the Miers nomination offered the prospect of a long and protracted battle. On October 27, Miers asked the president to withdraw her nomination, a request that Bush "reluctantly accepted." Her withdrawal not only avoided a confirmation battle, but prevented a difficult legal dispute between the Senate and White House over access to papers and documents she prepared as White House counsel.

Four days later, Bush nominated Samuel Alito, a member of the Third Circuit Court of Appeals, to replace Justice O'Connor. The baying of the Christian Right quickly ceased: even more clearly than Chief Justice Roberts, Alito was viewed as a solidly conservative justice, so much so that he was once nicknamed Scalito in recognition of his intellectual similarity to the Court's other Italian American member, Antonin Scalia. Despite a 10–8 party-line vote by the Senate Judiciary Committee and formal opposition by the American Civil Liberties Union (only the third time the ACLU had voted to oppose a Supreme Court nominee), Alito was confirmed by the Senate on January 31, 2006. Senator John Kerry (D-Mass.) tried to organize a filibuster against the Alito nomination, but thanks in part to the Gang of 14, which did not consider the Alito nomination to fall within the "exceptional circumstances" clause of their agreement, the attempt failed.

Whether the Religious Right's long-standing goal of an anti-*Roe* Court is at hand remains to be seen. It may be some time before the issue is presented squarely to the Court, and early rulings by the Roberts Court suggest that there are still only two justices, Scalia and Thomas, who unequivocally would vote to overturn *Roe* today. There is no doubt, however, that the various judicial appointments by George W. Bush, including Roberts and Alito, have gone a long way toward satisfying the hopes and expectations of the Christian Right.

CHAPTER FIVE

The First Freedom

Separation of Church and State

A FEW MONTHS FOLLOWING her retirement from the United States
Supreme Court in January 2006, Sandra Day O'Connor took
part in a panel discussion on religious rights and freedoms at the
Institute of Bill of Rights Law at William and Mary School of Law.
During the course of her remarks, she compared the Supreme Court's
rulings on religious issues over the years to the famous serpentine brick
walls designed nearly two hundred years ago by Thomas Jefferson for
the University of Virginia.

"I think the Court has tried to walk this fine line but it's hard to
draw the line with any precision," O'Connor said. Nonetheless, she argued that the goal of keeping church and state separate was a worthy
one and one that has worked well for the country.

O'Connor's allusion to Jefferson and his elegant garden walls was
particularly apt, for it is Jefferson who laid the foundation for the long
line of Supreme Court cases that firmly removed religious expression
and promotion from various government institutions (notably public
schools) and programs. Shortly after Jefferson became president in 1801,
he received a letter of congratulation from the Danbury Baptist Association in Connecticut. Apart from its warm praise of Jefferson and
his "glow of philanthropy and good will," the purpose of the letter

was to complain that, under Connecticut's constitution, "what religious privileges we [the Baptists] enjoy (as a minor part of the State) we enjoy as favors granted, and not as inalienable rights." While recognizing that Jefferson was not "the national legislator," they nonetheless hoped that he would prevail upon Connecticut to relieve them of the legal burdens imposed on their exercise of religion. As is so often the case, this was at its core a tax issue: what the Baptists were actually complaining about was the fact that their tax dollars were used to support Connecticut's state-sponsored religion, the Congregationalist Church.

Without making any specific statement regarding Connecticut's tax policy, Jefferson warmly endorsed the Baptists' concept of religious liberty in his reply on January 1, 1802:

> Believing with you that religion is a matter which lies solely between Man & his God, that he owes account to none other for his faith or his worship, that the legitimate powers of government reach actions only, & not opinions, I contemplate with sovereign reverence that act of the whole American people which declared that their legislature should "make no law respecting an establishment of religion, or prohibiting the free exercise thereof," thus building a wall of separation between Church & State. Adhering to this expression of the supreme will of the nation in behalf of the rights of conscience, I shall see with sincere satisfaction the progress of those sentiments which tend to restore to man all his natural rights, convinced he has no natural right in opposition to his social duties.

As unequivocal as Jefferson's response was, it actually pales in comparison to his initial draft. According to James Hutson, former head of the Manuscript Division of the Library of Congress, Jefferson originally penned a longer and more emphatic reply to the Danbury Baptist Association, but crossed out much of his first draft on advice from his attorney general, Levi Lincoln. In 1998, when the Library of Congress was preparing an exhibit titled "Religion and the Founding of the American Republic," it asked the Federal Bureau of Investigation to use its forensic tools to examine the original manuscript and determine if Jefferson's deleted text could be reconstructed. The FBI was successful in doing so, and the recovered material underscores Jefferson's dim view of the blending of government and religion.

The original version of the famous "wall" sentence, for instance, read: "a wall of *eternal* separation between Church & State." Another large block of text removed by Jefferson was a defense of his controversial refusal to declare national days of thanksgiving and prayer (unlike his two predecessors, Washington and John Adams). Since the federal government is prohibited from passing laws respecting the establishment of religion, Jefferson said, he felt that the declaration of such days of devotion was the province of the country's individual religious sects. He distinguished his role as president from the practice of "the Executive of another nation as the legal head of its church," i.e., the king of England, from whom such declarations were expected.

Hutson argued that Jefferson's condemnation of such celebrations as "British" was a none-too-subtle dig at the Federalists and their alleged monarchical tendencies. The controversy underscores the rough-and-tumble nature of early-nineteenth-century politics: Jefferson was merely responding to Federalist charges that Republicans in general and Jefferson in particular were irreligious and even atheistic. Some Federalist preachers had gone so far as to suggest that Democratic-Republican godlessness was the cause of a yellow fever epidemic that beset Philadelphia in 1799. (Some two hundred years later both Pat Robertson and Jerry Falwell would similarly blame the 9/11 attacks on "Christ-haters," including pagans, abortionists, feminists, gays and lesbians, the ACLU, and People for the American Way.)

Levi, a native of New England, persuaded Jefferson that his broad criticism of days of thanksgiving and prayer would not play well in the region, and might dampen the steady rise of New England Republicanism. Jefferson took Levi's advice and struck the passage from his letter. But the core message of his reply to the Danbury Baptists, that the passage of the First Amendment erected a wall of separation between government and religion, remained untouched.

Thomas Jefferson optimistically thought that the American Constitution had put the issue of religious divisiveness to rest. In a May 28, 1818, letter to Mordecai Manuel Noah—journalist, playwright, New York University founder, and at the time the nation's most prominent

Jew—Jefferson wrote, "Your sect by its sufferings has furnished a remarkable proof of the universal spirit of religious intolerance, inherent in every sect, disclaimed by all while feeble and practiced by all when in power. Our laws have applied the only antidote to the vice, protecting our religious, as they do our civil rights by putting all on an equal footing. But more remains to be done."

Much more needed to be done than Jefferson could easily have imagined, and still needs to be done. For the last three decades the Christian Right has labored mightily to elect politicians and appoint judges willing to disregard the rational balance among the various sects struck by Jefferson and the other framers, and to elevate one—evangelical Christianity—above all others. For generations, Jefferson's own words served as a valuable guide to the Supreme Court, but as its membership has grown steadily more conservative, the Court has countenanced greater governmental promotion of and involvement in religion, to the detriment of both.

The Rediscovery of Jefferson's Wall

Jefferson's letter to the Danbury Baptists languished in historical obscurity for nearly a century before being briefly referenced by the Supreme Court in the case of *Reynolds v. United States* (1878). Reynolds, a Mormon, was charged with bigamy and defended himself in part by arguing that he believed it to be his religious duty to practice polygamy. The Court cited Jefferson's letter for the proposition that while the First Amendment protects opinions with respect to religion, it does not bar governmental regulation of actions.

> Coming as [the letter] does from an acknowledged leader of the advocates of the [First Amendment], it may be accepted almost as an authoritative declaration of the scope and effect of the amendment thus secured. Congress was deprived of all legislative power over mere opinion, but was left free to reach actions which were in violation of social duties or subversive of good order.

Finding that polygamy has historically "been odious" in Western European culture and certainly subversive of good order, the Court concluded that Congress could legitimately outlaw the practice, and that Reynolds could not raise a First Amendment defense to his prosecution.

The first use of Jefferson's wall metaphor as an appropriate description of the boundary between church and state occurred in *Everson v. Board of Education* (1947), a case in which a group of New Jersey parents challenged the use of taxpayer funds to reimburse the parents of children attending Catholic school for the cost of public bus fare. Writing for a narrow 5–4 majority, Associate Justice Hugo Black offered a sweeping interpretation of the First Amendment's establishment clause:

> No tax in any amount, large or small, can be levied to support any religious activities or institutions, whatever they may be called, or whatever form they may adopt to teach or practice religion. Neither a state nor the federal government can, openly or secretly, participate in the affairs of any religious organizations or groups and vice versa. In the words of Jefferson, the clause against establishment of religion by law was intended to erect "a wall of separation between church and state."

Even the dissenters agreed with Black's broad characterization of the intent of the establishment clause; what they disagreed with was the majority's resolution of the case itself. Black anticipated later rulings on the separation of church and state by concluding that the transportation reimbursements did not constitute a breach of the wall of separation: "[The First] Amendment," Black wrote, "requires the state to be a neutral in its relations with groups of religious believers and nonbelievers; it does not require the state to be their adversary. State power is no more to be used so as to handicap religions than it is to favor them."

A year later, the Court leaned heavily on Jefferson's wall metaphor in striking down, by a vote of 8–1, an Illinois public school program that hired instructors to give religious lessons in public schools during the regular school day. In a concurring opinion, Associate Justice Felix Frankfurter, one of the dissenters in the *Everson* case, strongly reaffirmed the Court's support for Jefferson's phrase, and concluded by quoting from Robert Frost's famous 1915 poem, "Mending Wall":

Separation means separation, not something less. Jefferson's metaphor in describing the relation between church and state speaks of a "wall of separation," not of a fine line easily overstepped.... We renew our conviction that "we have staked the very existence of our country on the faith that complete separation between the state and religion is best for the state and best for religion." If nowhere else, in the relation between church and state, "good fences make good neighbors."

Despite Frankfurter's ringing endorsement, the boundary disputes between religion and civil government have intensified over the last half century, particularly since the politicization of the Christian Right in the late 1970s. The repeated assaults on Jefferson's wall have left it cracked and crumbling, and recent Courts have shown little inclination to shore it up. As early as 1971, in *Lemon v. Kurtzman*, Chief Justice War-ren Burger referred to the wall as "a blurred, indistinct, and variable barrier depending on all the circumstances of a particular relationship." Although the Court reached a wall-like decision, holding that a Penn-sylvania law allowing reimbursement of religious schools for some expenses was unconstitutional, it was clear that the Court's more con-servative members were uncomfortable with Jefferson's view of the proper boundary between church and state.

The chief justice showed a little more deference to the concept in *Larkin v. Grendel's Den, Inc.* (1982): he referred to Jefferson's wall as "a useful signpost" for determining excessive "entanglement between church and state authority" in a decision that struck down a Massa-chusetts law that gave schools and churches within five hundred feet of a bar the ability to block liquor licenses by simply objecting to the li-cense application. But in *Lynch v. Donnelly* (1984), the case in which the Burger Court upheld the legality of a Pawtucket, Rhode Island, Na-tivity scene by a narrow 5–4 vote, the wall finally came tumbling down.

"The concept of a 'wall' of separation is a useful figure of speech probably deriving from views of Thomas Jefferson," Burger wrote. "The metaphor has served as a reminder that the establishment clause forbids an established church or anything approaching it. But the metaphor itself is not a wholly accurate description of the practical aspects of the relationship that in fact exists between church and state." Burger went on to argue that the Constitution "affirmatively mandates accommodation, not merely tolerance, of all religions, and forbids hostility toward any."

Replacing Jefferson's Wall with a Lemon

It has been almost four decades since Jefferson's wall was the prevailing analytical tool for determining if a particular state action violates the establishment clause of the First Amendment. Even before the political resurgence of the Religious Right in the late 1970s, the increasingly conservative Courts under Chief Justices Warren Burger and William Rehnquist had replaced the church-state "wall" with what can best be described as a poorly maintained picket fence. Rejecting the compelling clarity of Frankfurter's phrase "separation means separation," the Burger Court in *Lemon v. Kurtzman* chose to establish a more nuanced but much less easily applied standard that has come to be known, logically enough, as the *Lemon* test.

As it often does, the Court consolidated *Lemon* with two other similar appeals, since all three cases involved challenges to legislation that provided state financial support to nonpublic schools. The Commonwealth of Pennsylvania had adopted a statute (the one challenged by plaintiff Alton Lemon) that reimbursed nonpublic schools for the cost of "teachers' salaries, textbooks, and instructional materials in specified secular subjects." The State of Rhode Island took a more direct approach, adopting a law under which the state paid 15 percent of the salary of nonpublic-school teachers.

Chief Justice Burger, writing for a somewhat splintered 7–2 majority, conceded that ever since Justice Black's 1947 decision in *Everson v. Board of Education*, it had been very difficult for the Court to "perceive the lines of demarcation in this extraordinarily sensitive area of constitutional law." He declared that the relevant guideposts for the Court were "the three main evils against which the establishment clause was intended to afford protection: 'sponsorship, financial support, and active involvement of the sovereign in religious activity.'"

Based on that analysis, Burger said, a three-part test can be extracted from the Court's many rulings on the separation of church and state: "First, the statute must have a secular legislative purpose; second, its principal or primary effect must be one that neither advances nor inhibits religion; finally, the statute must not foster 'an excessive government entanglement with religion.'" After enunciating the relevant factors to consider, Burger carefully applied them to the two challenged programs. The proposal by Rhode Island to provide direct salary supplementation to nonpublic-school teachers, Burger said, was the most problematic. The types of nonpublic-school support endorsed by the Court in the past, he pointed out, were for resources that were themselves clearly secular: "bus transportation, school lunches, public health services, and secular textbooks supplied in common to all students." But in order to prevent state-supported teachers from fostering religion, Rhode Island imposed a detailed list of restrictions that by their very nature, Burger said, would require "comprehensive, discriminating, and continuing state surveillance," thus violating the establishment clause by requiring excessive state entanglement with religion. As for Pennsylvania, not only did its aid program raise the same entanglement concerns, but it suffered from the additional defect, Burger maintained, "of providing state financial aid directly to the church-related school."

In the conclusion of his opinion, Burger raised additional concerns that are highly relevant to the battles over state support for religious activity. "Ordinarily political debate and division, however vigorous or even partisan," he said, "are normal and healthy manifestations of our democratic system of government, but political division along religious lines was one of the principal evils against which the First Amendment was intended to protect." The two challenged statutes would exacerbate those divisions, he wrote, because they provided for annual appropriations for the benefit of just a few religious groups. Moreover, there was every indication that the size of the appropriations would grow in the years to come.

Burger also acknowledged that the type of appropriation authorized by Pennsylvania and Rhode Island could easily be the nose of the camel when it comes to the establishment of religion by the state. "A certain momentum develops in constitutional theory," he warned, "and it can be a 'downhill thrust' easily set in motion but difficult to retard or stop." After paying homage to the "enormous role" that church-related schools have played in American life, Burger concluded with a passage that, consciously or not, hearkened back to a less complicated and more wall-like view of church-state separation:

> The sole question is whether state aid to these schools can be squared with the dictates of the religion clauses. Under our system the choice has been made that government is to be entirely excluded from the area of religious instruction and churches excluded from the affairs of government. The Constitution decrees that religion must be a private matter for the individual, the family, and the institutions of private choice, and that while some involvement and entanglement are inevitable, lines must be drawn.

Although the Religious Right was only just emerging from its Scopes-induced disdain of political activism when the Supreme Court handed down the *Lemon* decision, the case quickly became a focal point of the movement's assault on the separation of church and state. Underlying the Christian Right's dissatisfaction with *Lemon* is the movement's disagreement with Burger's two key premises: that religion is a private, individual matter, and that "lines must be drawn." While its leaders mouth platitudes of religious pluralism, there is no question that the goal of the Religious Right is to erase the lines between church and state rather than draw them. Not surprisingly, that makes the modification or outright abandonment of the *Lemon* test one of the Right's primary goals.

The Battle to Overturn Lemon

It did not take long for Chief Justice Burger himself to regret his promulgation of the *Lemon* test. Just two years later, he wrote a dissent in *Committee for Public Education v. Nyquist* (1973) in which he criticized the majority's use of his test to strike down a New York statute that pro-

vided various types of aid, including tuition reimbursements, to sectarian schools. Burger was particularly dismayed that the majority had
measured the challenged law's "primary effect" in part by looking at
where parents chose to spend the money provided by the state. Instead,
he argued, once the majority recognized New York's "legitimate interest in promoting 'diversity and pluralism,'" any further inquiry should
have ended. In effect, Burger was suggesting an analysis that would have
reduced the *Lemon* test to just its first prong.

A decade later in *Marsh v. Chambers* (1983), when the Court considered a challenge to the Nebraska legislature's practice of opening its
legislative sessions with a prayer, Chief Justice Burger took an even
more minimalist approach to the *Lemon* test: he and five of his colleagues ignored it altogether. Instead, Burger effectively replaced the
Lemon test with what can best be described as "the weight of history"
test.

"The opening of sessions of legislative and other deliberative public bodies with prayer is deeply embedded in the history and tradition
of this country," Burger said. "From colonial times through the founding of the Republic and ever since, the practice of legislative prayer has
coexisted with the principles of disestablishment and religious freedom." He pointed out that among other things, each of the courts
hearing the *Marsh* case opened their proceedings with the traditional
invocation, "God save the United States and this Honorable Court."

Burger did concede that "standing alone, historical patterns cannot
justify contemporary violations of constitutional guarantees." However, he pointed to the fact that just three days before the First Congress agreed on the final language of the First Amendment, that same
body passed a statute authorizing the payment of chaplains to open
the sessions of the Senate and House of Representatives. "This unique
history," Burger concluded, "leads us to accept the interpretation of
the First Amendment draftsmen who saw no real threat to the establishment clause arising from a practice of prayer similar to that now
challenged."

Writing in dissent with Associate Justice Thurgood Marshall, Associate Justice William Brennan analyzed the constitutionality of Nebraska's legislative chaplain under the *Lemon* test and, for him, the

outcome was clear: "In sum, I have no doubt that, if any group of law students were asked to apply the principles of *Lemon* to the question of legislative prayer, they would nearly unanimously find the practice to be unconstitutional." But Brennan did not stop there; he continued on in his lengthy dissent to explain why, even apart from the *Lemon* test, the practice of legislative prayer violates the establishment clause.

At the core of the clause, Brennan said, are the principles of "separation" and "neutrality." Those principles serve a variety of functions, not least of which is diminishing the divisiveness of political battles over religion. "With regard to matters that are essentially religious . . . the establishment clause seeks that there should be no political battles," Brennan argued, "and that no American should at any point feel alienated from his government because that government has declared or acted upon some 'official' or 'authorized' point of view on a matter of religion."

Associate Justice John Paul Stevens contributed a separate dissent, one that was much briefer and more direct. "It seems plain to me," Stevens said, "that the designation of a member of one religious faith to serve as the sole official chaplain of a state legislature for a period of sixteen years constitutes the preference of one faith over another in violation of the establishment clause of the First Amendment."

The Court returned to *Lemon* in the following term, when it applied the test halfheartedly to the question of whether Pawtucket's Nativity scene violated the establishment clause. Writing again on the subject, Chief Justice Burger acknowledged that the Court has "often found it useful" to apply the *Lemon* criteria, but added, "We have repeatedly emphasized our unwillingness to be confined to any single test or criterion in this sensitive area." On behalf of the four dissenters, Associate Justice Brennan wrote:

The Court's less-than-vigorous application of the *Lemon* test suggests that its commitment to those standards may only be superficial. After reviewing the Court's opinion, I am convinced that this case appears hard not because the principles of decision are obscure, but because the Christmas holiday seems so familiar and agreeable. Although the Court's reluctance to disturb a community's chosen method of celebrating such an agreeable holiday is understandable, that cannot justify the Court's departure from controlling precedent. In my view, Pawtucket's maintenance and display at public expense of a symbol as distinctively sectarian as a crèche simply cannot be squared with our prior cases.

The Court's most open battle over *Lemon* occurred in *Wallace v. Jaffree* (1985), when six justices agreed that an Alabama statute authorizing a one-minute period of silence in all public schools "for meditation or voluntary prayer" was unconstitutional. Writing for the majority, Associate Justice Stevens applied the criteria of the *Lemon* test and concluded that the Alabama statute failed the first prong, the requirement of "a secular legislative purpose." In rebuttal, Chief Justice Burger pointed once again to the practice of the Court and Congress to open their sessions with prayer and suggested that it was ironic, if not "bizarre," for the majority to reject a moment of silence for Alabama schools. The majority's application of *Lemon*, Burger suggested, reflects "a naive occupation with an easy, bright-line approach for addressing constitutional issues." Overlooked, of course, was the fact that the brightest line—the original "wall of separation" suggested by Jefferson—had been long since discarded.

Associate Justice William Rehnquist, dissenting separately, went much further than Burger. He took the opportunity to present a lengthy analysis on the origins of the First Amendment, and suggested that "the establishment clause has been freighted with Jefferson's misleading [wall] metaphor for nearly forty years." Above all else, Rehnquist said, while the First Amendment was intended to forestall the establishment of a national religion, there is nothing to suggest that the framers objected to a governmental preference for religion over irreligion.

In support of his argument, Rehnquist quoted from the *Commentaries on the Constitution of the United States*, a three-volume treatise on constitutional law first published in 1833 by Associate Justice Joseph Story. In Story's view, religious pluralism was not the goal of the First Amendment:

Probably at the time of the adoption of the Constitution, and of the amendment to it now under consideration [First Amendment], the general if not the universal sentiment in America was, that Christianity ought to receive encouragement from the state so far as was not incompatible with the private rights of conscience and the freedom of religious worship. An attempt to level all religions, and to make it a matter of state policy to hold all in utter indifference, would have created universal disapprobation, if not universal indignation. . . . The real object of the [First Amendment] was not to countenance, much less to advance, Mahometanism, or Judaism, or infidelity, by prostrating Christianity; but to exclude all rivalry among Christian sects, and to prevent any national ecclesiastical establishment which should give to a hierarchy the exclusive patronage of the national government.

"The 'wall of separation between church and state,'" Rehnquist concluded, "is a metaphor based on bad history, a metaphor which has proved useless as a guide to judging. It should be frankly and explicitly abandoned."

For the Religious Right, this was music to their ears, particularly when two promising signs appeared that the Court might be on the verge of formally abandoning the *Lemon* test: the first occurred in 1986, when President Reagan appointed Rehnquist as chief justice, and the second in 1989, when the Court handed down its decision in *Allegheny County v. Greater Pittsburgh ACLU.* The *Allegheny County* case involved establishment clause challenges to two holiday displays in downtown Pittsburgh, one a crèche on the Grand Staircase of the Allegheny County Courthouse, and the other a Hanukkah menorah outside the City-County Building, where it stood "next to a Christmas tree and a sign saluting liberty" (the substance of the case is discussed in Chapter 6). Contained in the Court's wildly fragmented opinion were the first concrete signs that Associate Justice Anthony Kennedy was ready to join the conservative bloc of the Court and jettison the *Lemon* test.

Even the majority in the *Allegheny County* case, led by Associate Justice Harry Blackmun, tweaked the *Lemon* test slightly; in deciding that a crèche violated the establishment clause (the menorah survived the Court's scrutiny), Blackmun put much greater emphasis on whether the challenged state action in some way "endorsed" religion. That type of analysis largely falls under the second prong of *Lemon*, and it is an approach that Associate Justice O'Connor had long advocated in church-state cases.

But the real surprise was the strength of Kennedy's objection to any use of the *Lemon* test as an analytical tool in establishment clause cases: "I am content for present purposes to remain within the *Lemon* framework," Kennedy said, "but do not wish to be seen as advocating, let alone adopting, that test as our primary guide in this difficult area. Persuasive criticism of *Lemon* has emerged." Kennedy went on to suggest that substantial revision of the *Lemon* test may be required, but even under its terms, both holiday displays should have survived constitutional scrutiny.

Although Kennedy did not prevail in *Allegheny County*, his dissent was precisely the type of opinion the Religious Right had been waiting for from President Reagan's last nominee, and the search was on for a case that could finally drive a stake through the *Lemon* test. The timing seemed propitious: religious conservatives were cautiously optimistic about President George H. W. Bush's first appointee, David Souter, and openly thrilled by the second, Clarence Thomas. Both had replaced liberal justices who had been in the plurality in *Allegheny County*—William Brennan and Thurgood Marshall, respectively. With the change in the Court's membership, the Religious Right was confident that the despised *Lemon* test finally would be abandoned by the new Court, a decision they hoped would usher in a new era of government-endorsed religious practices.

Lee v. Weisman: *The* Lemon *Test Survives*

The perfect case seemed to present itself in 1991. Daniel Weisman, the father of a student in a Providence, Rhode Island, middle school, sued the school board when it invited Rabbi Leslie Gutterman to offer a nondenominational prayer during the school's graduation ceremony. Both the U.S. District Court in Rhode Island and the First Circuit

Court of Appeals, applying the *Lemon* test, concluded that the school district had in fact violated the establishment clause of the First Amendment. When the Supreme Court agreed to hear the Providence School Board's appeal, there was widespread anticipation that the Court would use the case to substantially rewrite or even abandon the *Lemon* test.

The Court's willingness to take the case appeared to be a political boon for President George H. W. Bush. His brand of dry and unexcitable conservatism had never played particularly well among evangelicals, and although he saw the inside of a church far more often than Ronald Reagan, Bush lacked his predecessor's innate charisma and ability to seduce the Christian Right with well-delivered lines pitched perfectly to their fondest hopes. With a potentially challenging re-election pending, Bush viewed the *Weisman* case as an opportunity to demonstrate to the Christian Right that he could deliver on one of the movement's more important agenda items. The intensity of evangelical interest in the case was evident in the large number of amici curiae ("friends of the court") briefs filed by various conservative legal organizations, including the Christian Legal Society; Concerned Women for America; Focus on the Family; the Liberty Counsel; the Rutherford Institute; and the Southern Baptist Convention Christian Life Commission.

The Bush administration's own dutiful assault on *Lemon* was presented by Solicitor General Kenneth W. Starr, with briefing assistance from various members of his staff, including Deputy Solicitor General John Roberts. Starr argued that the Court should shift its interpretation of the establishment clause to a "liberty-focused principle" that would allow schools to include "a noncoercive, ceremonial acknowledgment of a deeply religious people." He told the justices that the chief problem with the *Lemon* test is that it is a "rigid doctrinal framework" that consistently "invalidate[s] practices with substantial historical sanction." But even here, the Bush administration did not go as far as Christian conservatives would have liked, since Solicitor General Starr refrained from arguing to the Court that prayer should be allowed in the classroom itself: "In that setting," Starr's brief conceded, "young children may be susceptible to influences that might be deemed indirectly coercive."

When the Court handed down its decision in June 1992, however, many were stunned to learn that the *Lemon* test had survived—and adding to the Religious Right's dismay was the fact that the 5–4 majority opinion upholding the test was written by none other than Associate Justice Anthony Kennedy. Rather than boosting Bush's standing among the Christian Right, the loss of *Weisman* and the vote of Associate Justice David Souter to uphold the *Lemon* test served as a stark reminder to evangelicals that neither Bush nor Reagan had delivered on their promises to effectively reshape either the judiciary or contemporary constitutional law. As former presidential candidate and Family Research Council president Gary Bauer said to the *Washington Post*'s Ruth Marcus, "Of the five new justices added to the court by Presidents Reagan and Bush, three joined in today's travesty. At that rate, one has to wonder why liberal interest groups bother fighting Republican nominees to the court. Why not just support them and watch them 'grow'?"

In the end, it turned out that *Weisman* was not in fact the ideal case on which to base a comprehensive challenge to the *Lemon* test. The dominant facts of the case, Kennedy said, were that a state official (the middle school principal) authorized and directed a "formal religious exercise" by Rabbi Gutterman during a public school graduation ceremony. As a result, the Court could resolve the case with a much narrower analysis than the administration and amici curiae were suggesting:

> This case does not require us to revisit the difficult questions dividing us in recent cases, questions of the definition and full scope of the principles governing the extent of permitted accommodation by the state for the religious beliefs and practices of many of its citizens. . . . We can decide the case without reconsidering the general constitutional framework by which public schools' efforts to accommodate religion are measured. Thus, we do not accept the invitation of petitioners and *amicus* the United States to reconsider our decision in *Lemon v. Kurtzman.* The government involvement with religious activity in this case is pervasive, to the point of creating a state-sponsored and state-directed religious exercise in a public

school. Conducting this formal religious observance conflicts with settled rules pertaining to prayer exercises for students, and that suffices to determine the question before us.

No doubt, the frustration of the Religious Right with the Republican appointees was heightened by news reports a couple of years later that Justice Kennedy had originally voted to uphold the nondenominational prayer, but then changed his mind. The revelation came following the release of the papers of Justice Blackmun, which included a note sent to him by Kennedy on March 30, 1992, that read: "After writing to reverse the high school graduation case, my draft looked quite wrong. So I have written it to rule in favor of the objecting student."

Of particular interest was the fact that *Weisman* was the first establishment clause case for Associate Justice David Souter, and his concurring opinion no doubt confirmed the darkest suspicions of the Christian Right. After a lengthy analysis of the drafting of the First Amendment, Souter concluded that "on balance, history neither contradicts nor warrants reconsideration of the settled principle that the establishment clause forbids support for religion in general no less than support for one religion or some." But Souter did not stop there; he went on to argue that even mere "ceremonial" or ecumenical acknowledgments of religion are often closely identified with a particular religion (i.e., Christianity) and, at the very least, are avowedly theistic.

"Many Americans who consider themselves religious are not theistic," Souter said. "Some, like several of the framers, are deists who would question Rabbi Gutterman's plea for divine advancement of the country's political and moral good. Thus, a nonpreferentialist who would condemn subjecting public school graduates to, say, the Anglican liturgy would still need to explain why the government's preference for theistic over nontheistic religion is constitutional."

Lemon *in the New Millennium:* *Ignored but Not Forgotten*

Eight years later, the issue of prayer at school-sanctioned events came before the Court again in the case of *Santa Fe Independent School District v.*

Doe (2000). Now the Religious Right was getting even more directly involved: representing the district was Jay Sekulow, of the American Center for Law and Justice, the legal advocacy group created by Pat Robertson to combat the efforts of the American Civil Liberties Union. Joining Sekulow on his brief were a number of conservative attorneys, including most notably Paul Clement, a former law clerk for Associate Justice Antonin Scalia who would go on to become U.S. solicitor general. The State of Texas was given permission to appear as amicus curiae, and was represented by then attorney general John Cornyn, who was elected to the U.S. Senate in 2002 and later appointed to the Senate Judiciary Committee.

The primary argument offered by the district was that the prayers in question were private speech by the students, and not government speech. Recognizing the concerns that had invalidated the middle school prayer in *Weisman*, the district adopted a policy that allowed the student body to hold two elections by secret ballot: one to determine if an invocation should be given over the loudspeaker prior to school football games, and if yes, then a second election to select the student to give the invocation.

Six members of the Court, however, viewed the student elections as little more than a sham. Writing for the majority, Associate Justice John Paul Stevens noted that the district's policy for football-game invocations was a direct descendant of earlier policies that established a "student chaplain" to lead "prayer at football games."

Given these observations, and in light of the school's history of regular delivery of a student-led prayer at athletic events, it is reasonable to infer that the specific purpose of the policy was to preserve a popular "state-sponsored religious practice." . . . School sponsorship of a religious message is impermissible because it sends the ancillary message to members of the audience who are nonadherents "that they are outsiders, not full members of the political community, and an accompanying message to adherents that they are insiders, favored members of the political community."

In the years between *Weisman* and *Santa Fe Independent School District*, the membership of the Court had changed slightly: in 1993 President

Clinton had appointed Ruth Bader Ginsburg, a member of the U.S. Court of Appeals for the D.C. Circuit, to replace Byron White, and in 1994, Stephen Breyer, the chief judge of the U.S. Court of Appeals for the First Circuit, to replace Harry Blackmun. The two new justices joined Associate Justice Stevens in not only striking down the district's invocation policy, but also reaffirming (at least in passing) the continued use of the *Lemon* test as an analytical tool for the Court in church-state cases. Perhaps in part because the district's efforts to offer prayer at the football game were so blatantly unconstitutional, even Associate Justice Kennedy was willing to put aside his skepticism of *Lemon* to join Stevens's opinion.

But any thoughts that the *Lemon* test had been buttressed by the ruling in *Santa Fe* were premature. Just nine days later, in *Mitchell v. Helms*, the Court's three most conservative members, Chief Justice Rehnquist and Associate Justices Scalia and Thomas, joined by Justice Kennedy, employed a diminished version of the *Lemon* test to uphold a Louisiana statute that funneled federal funds through state educational agencies to local educational agencies (LEAs), despite the fact that each year, roughly 30 percent of the LEAs receiving the funds were religiously affiliated. (Associate Justices O'Connor and Breyer concurred in the result, but not in the plurality's reasoning.)

Writing the lead opinion, Thomas asserted that in an earlier case, *Agostini v. Felton* (1997), the Court had essentially narrowed *Lemon* to just two factors: whether the challenged state action had a secular purpose and whether it had the primary effect of advancing or inhibiting religion. "We acknowledged," Thomas said, "that our cases discussing excessive entanglement had applied many of the same considerations as had our cases discussing primary effect, and we therefore recast *Lemon's* entanglement inquiry [the third prong of Burger's formulation] as simply one criterion relevant to determining a statute's effect."

A year after his opinion in the *Mitchell v. Helms* case, Thomas drafted the opinion for a 6–3 majority in *Good News Club v. Milford Central School* (2001), and no doubt pleased opponents of the *Lemon* test by simply omitting it altogether. At issue was whether a New York school unconstitutionally denied access to its facilities to a private Christian youth organization, the Good News Club. The Court granted certiorari to resolve a conflict among the circuit courts as to "whether speech can be excluded from a limited public forum on the basis of the religious nature of the speech."

The best explanation for Thomas's failure to even mention the *Lemon* test in the *Good News* case is that it is most naturally applied in cases in which government affirmatively adopts a policy that appears to have the effect of establishing religion. The *Lemon* test is arguably less useful in analyzing actions taken by a government to *avoid* the possible establishment of religion. Milford, for instance, argued that it would have violated the establishment clause if it allowed the Good News Club to use school facilities for its meetings. However, Justice Thomas and the rest of the majority found little merit in the city's argument.

But that explanation does not satisfactorily illuminate how Chief Justice Rehnquist could completely ignore *Lemon* when addressing an establishment clause challenge to a pilot program set up by the state of Ohio to give "educational choice" to residents of the Cleveland City School District, as he did in *Zelman v. Simmons-Harris* (2002). By a 5–4 vote, the Court ruled that the program was in fact constitutional.

To be fair, a pale shadow of the Court's still-valid *Lemon* standard can be found in the majority opinion: citing Justice Thomas's earlier opinion in *Agostini*, Rehnquist wrote, "We continue to ask whether the government acted with the purpose of advancing or inhibiting religion [and] whether the aid has the 'effect' of advancing or inhibiting religion." That is at least a nod to the first two prongs of the *Lemon* test. In the case of Ohio's educational choice program, Rehnquist said, it was clear that the law had a secular purpose. As for whether it "advanced religion," the majority concluded that the private choices of the aid recipients—the parents—insulated the state from any possible establishment clause violations:

> Where a government aid program is neutral with respect to religion, and provides assistance directly to a broad class of citizens who, in turn, direct government aid to religious schools wholly as a result of their own genuine and independent private choice, the program is not readily subject to challenge under the establishment clause.

The final two establishment clause cases relevant to this discussion of the *Lemon* test were both handed down the same day, on June 27, 2005: *McCreary County v. American Civil Liberties Union of Kentucky*, declaring the display of the Ten Commandments in the county courthouse to be unconstitutional, and *Van Orden v. Perry* (2005), rejecting a claim that a granite Ten Commandments monument on the state capitol grounds violates the establishment clause. Not surprisingly, the role that *Lemon* played in the analysis of the challenged action depended in large part on which wing of the Court controlled the outcome of the case. Given the fractured nature of the Court's ruling in this area, it is also not surprising that both decisions were decided by a vote of 5–4, with Associate Justice Stephen Breyer providing the swing vote in each case.

In *McCreary*, Associate Justice David Souter wrote the majority opinion, and *Lemon* once again returned to the forefront of church-state analysis. "Ever since *Lemon v. Kurtzman* summarized the three familiar considerations for evaluating establishment clause claims," Souter said, "looking to whether government action has 'a secular legislative purpose' has been a common, albeit seldom dispositive, element of our cases." Although Souter noted that a finding of "illegitimate purpose" had rarely served as a basis for overturning government action, he cited Associate Justice Brennan's dissent in *Zelman v. Simmons-Harris* to underscore the importance of the inquiry: "Manifesting a purpose to favor one faith over another, or adherence to religion generally, clashes with the 'understanding, reached . . . after decades of religious war, that liberty and social stability demand a religious tolerance that respects the religious views of all citizens.'"

As part of their defense for the practice of posting the Ten Commandments, the counties in *McCreary* urged the Court to abandon the "legislative purpose" inquiry of *Lemon*, on the grounds that the difficulty of divining such purpose allows the Court to impose its own view. Souter sternly disagreed, noting that such examinations of legislative purpose are a familiar part of appellate practice.

"With enquiries into purpose this common," Souter sarcastically concluded, "if they were nothing but hunts for mares' nests deflecting attention from bare judicial will, the whole notion of purpose in law would have dropped into disrepute long ago."

The majority in *McCreary* also rejected the alternative argument of the counties, that the "legislative purpose" inquiry of *Lemon* can be satisfied with a simple legislative pronouncement, regardless of the history behind the pronouncement or the actual effect of the legislation. "The Court often does accept governmental statements of purpose," Souter said, "in keeping with the respect owed in the first instance to such official claims. But in those unusual cases where the claim was an apparent sham, or the secular purpose secondary, the unsurprising results have been findings of no adequate secular object, as against a predominantly religious one." The majority concluded that there was "ample support for the district court's finding of a predominantly religious purpose behind the counties' . . . display," and upheld the injunction ordering its removal.

Between *McCreary* and *Van Orden*, however, the *Lemon* test went from a starring role to a bit player. Associate Justice Stephen Breyer wrote a concurring opinion supporting the constitutionality of the granite Ten Commandments at the Texas State Capitol, thus enabling Chief Justice Rehnquist to write the lead opinion for a conservative plurality. He quickly made it clear that the *Lemon* test would not be part of his analysis:

> Whatever may be the fate of the *Lemon* test in the larger scheme of establishment clause jurisprudence, we think it not useful in dealing with the sort of passive monument that Texas has erected on its capitol grounds. Instead, our analysis is driven both by the nature of the monument and by our nation's history.

Rehnquist's suggestion that *Lemon* is of little use in analyzing a "passive monument" is clearly contradicted by Justice Souter's thoughtful application of the test to the equally passive wall-mounted version of the Ten Commandments in Kentucky.

What was really at issue was the willingness of Rehnquist and his conservative colleagues to countenance a far greater degree of church-state interaction than was contemplated by the framers. The perils of that approach were amply summed up by what Associate Justice John

Paul Stevens wrote in his brief dissent in *Zelman*, the Ohio school-choice case:

> I am convinced that the Court's decision [in *Zelman*] is profoundly misguided. Admittedly, in reaching that conclusion I have been influenced by my understanding of the impact of religious strife on the decisions of our forbears to migrate to this continent, and on the decisions of neighbors in the Balkans, Northern Ireland, and the Middle East to mistrust one another. Whenever we remove a brick from the wall that was designed to separate religion and government, we increase the risk of religious strife and weaken the foundation of our democracy.

Stevens's concerns are well-founded. As the battles over the *Lemon* test themselves illustrate, one of the chief consequences of abandoning Jefferson's wall of separation has been a steadily growing divisiveness in American politics and society over religious issues. Since it has never been formally overruled, the *Lemon* test remains a viable standard for lower courts, where the vast majority of the controversies over separation of church and state are resolved (which is the chief reason Religious Right attorneys pushed so hard for its modification in *Lee v. Weisman*). But it may well be that there are finally five justices on the Court at the same time—Chief Justice Roberts and Associate Justices Scalia, Kennedy, Thomas, and Alito—who would be willing to replace *Lemon* with some other standard.

During his confirmation hearing, Chief Justice Roberts told the Senate Judiciary Committee that one of the reasons that the *Lemon* test has survived for the last three and a half decades is that no one has suggested a compelling replacement. There is a logical candidate, of course: the sturdy wall described by Jefferson more than two hundred years ago. But it is doubtful that this Court is likely to embrace either Jefferson's metaphor or his broader philosophical views about the proper balance between religion and government. Just how far the Roberts Court will go in allowing government and religion to interact remains to be seen, but it almost certainly will place a greater emphasis on the nominal neutrality of state action regardless of its actual effect (as in the case of the Ohio school-choice program) and show a greater willingness to accept state or federal assertions of secular purpose, even in cases in which a simple inquiry would make it clear that the purpose was a sham or overwhelmingly outweighed by the action's religious purpose. In the end, it is a safe bet that the boundary between religion and government will be far more blurred with a justice like Samuel Alito on the Court than someone in the mold of Sandra Day O'Connor. And that fact alone underscores why the Christian Right has focused so much time and attention on influencing the nomination and confirmation of Supreme Court justices.

CHAPTER SIX

Roy's Rock

The Battle over Public Display of Religious Symbols

ONE OF THE MORE INTERESTING cultural trends recently has been Hollywood's rediscovery of the Christian filmgoer. It is no secret, of course, that the Religious Right has long viewed Hollywood as a toxic mix of both Sodom and Gomorrah. But in the eyes of many Christian conservatives, Hollywood earned a little bit of redemption with the release of *The Passion of the Christ*, Mel Gibson's retelling of the final hours of Jesus of Nazareth. Numerous critics questioned the film's graphic violence; *Newsweek* film critic David Ansen, for instance, wrote, "Instead of being moved by Christ's suffering or awed by his sacrifice, I felt abused by a filmmaker intent on punishing an audience, for who knows what sins." *Chicago Sun-Times* critic (and former altar boy) Roger Ebert said flatly, "This is the most violent film I have ever seen." Nonetheless, the film was a tremendous financial success, pulling in more than $370 million in the U.S. and another $240 million worldwide (against a production and advertising budget of just $35 million). Given those kinds of numbers, it's not surprising that Hollywood has been panting after projects that will appeal to Christian moviegoers. The venerable studio Twentieth Century Fox has even launched a Christian-oriented studio called Fox Faith, which requires that all of its titles "have overt Christian content or be derived from the work of a Christian author."

This is not the first time that Hollywood has turned to Christian themes to fill movie theater seats. In the mid-1950s, faced with shrinking audiences due to the growing popularity of television, studios invested heavily in widescreen movie formats like Twentieth Century Fox's CinemaScope and Paramount Picture's VistaVision. The new technology was particularly suited to stories with expansive panoramas, so not surprisingly, screenwriters and directors turned to the Bible for material (and of course, there was the added benefit that the Good Book's stories are all in the public domain). Over the next decade or so, studios cranked out a stream of testamentary films, with titles like *The Robe* (1953); *Demetrius and the Gladiators* (1954), advertised with the slogan "It begins where *The Robe* left off!"; *Salome* (1953); *Slaves of Babylon* (1953); and *The Prodigal* (1955). Most were largely forgettable, but in 1956 Paramount produced the most famous biblical epic of them all: Cecil B. DeMille's *The Ten Commandments,* starring as Moses the inimitable Charlton Heston, whom the seventy-five-year-old DeMille said was cast because of his resemblance to artist renderings of the Old Testament leader.

There's no question that DeMille created a masterpiece of cinema, a nearly four-hour epic with some of Hollywood's finest talent of the time: Heston was joined by Yul Brynner, Anne Baxter, Edgar G. Robinson, and Vincent Price, to name just a few.

However, there is something curiously American about the fact that much of the litigation over religious monuments in public spaces today stems from a publicity stunt for *The Ten Commandments.* During production of the film, DeMille contacted the Fraternal Order of the Eagles, which already had a well-established "youth guidance program" for distributing framed copies of the Ten Commandments. He suggested that the Eagles distribute stone monuments engraved with the Commandments, and offered to have actors from his movie appear at their unveilings—Charlton Heston, for instance, traveled to the International Peace Garden on the border of North Dakota and Manitoba in June 1956 to help unveil one of the monuments.

A "Suggested Program for Ten Commandments Monolith Dedication," introduced by the Eagles themselves as evidence in a later federal court trial, underscored the religious motivation of the organization in erecting its monuments:

> We, of the Fraternal Order of Eagles, in searching for a youth guidance program recognized that there can be no better, no more defined program of Youth Guidance, and adult guidance as well, than the laws handed down by God Himself to Moses more than 3,000 years ago, which laws have stood unchanged through the years. They are a fundamental part of our lives, the basis of all our laws for living, the foundation of our relationship with our Creator, with our families and with our fellow men. All the concepts we live by— freedom, democracy, justice, honor—are rooted in the Ten Commandments. . . . The erection of these monoliths is to inspire all who pause to view them, with a renewed respect for the law of God, which is our greatest strength against the forces that threaten our way of life.

There's no solid figure as to how many *Ten Commandments*–inspired monuments and plaques the Eagles ultimately installed—one estimate puts the total around 150, but others suggest as many as 4,000—but regardless of the precise number, there is no question that they continue to play a leading role in one of the country's most closely watched constitutional dramas.

Thou Shalt Not . . .

Appropriately enough, the first federal court challenge of a Ten Commandments display involved one of the granite monuments installed by the Eagles, although it was not part of the actual publicity blitz for DeMille's film. In 1969 or 1970, the Salt Lake City and County Boards of Commissioners voted to accept a Ten Commandments monument from the Eagles and install it in a particularly public location: near the front entrance of the Hall of Justice in Salt Lake, which houses both the city and the county's courts. Although the Eagles paid for the monument, Salt Lake taxpayers paid for its installation and some landscaping—a light over the monument, a walkway, and a bench for contemplation—and over the years have also paid for the monument's upkeep.

"The stone is granite," Chief Judge Willis Ritter wrote in *Anderson v. Salt Lake City Corp.* (D. Utah 1972), "five feet by three feet, set in cement for permanence, and is of the cleft tombstone shape of common depictions of the tablets bearing the biblical Ten Commandments."

Judge Ritter, who was appointed by President Harry Truman in 1949, began his constitutional analysis by noting that the First Amendment is a direct descendant of Virginia's Statute of Religious Liberty, which was drafted in large part by Thomas Jefferson. The language of the statute, Ritter said, makes it clear that Jefferson was firmly opposed to *any* state support of religious activity: "Well aware that almighty God hath created the mind free; that to compel a man to furnish contributions of money for the propagation of opinions which he disbelieves, is sinful and tyrannical." Ritter noted Jefferson's use of the wall metaphor in his letter to the Danbury Baptists, and said that his use of the phrase "verifies and confirms the inner logic of the establishment clause itself which is absolute and uncompromising—'Congress *shall* make *no law* respecting an establishment of religion.'"

After reviewing the Supreme Court's ruling in *Everson v. Board of Education* at length, the seventy-three-year-old Judge Ritter posed the fundamental question: "What are the purpose and the primary effect of the Ten Commandments monument?" To which he answered: "The purpose *and* the primary effect of the action of the Boards of Commissioners is the advancement of religion. The purposes of the Eagles must be deemed to have been adopted by the commissioners when they authorized the erection of this stone." By affirmatively aiding the religious objectives of the Eagles and preferring one religion over another, Judge Ritter said, the Boards of Commissioners violated not merely the establishment clause of the First Amendment but also the equal protection clause of the Fourteenth: "If all such religions, lodges or institutions are allowed to plant tombstone-like slabs on the courthouse grounds, the lawns will resemble a disorderly and unsightly cemetery. The commissioners may be in the unenviable position of being obliged to face up to this dilemma."

Judge Ritter's order for the removal of the Ten Commandments monument, however, was never carried out. Just six months later, the Tenth Circuit Court of Appeals reversed his decision, relying in large

part on the Supreme Court's recently issued decision in *Lemon v. Kurtzman* (1971). Like Judge Ritter, the Tenth Circuit focused on "'purpose
and primary effect' of the subject monolith," but it reached the opposite conclusion from the court below, in part because of its willingness
to ignore trial testimony on the obvious point that "a large portion of
our population believes [the Ten Commandments] are Bible based."

In support of its conclusion that the Decalogue is at least as secular as it is religious, the Tenth Circuit relied on two fairly flimsy items:
an offhand comment by an attorney during oral argument that the Ten
Commandments are an early legal code, and the allegedly "noteworthy"
fact that the Order of Eagles "is not a religious organization—it is
a fraternal order." The Court brushed aside the fact that the primary
mission of the Order of Eagles is to advocate "ecclesiastical law as the
temporal foundation on which all law is based," noting that it does not
carry out that mission through coercion. "So," the Court grandly concluded, "the Decalogue is at once religious and secular.... It does not
seem reasonable to require removal of a passive monument, involving
no compulsion, because its accepted precepts, as a foundation for law,
reflect the religious nature of an ancient era."

Sixteen years later, the Tenth Circuit conceded in the case of *Summum v. Callaghan* (1997) that its earlier *Anderson* decision might have been
erroneous. Before the appellate court was an appeal by Summum, a
church established in Utah in 1975, from a district court decision that
dismissed its lawsuit against Salt Lake County. Summum made several
requests to the county for permission to install a monolith with its religious tenets nearby and similar "in size, shape, and design" to the Ten
Commandments monument at the county courthouse; each request,
however, was denied.

The county commissioners argued that Summum's requests were
rejected to avoid the appearance of a "state endorsement" of the Summum religion. While that may have been at least partly true, it is likely
that the commissioners were more than a little uncomfortable with various aspects of Summum's philosophy, which includes a belief in psy-
chokinesis, consumption of "holy nectars in a small amount just prior
to meditation," and the promotion of "the Meditation of Sexual Ecstasy." According to its extensive website, "Summum treats sexuality as

a divine and integral part of spiritual evolution and defines 'ecstasy' as 'the state of union with God.'" Summum is also an active promoter of mummification, which, thanks to its IRS-approved religious standing, is available as a tax-free service.

In overturning the district court's dismissal, the Tenth Circuit noted that the validity of its ruling in *Anderson* was "called into question" by the Supreme Court's decision in *Stone v. Graham* (1980), which explicitly held that the Ten Commandments "are undeniably a sacred text." For procedural reasons, the Tenth Circuit did not reverse its earlier ruling, but it still sent Summum's case back to the district court, with instructions to determine if Salt Lake County created a "nonpublic or limited public forum" when it accepted the Eagles's Ten Commandments monument in the late 1960s. "If it is determined that the county discriminated against Summum based on Summum's religious viewpoint," the appellate court said, "it is highly unlikely the county could defend its actions on establishment clause grounds."

After the Tenth Circuit's decision in the *Summum* case, Salt Lake County chose to move its Ten Commandments monument rather than run the risk of being required to install a Summum monument. Four other communities also voluntarily moved their monuments to private property after receiving a letter from Summum's attorney; an additional monument stayed put, having been originally installed on private property.

Two other communities in Utah, Ogden and Pleasant Grove, continued fighting Summum's claim in court. In 2002, after extensive litigation, the Tenth Circuit ruled that Ogden in fact had violated Summum's First Amendment rights and held that "the free speech clause of the First Amendment compels the City of Ogden to treat with equal dignity speech from divergent religious perspectives. On these facts, the city cannot display the Ten Commandments monument while declining to display the Seven Principles monument." Rather than devote any public space to Summum's philosophy, Ogden moved its Ten Commandments monolith to private property.

The Ten Commandments monument in Pleasant Grove, Utah, may also face the crane. Summum sued the city, seeking a preliminary injunction to allow it to display its monument alongside the Ten Commandments. Summum's request was rejected by the district court, but in April 2007 a three-judge panel of the Tenth Circuit overturned that ruling. The appeals court concluded that Summum had met the standard for a preliminary injunction and ordered the district court to allow Summum to erect its monument. In August of that year, the entire Tenth Circuit split evenly on whether to rehear the case, which left the earlier decision intact. Attorneys for Pleasant Grove, including Edward White of the Thomas More Law Center and Francis J. Manion and Jay Sekulow of the American Center for Law and Justice, have said that they plan to appeal the Tenth Circuit's decision to the United States Supreme Court.

The Stone *Decision and Roy's Rock*

Somewhat remarkably, the Supreme Court's first specific ruling on the constitutionality of a Ten Commandments display did not occur until *Stone v. Graham* (1980), when the Court reviewed a Kentucky law requiring the posting of the Decalogue in each public school classroom. The state trial court had applied the Supreme Court's *Lemon* test and concluded that the law was constitutional; the Kentucky Supreme Court affirmed the decision, albeit by an evenly divided vote.

In a 6–3 decision issued per curiam—literally "by the court," or unsigned by a particular justice—however, the United States Supreme Court reversed the state court decisions. The majority rejected the trial court's conclusion that the legislature's "avowed purpose" was in fact secular. "The preeminent purpose for posting the Ten Commandments on schoolroom walls is plainly religious in nature," the Court said. "The Ten Commandments are undeniably a sacred text in the Jewish and Christian faiths, and no legislative recitation of a supposed secular purpose can blind us to that fact." The Court noted that while some of the commandments address secular issues—murder, stealing, bearing false witness, etc.—the rest deal with specific obligations of the Christian faith: "worshipping the Lord God alone, avoiding idolatry, not using the Lord's name in vain, and observing the Sabbath Day." Since the Kentucky law clearly violated the first prong of the *Lemon* test, the Court said, it was an unconstitutional violation of the establishment clause.

In his dissent, Chief Justice Rehnquist objected to the fact that the majority of the Court dismissed the Kentucky General Assembly's expressly stated purpose, particularly given the fact that the existence of a secular purpose was endorsed by the state courts. "It is…undeniable," Rehnquist said, "as the elected representatives of Kentucky determined, that the Ten Commandments have had a significant impact on the development of secular legal codes of the Western world." In his view, the Court should have deferred to the General Assembly's decision to install such an important document in the state's schools.

The same year that the *Stone* decision was handed down, Roy Moore, a deputy prosecutor in Etowah County, Alabama, carved the Ten Commandments onto two wooden tablets. In 1992, Republican governor Guy Hunt appointed Moore to serve as circuit court judge in Etowah County, and Moore brought his wooden tablets into the courtroom, hanging them on the wall behind the bench. Like former circuit court judge (and Alabama governor) George Wallace, Moore also made a practice of opening up each court session with a prayer.

After observing Moore's prayer practice, the Alabama ACLU threatened to sue Moore in 1994 for violating the doctrine of the separation of church and state, a charge that Moore angrily denied. He was up for reelection to the circuit court that fall, and although the ACLU had held off on its lawsuit, Moore still used the controversy to promote his campaign; when the results were in, Moore had won reelection in a landslide, and was well on his way to becoming a celebrity with the Religious Right.

When the ACLU carried through on its threat to sue Moore in the spring of 1995, the recently elected Republican governor Fob James threw his support behind the embattled judge. At a rally in support of Moore later that spring, James told the judge, "We stand behind you; we stand behind you come hell or high water." In addition to authorizing forty thousand dollars in state funds to help pay Moore's legal bills, James also said that if a federal judge ordered the plaque removed, he would send in the National Guard to protect it. But James never had occasion to send soldiers into Etowah County; the litigation over Moore's hand-carved Ten Commandments bounced between federal and state court for a few years before petering out at the Alabama Supreme Court without any real resolution.

In the interim, a group of Alabama residents formed the Christian Family Association and recruited Moore to enter the 2000 race for the vacant position of chief justice of the Alabama Supreme Court. Although his chief primary opponent, Harold See, was already a member of the court and the recipient of campaign advice from none other than Karl Rove, Moore easily beat See and went on to win the general election, largely on the strength of his name recognition as the "Ten Commandments judge." Moore was sworn in as the chief justice of the Alabama Supreme Court on January 15, 2001.

During his campaign, Moore promised supporters that he would install the Ten Commandments in a "public place" within the state supreme court building; not long after taking office, Moore hung his wooden Ten Commandments in the waiting room of his office, but his Religious Right supporters argued that the location was not public enough. Moore had an answer to that complaint: a 5,280-pound monument carved out of Vermont granite, with the Ten Commandments on two tablets at the top and inspirational quotations around the sides. On the night of July 31, 2001, Moore and some supporters rolled the monument up the supreme court's limestone steps on wooden rollers and installed it in the building's rotunda. The installation of the monument was filmed by representatives of Rev. D. James Kennedy's Coral Ridge Ministries, an evangelical Christian church that used the footage to raise funds for Moore's legal defense fund.

Not surprisingly, a federal lawsuit seeking the removal of the monument was soon filed in federal court. During the trial in October 2002, Moore testified that he would not remove the monument:

> [The monument] serves to remind the appellate courts and judges of the circuit and district court of this state and members of the bar who appear before them, as well as the people of Alabama who visit the Alabama Judicial Building, of the truth stated in the Preamble to the Alabama Constitution that in order to establish justice we must invoke "the favor and guidance of almighty God."

In mid-November, U.S. District Court Judge Myron Thompson ruled that Moore had violated the establishment clause by imposing his belief in the Judeo-Christian God on all residents of Alabama, regardless of their personal beliefs. He ordered the monument removed, but stayed execution of his order when Moore appealed the decision to the Eleventh Circuit Court of Appeals.

The court of appeals unanimously affirmed the district court's decision, noting that the Supreme Court in *Stone* had stated that "the Ten Commandments are undeniably a sacred text." While it is possible for a government to present the Ten Commandments in a secular fashion (as in a study of history, for instance), any such use must be scrutinized under the *Lemon* test, which the court of appeals cited as the prevailing legal standard. As the district court had noted, there was no need to go past the first prong of the test: whether there was a valid secular purpose for installing the monument. Based largely on Moore's own unapologetic testimony about the need to "acknowledge the law and sovereignty of the God of the Holy Scriptures," the district court had concluded there was no valid secular purpose, and the court of appeals agreed.

Moore's other main argument on appeal was that his monument was constitutional in light of *Marsh v. Chambers* (1983), in which the Supreme Court upheld Nebraska's practice of opening legislative sessions with prayer. The court of appeals rejected that claim, however: "That there were some government acknowledgments of God at the time of this country's founding and indeed are some today, however, does not justify under the establishment clause a 5,280-pound granite monument placed in the central place of honor in a state's judicial building." Following the appeals court's decision, District Judge Thompson ordered the removal of the monument by August 20, 2003. Three days before the deadline, a rally was organized outside the court building in support of Judge Moore, with appearances by conservative presidential candidate Alan Keyes and the Reverend Jerry Falwell. Moore was bluntly unapologetic; "Let's get this straight," he said. "[The monument] is about the acknowledgment of God." Echoing the words of his mentor, Francis Schaeffer, Falwell told the audience that Moore was justified in his defiance of the federal court. "Civil disobedience," he said, "is the right of all men when we believe breaking man's law is needed to preserve God's law."

Judge Thompson's order specified that if the monument was still in place on August 20, the state would start incurring fines of five thousand dollars per day. On August 21, the other eight members of the state supreme court met and overruled Moore's refusal to obey the federal court. The monument was put in storage, and later that fall, Moore was removed from his position by the Alabama Court of the Judiciary. The loss of his position as chief justice helped make Moore a martyr in the eyes of the Christian Right, and both he and the monument (dubbed "Roy's Rock") remain popular attractions for evangelical Christians around the country.

In 2006 Moore tried to capitalize on his notoriety as the Ten Commandments judge and keeper of the Rock by running in the Republican gubernatorial primary in Alabama against incumbent Bob Riley. In the opening months of the contest, poll numbers suggested that Moore might prevail, but Riley ended up defeating Moore handily by a 2–1 margin. There were numerous calls for Moore to run as an Independent, but he declined to do so. Since losing the gubernatorial election, he has concentrated on writing articles for the libertarian publication WorldNetDaily, and serving as chairman of a conservative advocacy group he helped establish called the Foundation for Moral Law.

Take Two Tablets...

Just six years after DeMille's *The Ten Commandments* was released in theaters, the Fraternal Order of Eagles presented a granite copy of the Decalogue to "The People and Youth of Texas." The state accepted the gift and selected a site for the six-foot-tall monument on the grounds of the Texas State Capitol. The cost of installing the monument was paid by the Eagles, but ongoing maintenance has been paid by the state.

Some forty years later, a Texas attorney by the name of Thomas van Orden filed a lawsuit against the State of Texas, alleging that the installation and maintenance of the monument was a violation of the establishment clause of the First Amendment. His lawsuit was rejected by the both the U.S. District Court in Texas and the Fifth Circuit Court of Appeals; the Supreme Court granted certiorari and heard arguments in the case on March 2, 2005. The case, *Van Orden v. Perry* (2005), attracted a huge amount of attention and a remarkable number of amici curiae briefs, particularly from Religious Right organizations. Among those urging the Supreme Court to uphold the constitutionality of the monument were:

- eighteen states, ranging from Alabama to Wyoming;
- the American Center for Law and Justice;
- the American Family Association Center for Law & Policy;
- the Claremont Institute Center for Constitutional Jurisprudence, which featured former attorney general Ed Meese on the brief;
- the Eagle Forum Education & Legal Defense Fund, the legal arm of Phyllis Schlafly's advocacy group;
- the Ethics and Public Policy Center, a conservative think tank whose members include former senator Rick Santorum (R-Pa.), serving as a senior fellow;
- the Foundation for Moral Law, Inc., the Reconstructionist legal organization inspired by Judge Moore's battle over his own Ten Commandments monument in Alabama;
- the Rutherford Institute;
- Faith and Action, a Christian missionary outreach to bring the Gospel of Jesus Christ to America's elected officials;
- Focus on the Family;
- the Thomas More Law Center;
- Wallbuilders, Inc., the organization founded by David Barton, a historian who has written extensively on the theory that America was founded as a Christian nation.

In the end, the Ten Commandments monument did survive, but it was a narrow decision. Chief Justice Rehnquist, who wrote the lead opinion, was able to persuade only three others to join him: Associate Justices Scalia, Thomas, and Kennedy. The fifth vote to uphold the monument was cast by Associate Justice Breyer, but he wrote a separate concurring opinion, which limited the precedential value of Rehnquist's opinion.

Hearkening back to *Lynch v. Donnelly*, the case in which the Court upheld the constitutionality of a crèche display in Pawtucket, Rhode Island, Rehnquist reiterated the argument that "there is an unbroken history of official acknowledgment by all three branches of government of the role of religion in American life from at least 1789," and he quoted at length from President Washington's first Thanksgiving Day proclamation. Rehnquist also listed numerous displays of the Ten Commandments in government buildings in Washington, including the courtroom of the Supreme Court, the rotunda of the Library of Congress, the Jefferson Building's Great Reading Room, the floor of the National Archives, in front of the Ronald Reagan Building, and in the Great Hall of the Justice Department, where "a statue entitled *The Spirit of Law* has two tablets representing the Ten Commandments lying at its feet."

Rehnquist distinguished the Texas monument from the invalidated Ten Commandments display in *Stone*, "where the text confronted elementary school students every day"; the Court is typically more cautious when elementary and secondary school children are involved, Rehnquist said. But given the fact that the monument was one of seventeen such installations designed to show the various strands of Texas political and legal history, it did not in Rehnquist's view violate the establishment clause.

In his decisive concurrence, Breyer recounted the Court's erratic history on church and state issues. "The Court has found no single mechanical formula," Breyer said, "that can accurately draw the constitutional line in every case." As he quite correctly pointed out, no test adopted by the Court can easily explain

the establishment clause's tolerance, for example, of the prayers that open legislative meetings . . . ; certain references to, and invocations of, the deity in the public words of public officials; the public references to God on coins, decrees, and buildings; or the attention paid to the religious objectives of certain holidays, including Thanksgiving.

Breyer did not propose a new test that would somehow justify the continued presence of the Ten Commandments on the Texas State Capitol grounds. Instead, he argued that in a "border-line case" such as this, the only appropriate approach is the application of "legal judgment." The judgment required is not "personal," Breyer insisted; instead, it is a judgment that "must reflect and remain faithful to the underlying purposes of the clauses, and it must take account of context and consequences measured in light of those purposes."

For Breyer, the exercise of "legal judgment" involves a close examination of the facts of the case, including the setting of the monument, its source (the Eagles, a group he described as "primarily secular"), and the purportedly "determinative" fact that the monument stood unchallenged for forty years. To Breyer, that indicated a general understanding in the community that the monument was primarily secular in nature, a conclusion that overlooks the obvious fact that it can take considerable time for sufficient cultural awareness to develop before certain practices are challenged (e.g., slavery, denying women the right to vote, child labor, etc.).

In a passionate dissent, Associate Justices Stevens and Ginsburg excavated Jefferson's wall metaphor and used it to answer the question of whether Texas may promote the Ten Commandments without violating the establishment clause. "If any fragment of Jefferson's metaphorical wall of separation between church and state is to be preserved—if there remains any meaning to the wholesome neutrality of which this Court's [establishment clause] cases speak,—a negative answer to that question is mandatory."

At length and in great detail, Stevens dissected both Rehnquist's plurality opinion and Breyer's concurrence. After reciting the Hollywood-inspired origins of the granite monuments, he underscored the monotheistic, religious nature of the Decalogue, with its unequivocal opening: "I AM the LORD thy God." It is not, as Stevens pointed out, a message that is likely to make "nonmonotheists and nonbelievers" feel like part of the political community. He rejected Rehnquist's tour-guide approach to religious displays in government buildings as largely irrelevant—none contain the full text of the Ten Commandments, for instance—and agreed with Associate Justice Souter that the prominent and public setting of the Texas Ten Commandments monument "enhances the religious content of its message." His last two paragraphs are particularly compelling:

> The judgment of the Court in this case stands for the proposition that the Constitution permits governmental displays of sacred religious texts. This makes a mockery of the constitutional ideal that government must remain neutral between religion and irreligion. If a state may endorse a particular deity's command to "have no other gods before me," it is difficult to conceive of any textual display that would run afoul of the establishment clause.
>
> The disconnect between this Court's approval of Texas's monument and the constitutional prohibition against preferring religion to irreligion cannot be reduced to the exercise of plotting two adjacent locations on a slippery slope. Rather, it is the difference between the shelter of a fortress and exposure to "the winds that would blow" if the wall were allowed to crumble. That wall, however imperfect, remains worth preserving.

Not surprisingly, the Court's lack of clarity on the Ten Commandments issue affects how such controversies are handled by the lower federal courts. For instance, in Kentucky, U.S. District Court Judge Karl Forester, a Reagan appointee, ruled in September 2007 that a Ten Commandments display in Rowan County was constitutional. That Decalogue, he concluded, is part of an exhibit "on the foundations of American law and government" and thus protected. Intellectually, this is an approach not terribly dissimilar from surrounding photos of nude women with pages of highbrow fiction and contemporary political interviews to defeat an obscenity charge. However, just two weeks earlier, Judge Forester refused to dismiss a lawsuit against a display in Garrard County on the grounds that "a reasonable person would conclude that the county's display has the effect of endorsing religion." He also found that the county's "officially stated purpose" is a "sham" intended to hide a religious intent behind the display.

The fight to continue taxpayer support for Ten Commandment monuments remains one of the Religious Right's favorite fund-raising topics. In mid-September 2007, attorney Jay Sekulow sent out an e-mail appeal titled "[American Center for Law and Justice] taking two critical cases to Supreme Court." The message was larded with links to donation pages to support the ACLJ's briefing efforts on behalf of the Ten Commandments monuments in Ogden and Pleasant Grove, Utah, and dire descriptions of the pending litigation. "Here are the facts," Sekulow wrote:

> An organization called Summum says if you display the Ten Commandments, you should also be required to display an alternative message...in this case, Summum's new-age "Seven Aphorisms" ...for the sake of "balance"!
>
> We're representing both cities in separate cases—arguing against this outrageous and dangerous view.
>
> Although this case sounds almost absurd...IT HAS BEEN ENDORSED BY THE TENTH CIRCUIT COURT OF APPEALS—they actually mandated the placement of these opposing monuments.

Sekulow warns that if the Supreme Court refuses to take the Summum cases, "the consequences are grave." He predicts that Summum will file similar suits around the country, "and there will be nothing to stop groups with an anti-American, unpatriotic agenda from utilizing the same strong-arm strategy."

The Court Adopts the "Three Reindeer Rule"

When the leaves begin falling from the trees, the time is near for another of the Christian Right's reliable annual fund-raisers: the so-called War on Christmas. As *Kingdom Coming* author Michele Goldberg pointed out in a 2005 *Salon* article, the idea of a secular attack on Christmas has been around since the late 1950s, when the ultraconservative John Birch Society accused the Communists of "denud[ing] the event of its religious meaning." American materialism has done a pretty good job of that on its own, but still, the idea that secularists are actively plotting to strip Christ from Christmas remains a popular Christian Right shibboleth.

No one is a more adamant believer in the mythical war than Fox News Channel host Bill O'Reilly, who for the last few years has run a special holiday segment called "Christmas Under Siege." O'Reilly, whose on-air persona is generally reminiscent of the pre–Mt. Crumpet Grinch, uses the segment to highlight reports from around the country allegedly demonstrating the secularization of Christmas: municipal "holiday trees," department chains favoring "Happy Holidays" over "Merry Christmas," secular celebrations in public schools, etc.

Given the importance of Christmas in American culture, it is not surprising that its celebration has generated cases for the Supreme Court's docket. In light of the First Amendment's prohibition against the establishment of religion, the issue is just how far government can go in acknowledging Christmas, Hanukkah, Kwanzaa, Saturnalia, or other midwinter festivals.

The Court's first significant Christmas case originated in Pawtucket, Rhode Island. One of the main attractions of the small New England city is the Slater Mill, a re-creation of the nation's first water-powered cotton mill, constructed at the very dawn of the region's industrial revolution (1793). Visitors to the mill, a National Historic Landmark Site, can learn about the growth of the textile industry, the often oppressive working conditions for young women and children, and the impact of mechanization on the region's cottage manufacturing.

The Slater Mill Historic Site is located at Hodgson Park, a privately owned five-acre piece of property that straddles the Blackstone River in downtown Pawtucket. On the east side of the river, the park is bounded by Roosevelt Avenue, one of the city's main streets; the Pawtucket City offices are also located on Roosevelt Avenue, approximately three hundred feet north of Hodgson Park. Beginning in 1973, the city contracted with the property owners to put a lighted Christmas display on the east side of Hodgson Park, facing Roosevelt Avenue. One week before Christmas in 1980, the ACLU and several Pawtucket taxpayers sued the city in U.S. District Court for the District of Rhode Island, alleging that a Nativity scene included in the Christmas display violated the establishment clause of the First Amendment.

As described by Chief District Court Judge Raymond Pettine, the city's Christmas display was a motley collection of midwinter symbolism: a "talking" wishing well, a Santa's House with a live Santa distributing candy, three painted cutout Christmas trees, a forty-foot fresh Christmas tree with lights, an elevated runway with reindeer pulling Santa's sleigh, assorted cutouts ranging from a dancing elephant to a robot, a large sign proclaiming "Season's Greetings," and in the center foreground of the display, a life-sized Nativity scene with representations of Mary, Joseph, and other visitors in reverential poses around a manger. The display, Judge Pettine found, was owned, maintained, and installed by the city, and each year, the mayor held a well-publicized ceremony to light the display.

Both the district court and the First Circuit Court of Appeals concluded that the "primary effect" of Pawtucket's inclusion of a crèche scene was the advancement of religion, and thus an unconstitutional violation of the establishment clause. Judge Pettine's assessment of the display is particularly powerful:

In sum, the Court does not understand what meaning the crèche, as a symbol, can have other than a religious meaning. It depicts the birth of Christ in a way that is not merely historical. It has not been so altered over the years as to relegate its religious connection to a matter of historical curiosity. It is the embodiment of the Christian view of the birth and nature of Christ. Unless that view has itself lost its religious significance, an artifact that portrays that view simply and unambiguously cannot be other than religious.

Following the First Circuit's affirmation of Judge Pettine, Pawtucket filed a petition for certiorari and the Supreme Court agreed to hear the case. When the case was argued before the justices on October 4, 1983, Pawtucket's attorney was joined by Solicitor General Rex E. Lee, who appeared as amicus curiae. Lee's appearance before the Court in defense of the Pawtucket crèche was intended as a signal of support by the Reagan administration to religious conservatives, who considered this a particularly important case. Joining Lee as amici curiae were a number of Christian legal groups, including John Whitehead's Coalition for Religious Liberty, the Legal Foundation of America, and the Washington Legal Foundation.

The display, Lee told the Court, is a "constitutionally permissible governmental acknowledgment of an important part of the American heritage." It would be "cultural censorship," Lee suggested, for the federal courts to prohibit local governments from recognizing the Christian origins of the "most joyous of our holidays."

The Court agreed, but the justices were sharply divided on the issue. Writing for the 5–4 majority in *Lynch v. Donnelly* (1984), Chief Justice Warren Berger took the opportunity to review what he described as "an unbroken history of official acknowledgment by all three branches of government of the role of religion in American life from at least 1789." His recitation included the practice of presidential Thanksgiving proclamations (conveniently overlooking the fact that a number of presidents, including most notably Thomas Jefferson, declined to issue them), the implicit public subsidization of religious holidays by giving government employees paid days off, the adoption of the national motto "In God We Trust," and the funding of national galleries with displays of religiously themed art. Given all of those examples, Burger said, it should be clear "why the Court consistently has declined to take a rigid, absolutist view of the establishment clause. . . . In our modern, complex society, whose traditions and constitutional underpinnings rest on and encourage diversity in all areas, an absolutist approach in applying the establishment clause is simplistic and has been uniformly rejected by the Court."

But Burger's own approach was fairly simplistic. He boiled the case down to one narrow question: "whether there is a secular purpose for Pawtucket's display of the crèche." Not surprisingly, he was able to find one: "to celebrate the holiday and to depict the origins of that holiday." Burger acknowledged that District Court Judge Pettine had concluded that the primary effect of the crèche display was "to confer a substantial and impermissible benefit on religion in general and on the Christian faith in particular." But if the Pawtucket crèche violates the establishment clause, Burger argued, then it must somehow be more beneficial to religion than a variety of other entanglements the Court has approved, including the use of public money for secular textbooks in church-sponsored schools, reimbursement of transportation costs to church-sponsored schools, federal grants for nonreligious buildings on church-sponsored campuses, etc. "We are unable to discern a greater aid to religion deriving from inclusion of the crèche," Burger concluded, "than from these benefits and endorsements previously held not violative of the establishment clause."

Neither justification for the constitutionality of Pawtucket's crèche, however, is particularly compelling. An establishment test that hinges on whether a municipality or state has successfully articulated one secular purpose amid other unstated but much more obvious religious motivations is close to no test at all. Moreover, arguing that the crèche is somehow less of a violation than previously approved entanglements merely begs the question of whether those earlier cases were wrongly decided. It is not in and of itself a basis for decision.

But by far the biggest error in Chief Justice Burger's opinion was his dismissal of the concerns that led to the adoption of the establishment clause in the first place. "We are unable to perceive," Burger said, "the Archbishop of Canterbury, the Bishop of Rome, or other powerful religious leaders behind every public acknowledgment of the religious heritage long officially recognized by the three constitutional branches of government. Any notion that these symbols pose a real danger of establishment of a state church is farfetched indeed."

There is a saying that old generals always fight the last war, and Burger's argument is a good example of that. The framers certainly were concerned about the possibility of an established Anglican Church, since many of them had direct experience with the consequences of such an arrangement (the Roman Catholic Church was too inconsequential in America at the time to merit much attention). But when they drafted the establishment clause of the First Amendment, they did not bar state sponsorship of particular creeds; they prohibited the establishment of *any* religion. Even in 1984, it should have been obvious that there was a very real establishment threat rising in the United States—not, as Burger pointed out, from either the Most Reverend Robert Runcie or Pope John Paul II, but from increasingly powerful homegrown evangelical Christians and Reconstructionists like Jerry Falwell, Pat Robertson, Timothy LaHaye, and others. It is a threat that has only intensified over the nearly twenty-five years that have passed since.

Over time, the Court's decision in *Lynch* has become known as "the Three Reindeer Rule," in recognition of the fact that the constitutionality of the Pawtucket crèche display hinged on the fact that it was surrounded by so many clearly secular symbols. Still, left to the lower courts is the challenge of determining whether a particular Nativity display is sufficiently sanitized by secular elements to remain constitutional. The irony for the Supreme Court is that by straining to find a basis to preserve unchanged an obviously treasured holiday display, it has entangled the federal courts in the church-state debate to an extent that the *Lemon* Court would have found laughably unconstitutional.

Allegheny County: *The Crèche on the Stairs*

The Court's struggles in this area were amply demonstrated by its complicated and confusing decision five years later in *Allegheny County v. Greater Pittsburgh ACLU* (1989). Before the Court were various challenges to two holiday displays in Pittsburgh: a crèche scene installed on the Grand Staircase of the Allegheny County Courthouse, and a Hanukkah menorah installed each year by the city next to a Christmas tree on the grounds of the City-County Building. The nine justices filed five separate opinions, with various justices joining in some portions of their colleagues' work and peevishly criticizing others. Indeed, the opinions in *Allegheny* are notable for their sharp tone, a tendency only recently matched in some of the Court's abortion decisions.

When the printers stopped churning and the dust settled, the upshot was that five justices (Blackmun, Brennan, Marshall, Stevens, and O'Connor) agreed that the county's crèche display violated the establishment clause. The other four justices (Rehnquist, Kennedy, White, and Scalia) would have permitted the crèche to remain. As for the menorah, both Blackmun and O'Connor sided with the Court's more conservative wing and ruled that in its context, it was constitutional.

The three sections of Blackmun's opinion that attracted the support of a majority of the Court were his discussion of the establishment clause's prohibition of "endorsement" of religion by government, his conclusion that the crèche in fact constituted "endorsement" by Allegheny County, and his detailed dissection of Associate Justice Kennedy's dissent.

After citing Associate Justice Black's strong language on the meaning of "establishment of religion" in church-state issues, Blackmun turned to the *Lemon* test and with a nod to Justice O'Connor's long-standing argument, said that the Court had further refined the test by focusing on whether a challenged government practice has the effect of "endorsing" religion. While the term itself is subject to varying definitions, Blackmun said, the core principle is that government is prohibited "from appearing to take a position on questions of religious belief" or from "making adherence to a religion relevant in any way to a person's standing in the political community."

Unlike the crèche in *Lynch*, which was surrounded by diverse and even eclectic secular images, the Allegheny County crèche stood alone on the Grand Staircase of the County Courthouse, with nothing to diminish the full impact of its religious message. Indeed, across the top of the crèche an angel was suspended with a banner reading "Glory to God in the Highest!"

"This praise to God in Christian terms," Blackmun concluded, "is indisputably religious—indeed sectarian—just as it is when said in the Gospel or in a church service." Since the county chose to endorse a patently Christian message, it violated the establishment clause, and the display must be permanently enjoined.

Before moving on to his analysis of the constitutionality of the city's menorah, Blackmun took the time to respond in detail to Justice Kennedy's dissent. He took particular exception to Kennedy's argument that, when the Court upheld the constitutionality of opening legislative sessions with prayer in *Marsh v. Chambers* (1983), it effectively endorsed any governmental practice that does not rise to the level of proselytization. But the actual test, Blackmun said, is whether a governmental practice has the effect of "endorsing" religion, not whether it constitutes proselytization.

Blackmun clearly took the strongest exception to Kennedy's suggestion that his analysis of the crèche constituted "an unjustified hostility toward religion." Kennedy, Blackmun said, "apparently has misperceived a respect for religious pluralism, a respect commanded by the Constitution, as hostility or indifference to religion. No misperception could be more antithetical to the values embodied in the establishment clause."

Kennedy argued that if a government is limited to recognizing the secular aspects only of a holiday with both secular and religious aspects, that constitutes "a callous indifference toward religious faith that our cases and traditions do not require." By limiting celebrations to nonadherents, Kennedy said, the Court would be forcing government to ignore "the plain fact, and the historical reality, that many of its citizens celebrate its religious aspects as well."

Blackmun rejected Kennedy's argument in terms that are applicable to the broad claims of the Religious Right and its Reconstructionist wing. A secular government, he pointed out, "is not the same as an atheistic or antireligious state. A secular state establishes neither atheism nor religion as its official creed." The Constitution mandates a secular government, Blackmun said, to avoid discrimination on the basis of religious faiths. But he recognized that some seek a more religious government:

> To be sure, in a pluralistic society there may be some would-be theocrats, who wish that their religion were an established creed, and some of them perhaps may be even audacious enough to claim that the lack of established religion discriminates against their preferences. But this claim gets no relief, for it contradicts the fundamental premise of the establishment clause itself. The antidiscrimination principle inherent in the establishment clause necessarily means that would-be discriminators on the basis of religion cannot prevail.... Some Christians may wish to see the government proclaim its allegiance to Christianity in a religious celebration of Christmas, but the Constitution does not permit the gratification of that desire, which would contradict the logic of secular liberty it is the purpose of the establishment clause to protect.

After the intensity of Blackmun's response to Kennedy, his discussion of the menorah seemed anticlimactic. Although there were a total of six votes to uphold the constitutionality of the display, no one else joined in Blackmun's analysis. In large part, that had to do with the fact that Blackmun proffered a new criteria to help determine a display's constitutionality: whether there is a reasonable alternative to the display in question. There are nonreligious symbols for Christmas—snowmen, reindeer, elves, Santa, or the Christmas tree erected by the county— but as Blackmun pointed out, it is difficult to come up with a "predominantly secular symbol of Hanukkah." But none of his colleagues found this line of reasoning particularly compelling.

The Supreme Court's difficulty in articulating a clear and easily followed standard governing the display of the Ten Commandments and religious holiday symbols underscores the innate wisdom of Jefferson's wall of separation. It is both unseemly and ultimately unsatisfying for the Court to be engaged in the exercise of parsing the layout and composition of Ten Commandments or holiday displays for the sole purpose of determining whether taxpayer money can be used to pay for them.

In this sense, Justice Blackmun's analysis is compelling: given the myriad nongovernmental but still public locations in which the Ten Commandments or religious holiday symbols can be displayed, it would seem that the only reason to involve government at all is to indicate some endorsement of Christian religious tenets, however slight. Through its efforts, the Religious Right has already succeeded in building a bench that has reduced the framer's intended neutrality on the subject of religion from a bedrock principle to little more than a balancing test, and there are clearly members of the current Court who would go much further.

CHAPTER SEVEN

Of Pandas and Prayer

Religion in the Public Schools

IN MAY 2007, American Vision, an aggressively Christian Reconstructionist organization, convened a gathering in North Carolina
called the Worldview Super Conference II. Led by Gary DeMar, a pro-
lific proponent of Reconstructionism, American Vision is committed
to "restoring America's biblical foundation—from Genesis to Revelation." Speaking in a sepulchral tone, the narrator of the video trailer for
the conference offers a grim view of the history of the evangelical
movement:

> Christianity in America was dealt a serious blow at the infamous
> Scopes Trial of 1925. After our hollow victory, Christians retreated
> from American public life with their tails tucked between their legs.
> Over the next fifty years, we allowed secular humanism to replace
> Christianity as the official religion of America. As a result, cher-
> ished freedoms to express our Christian faith were eroded before
> our eyes. The killing of preborn babies was legalized. Violent crime
> rose to staggering levels in our nation's history. The quality of ed-
> ucation plummeted to new depths. It wasn't until 1975, and the
> born-again era, that Christians began to reemerge and reengage
> the culture once again.

"If America is to be restored to the godly nation it was," the narrator says, "we must prepare this generation to capture the future."

The narrator's lugubrious reference to the 1925 Scopes Trial is understandable. Few events were more destructive to the progress of the evangelical movement than the so-called Monkey Trial, the case that made "evolution" a household word across America. The origins of the litigation can be traced in part to one state legislator's intense dislike of a then-popular book on human history, and in part to the determination of a handful of Tennessee businessmen to put their small rural town on the map.

Sometime during 1924, John W. Butler, a member of the Tennessee House of Representatives from Lafayette, learned that some Tennessee schools were using Hendrik Van Loon's popular five-hundred-page tome, *The Story of Mankind*, to teach the history of humanity. Butler strongly objected to Van Loon's opening chapter, in which the author described humanity's distant ancestor, a clever mammal that surpassed others by using its forefeet to hold prey and learning to walk on its hind legs:

> This creature, half ape and half monkey but superior to both, became the most successful hunter and could make a living in every clime. For greater safety, it usually moved about in groups. It learned how to make strange grunts to warn its young of approaching danger and after many hundreds of thousands of years it began to use these throaty noises for the purpose of talking.
>
> This creature, though you may hardly believe it, was your first "man-like" ancestor.

Butler was so outraged by Van Loon's thesis that he sponsored legislation, called the Butler Act, to make it unlawful for any teacher in a state-supported school "to teach any theory that denies the story of the Divine Creation of man as taught in the Bible, and to teach instead that man has descended from a lower order of animals."

"Darwin says that man is an offshoot of the Old World monkeys," Butler told a reporter for the *New York Times* just before the Scopes Trial, "and so his theory denies the Bible story that God created man in His own image. The teaching of this theory of evolution breaks the hearts of fathers and mothers who give their children the advantages of higher education in which they lose their respect for Christianity and become infidels."

Following the passage of the Butler Act, the American Civil Liberties Union ran advertisements in newspapers throughout Tennessee, looking for a teacher willing to challenge the law. To Dayton mine manager and civil engineer George W. Rappleyea, the passage of the Butler Act was a great opportunity to boost the profile of the small Tennessee town by challenging the constitutionality of the new law. While discussing the act at a downtown soda fountain, Rappleyea asked a tall, slim, shy twenty-four-year-old Dayton high school science teacher named John Scopes if he would be willing to test the new law. Scopes reluctantly agreed, and Rappleyea swore out a complaint against him for violating the Butler Act. If convicted on the misdemeanor charge, Scopes faced a possible fine of one hundred to five hundred dollars. "It isn't very much," Scopes conceded to a reporter during a pretrial trip to New York to consult with the ACLU, "but it would be a lot to me."

Scopes needn't have worried about losing what amounted to a month's wages; the one hundred dollar fine assessed by Judge John T. Raulston following his conviction was thrown out by the Tennessee Supreme Court on a technicality (the amount of the fine should have been determined by the jury, not the judge). And even if the fine had survived appeal, prosecuting attorney William Jennings Bryan had generously offered to pay it on Scopes's behalf if the ACLU did not do so—Bryan, a lifelong champion of the people, was philosophically opposed to fines for low-paid workers like teachers. The barely perceptible slap on the wrist that Scopes received was only part of the "hollow victory" for evangelicals; the real loss was in the court of public opinion, and the lead prosecutor against fundamental Christianity in that venue was the brilliant but sardonic journalist H. L. Mencken.

In a series of columns filed from Dayton for the *Baltimore Sun*, Mencken depicted a social and educational backwater filled with what he harshly described as "local primates." The people of Dayton, Mencken wrote, "are simply unable to imagine a man who rejects the literal authority of the Bible. The most they can conjure up, straining until they are red in the face, is a man who is in error about the meaning of this or that text."

As the trial wore on, Mencken became increasingly sarcastic and scathing in his depiction of the trial and the local defenders of the Butler Act. He blamed the "intelligentsia of Tennessee" for failing to oppose the passage of the law in the first place, and then for failing to come to Scopes's aid as the trial got under way. Watching the epic legal battle between Bryan and defense counsel Clarence Darrow, Mencken saw the emergence of a national threat:

> Darrow has lost this case. It was lost long before he came to Dayton. But it seems to me that he has nevertheless performed a great public service by fighting it to a finish and in a perfectly serious way. Let no one mistake it for comedy, farcical though it may be in all its details. It serves notice on the country that Neanderthal man is organizing in these forlorn backwaters of the land, led by a fanatic, rid of sense and devoid of conscience. Tennessee, challenging him too timorously and too late, now sees its courts converted into camp meetings and its Bill of Rights made a mock of by its sworn officers of the law. There are other States that had better look to their arsenals before the Hun is at their gates.

But thanks in no small part to the derision and mockery of Christian fundamentalists that his own writing helped inspire, "the Huns," as Mencken described them, left the public arena for more than half a century.

Epperson v. Arkansas *and* Edwards v. Aguillard

Just three years after Tennessee passed the Butler Act, Arkansas passed its own version, which made it a misdemeanor for any person "to teach the theory or doctrine that mankind ascended or descended from a lower order of animals," or "to adopt or use in any such institution a textbook that teaches" such a theory. As a result, for nearly forty years, the textbook used in Little Rock high school biology classrooms made no mention of evolution at all. In 1965, however, the school district purchased a biology text that included Darwin's theory, and instructed its high school teachers to use it.

Faced with the real risk of prosecution under Arkansas's "monkey law," a tenth-grade biology teacher named Susan Epperson filed a lawsuit challenging the statute as unconstitutional. A lower court agreed, but the Arkansas Supreme Court reversed the decision with a two-sentence opinion which declared that each state had the power to establish the curriculum for its public schools and expressed "no opinion on the question whether the act prohibits any explanation of the theory of evolution or merely prohibits teaching that the theory is true..." The United States Supreme Court agreed to hear Epperson's appeal.

Writing for a unanimous Court, Associate Justice Abe Fortas laid out the standard by which the Arkansas statute would be judged:

> Government in our democracy, state and national, must be neutral in matters of religious theory, doctrine, and practice. It may not be hostile to any religion or to the advocacy of no-religion; and it may not aid, foster, or promote one religion or religious theory against another or even against the militant opposite. The First Amendment mandates governmental neutrality between religion and religion, and between religion and nonreligion.

The Arkansas law, Fortas ruled, violated the First Amendment's prohibition against tailoring education "to the principles or prohibitions of any religious sect or dogma."

"In the present case," he concluded, "there can be no doubt that Arkansas has sought to prevent its teachers from discussing the theory of evolution because it is contrary to the belief of some that the Book of Genesis must be the exclusive source of doctrine as to the origin of man.... Plainly, the law is contrary to the mandate of the First, and in violation of the Fourteenth, Amendment to the Constitution."

The Court's decision did not come as a huge shock to the nation. By the time *Epperson* was decided, in 1968, only two states still prohibited the teaching of evolution: Arkansas and Mississippi. Even Tennessee, the model for the prohibition against Darwin, had repealed the Butler Act in 1967. But despite the unanimity of the Court's decision in *Epperson,* the efforts to slide some version of creationism into public school curricula persisted.

The most powerful movement was the rise of scientific creationism, or as it is better known today, "creation science." First introduced as a theory in the 1920s by George McCready Price, whose 1923 book, *The New Geology,* was cited at the Scopes Trial, creation science was further popularized in 1961 by the publication of *The Genesis Flood* by Henry M. Morris and John C. Whitcomb. In 1972 Morris founded an organization called the Institute for Creation Research (ICR) in California, which continues to support research and publications furthering creation science and "young-earth creationism." In September 2007, for instance, ICR hosted a conference in Denver, Colorado, called "Thousands...Not Billions," described as "a young-earth conference confronting worldviews: Evolution or Creation?"

Paul Ellwanger, the founder of a South Carolina group called Citizens for Fairness in Education, used ICR materials to draft a model state law that mandated the teaching of creationism as science alongside evolution. In 1981 the State of Arkansas adopted Ellwanger's creation-science law without alteration. The act opens with the following definition:

(a) "Creation-science" means the scientific evidences for creation and inferences from those scientific evidences. Creation-science includes the scientific evidences and related inferences that indicate:

(1) Sudden creation of the universe, energy, and life from nothing;

(2) The insufficiency of mutation and natural selection in bringing about development of all living kinds from a single organism;

(3) Changes only within fixed limits of originally created kinds of plants and animals;

(4) Separate ancestry for man and apes;

(5) Explanation of the earth's geology by catastrophism, including the occurrence of a worldwide flood; and

(6) A relatively recent inception of the earth and living kinds.

The Arkansas law was challenged in U.S. District Court by a wide range of religious organizations and state residents in the case of *McLean v. Arkansas Board of Education* (1982). Applying the version of the *Lemon* test set out by the United States Supreme Court in *Stone v. Graham*, the district court concluded that creation-science law violated the test's first prong in lacking any secular legislative purpose: "It was simply and purely an effort to introduce the biblical version of creation into the public school curricula," the court said. "The only inference which can be drawn from these circumstances is that the act was passed with the specific purpose by the General Assembly of advancing religion."

The district court also noted that the law relied heavily on ICR materials, and concluded that it "is an extension of Fundamentalists' view that one must either accept the literal interpretation of Genesis or else believe in the godless system of evolution. The two model approach of the creationists is simply a contrived dualism which has no scientific factual basis or legitimate educational purpose." The district court entered a permanent injunction barring Arkansas from enforcing its creation-science law. Since Arkansas did not appeal the decision, however, the legal impact of the decision was limited to that state.

The issue of creation science reached the Supreme Court in December 1986, when the justices heard oral arguments on the constitutionality of Louisiana's Balanced Treatment for Creation-Science and Evolution-Science in Public School Instruction Act, also called simply the Creationism Act. Under the terms of the Creationism Act, no school was required to teach evolution or any other theory of human origin. However, the law also stated that if a school decided to teach evolution, then it was also required to teach creation science. Both the U.S. District Court in Louisiana and the Fifth Circuit Court of Appeals concluded that the Creationism Act was intended to promote the beliefs of a particular religion and thus violated the establishment clause of the First Amendment.

The State of Louisiana appealed the decision to the Supreme Court, which granted certiorari. Three amici briefs were filed supporting the state's position, including one written by Michael Farris on behalf of Concerned Women for America. A much larger number of groups filed briefs asking the Court to affirm the lower court decisions, including several states; the American Federation of Teachers; Americans United for Separation of Church and State; the National Academy of Sciences; People for the American Way; and a group of seventy-two Nobel Prize winners.

In a 7–2 decision issued six months later in *Edwards v. Aguillard* (1987), the Court agreed that the law was unconstitutional. The majority opinion, written by Associate Justice William Brennan, concentrated almost exclusively on the first prong of the *Lemon* test: "whether [Louisiana's] actual purpose is to endorse or disapprove of religion." Brennan noted that the ostensible purpose of the Louisiana law was to promote academic freedom, but the Court, he added firmly, was not required to give deference to a legislative purpose that is clearly a sham.

"The goal of providing a more comprehensive science curriculum is not furthered," Brennan said, "either by outlawing the teaching of evolution or by requiring the teaching of creation science." The state's academic-freedom argument was also undercut by the bill's sponsor, state senator Bill Keith, who said during legislative hearings on the bill, "My preference would be that neither [creationism nor evolution] be taught." Senator Keith also made it clear during the hearings that his decision to sponsor the Creationism Act stemmed from the fact that evolution is contrary to his religious views.

Additional evidence of the legislature's real intent, Brennan said, could be found in the fact that creation science is not an open-ended inquiry, but instead is intended to promote the belief of one religion in a supreme being. "Out of many possible science subjects taught in the public schools," he noted, "the legislature chose to affect the teaching of the one scientific theory that historically has been opposed by certain religious sects.... Because the primary purpose of the Creationism Act is to advance a particular religious belief, the act endorses religion in violation of the First Amendment."

Associate Justice Antonin Scalia's lengthy and frequently sarcastic dissent, which was joined by Chief Justice Rehnquist, offered two main responses to the majority's decision. First, quoting former chief justice Burger, Scalia said that all Louisiana was required to do was show a secular purpose, and that invalidation was only appropriate when or

if the challenged statute was "motivated wholly by religious considerations." In Scalia's view, there was ample evidence of a secular motive,
not least of which was the legislature's own clear statement of purpose.
He described himself as "astonished" by the majority's decision,
"which I can only attribute to an intellectual predisposition created by
the facts and the legend of *Scopes v. State* (1927)—an instinctive reaction
that any governmentally imposed requirements bearing upon the teaching of evolution must be a manifestation of Christian fundamentalist
repression."

Scalia also took the opportunity in his dissent to suggest that given
the difficulty of applying the first prong of the *Lemon* test—the search
for governmental intent—the time had come to abandon the test altogether. Without specifically saying so, Scalia essentially argued that
Chief Justice Burger replaced the use of Jefferson's wall metaphor with
the *Lemon* test to give the Court more flexibility in its application of the
establishment clause. "I think it time," Scalia wrote, "that we sacrifice
some 'flexibility' for 'clarity and predictability.'" One way to accomplish that, of course, would be to unearth the establishment-clause
analysis in place for the half century prior to *Lemon*: Jefferson's wall of
separation.

Kitzmiller *and the Shift from* "Creation Science" *to* "Intelligent Design"

The Court's rejection of the Louisiana Creationism Act did not put a
stop to the Religious Right's assault on evolution. In his opinion in
Edwards, Associate Justice Brennan made it clear that the Court's decision was not intended to foreclose all challenges to evolution, and
pointed to the fact that the Court had said in *Stone* that there might be
acceptable secular uses of the Ten Commandments in school curricula.
"In a similar way," Brennan said, "teaching a variety of scientific theories about the origins of humankind to schoolchildren might be validly
done with the clear secular intent of enhancing the effectiveness of science instruction."

At about the same time that *Edwards* was handed down, Drs. Perci-
val Davis and Dean Kenyon were working on a new biology book for
high school students titled *Of Pandas and People: The Central Question of Bi-*

ological Origins. The governing message of the book, which is published by the Texas-based Foundation for Thought and Ethics (FTE), is that life on earth is the result of "intelligent design" by some supernatural being. When the book was published in 1989, it quickly became a favorite of local Christian Right groups, who urged school boards and individual biology teachers to adopt the text. In communities across the country, Religious Right activists also ran low-key campaigns for school boards (part of the "stealth strategy" of Pat Robertson's Christian Coalition), with the goal of electing a pro-intelligent-design majority.

By itself, *Of Pandas and People* might have lapsed into obscurity, but it attracted the attention of the Discovery Institute (DI), a Religious Right think tank founded in 1990 by Bruce Chapman, a former director of the U.S. Census Bureau under President Ronald Reagan. In 1994, he met philosophy professor Stephen Meyer, who introduced him to the concept of intelligent design. Chapman quickly saw that the issue could be a powerful fund-raising tool for the DI. With the help of Meyer and DI board member George Gilder (who later owned the conservative magazine the *American Spectator* for a period of time), Chapman solicited funds from the Ahamnson family, a clan nearly as legendary in conservative political and social circles as the Pittsburgh-based Mellon Scaifes. The scion of the Ahmanson family, Howard Jr., is a particularly active supporter of the Christian Right and a follower of R. J. Rushdoony's Christian Reconstructionist movement. In fact, Ahmanson served as a board member for Rushdoony's Chalcedon Foundation for more than a decade.

Ahmanson pledged $750,000 over three years to the DI, which used the funds to establish what is now known as the Center for Science and Culture (CSC). The CSC's goals were outlined in a document titled "Wedge Strategy," in which the center laid out its plans to introduce intelligent design in part by portraying the mainstream scientific community as biased and unfairly restrictive. A central component of the wedge strategy (a copy of the document was leaked onto the Internet in 1999) is a campaign called "Teach the Controversy," in which intelligent-design supporters argue that the principle of academic freedom requires that their theory be presented alongside the theory of evolution. In August 2005, during a Q&A session with Texas reporters at the White House, President George W. Bush caused a stir by agreeing with the DI's position. "Both sides ought to be properly taught," Bush said, "so people can understand what the debate is about.... I think that part of education is to expose people to different schools of thought." The president's remarks demonstrated the remarkable success of the creationist/intelligent-design camp in creating the appearance of a legitimate scientific debate.

The School Board of Directors in Dover, Pennsylvania, evidently agreed with the president. In October 2004 the board had voted 6–3 that "students will be made aware of gaps/problems in Darwin's theory and of other theories of evolution including, but not limited to, intelligent design. Note: Origins of Life is not taught." According to a press release issued by the board the following month, the school district's biology teachers would be required to read a statement to their students, which said in part:

> Because Darwin's theory is a theory, it continues to be tested as new evidence is discovered. The theory is not a fact. Gaps in the theory exist for which there is no evidence.... Intelligent design is an explanation of the origin of life that differs from Darwin's view. The reference book *Of Pandas and People* is available for students who might be interested in gaining an understanding of what intelligent design actually involves.

If any teacher refused to read the statement, then a school administrator would do so. The district was sued almost immediately by a group of eleven parents, with the assistance of the ACLU and Americans United for Separation of Church and State. The board was represented pro bono by the conservative Catholic firm the Thomas More Law Center, which had been soliciting districts willing to promote intelligent design. The matter went to trial at the end of September 2005, but due to the complexity of the issues presented and the sheer amount of evidence, the trial did not end until November 4, 2005. Six weeks later, a lengthy and detailed decision in the case, *Kitzmiller v. Dover Area School District*, was handed down by U.S. District Court Judge John Jones III.

After reviewing applicable Supreme Court and Third Circuit law, Jones concluded that there were two tests to apply to Dover's intelligent-design policy: first, whether the policy "endorsed" religion (the approach suggested by Justice O'Connor in *Lynch* and largely accepted by the Court in *Allegheny*), and second, whether the policy then violated the remaining prongs of the *Lemon* test (the "purpose" and "effect" inquiries).

Judge Jones conducted a careful review of the history of evolution in the federal courts, and noted that the intelligent-design movement sprang up largely in response to the Supreme Court's ruling in *Edwards*. In fact, Jones noted, early editions of the biology text *Of Pandas and People* used the phrase "creation science," but after the *Edwards* decision, the phrase was systematically eliminated. From the testimony of the plaintiffs' expert, Jones said, "three astonishing points emerge: (1) the definition for creation science in early drafts is identical to the definition of ID [intelligent design]; (2) cognates of the word "creation" ("creationism" and "creationist"), which appeared approximately 150 times, were deliberately and systematically replaced with the phrase "ID"; and (3) the changes occurred shortly after the Supreme Court held that creation science is religious and cannot be taught in public school science classes in *Edwards*." It was absolutely clear, Jones concluded, "that ID is creationism relabeled."

Given that conclusion, Jones said, the next question is whether the disclaimer drafted by the district constitutes an "endorsement" of religion. In no uncertain terms, Jones said that it did:

> In summary, the disclaimer singles out the theory of evolution for special treatment, misrepresents its status in the scientific community, causes students to doubt its validity without scientific justification, presents students with a religious alternative masquerading as a scientific theory, directs them to consult a creationist text as though it were a science resource, and instructs students to forgo scientific inquiry in the public school classroom and instead to seek out religious instruction elsewhere.

Although the district's policy failed the "endorsement" test, Judge Jones went on to analyze the controversy under the *Lemon* test, and found that the district's policy was unconstitutional under that standard as well. After reciting the facts of the case at length, Jones found that any secular purpose enunciated by the board was a mere pretext, and that the effect of the policy "was to impose a religious view of biological origins into the biology course, in violation of the establishment clause."

The *Kitzmiller* decision was a bitter pill for the Religious Right to swallow. Although the Thomas More Law Center had been spoiling for a fight on this topic, the Discovery Institute was leery of a head-on confrontation for precisely this reason, that a federal judge would equate intelligent design with creationism. The DI's preferred approach was to persuade school boards to "teach the controversy," rather than actually teaching intelligent design itself. The precedential value of the *Kitzmiller* decision is limited to the Middle District of Pennsylvania, since the decision was not appealed by the school board. But there is no question that the thoroughness of Judge Jones's analysis is likely to be very persuasive.

Although he was appointed by President Bush in 2002, Judge Jones was harshly criticized by some Religious Right leaders. The associate director of the DI, John West, said that the opinion resulted from Jones's desire to get on "his soapbox to offer his own views of science, religion, and evolution. He makes it clear that he wants his place in history as the judge who issued a definitive decision about intelligent design. This is an activist judge who has delusions of grandeur." Attorney Phyllis Schlafly, president of the Eagle Forum, wrote in an e-mail to supporters that "Judge John E. Jones III could still be chairman of the Pennsylvania Liquor Control Board if millions of evangelical Christians had not pulled the lever for George W. Bush in 2000. Yet this federal judge, who owes his position entirely to those voters and the president who appointed him, stuck the knife in the backs of those who brought him to the dance in *Kitzmiller v. Dover Area School District.*"

Demonstrating his thorough grasp not merely of the legal issues in the case, but also the larger social battle taking place in America, Judge Jones clearly anticipated the objections of intelligent-design supporters:

Those who disagree with our holding will likely mark it as the product of an activist judge. If so, they will have erred as this is manifestly not an activist court. Rather, this case came to us as the result of the activism of an ill-informed faction on a school board, aided by a national public interest law firm eager to find a constitutional test case on [intelligent design], who in combination drove the board to adopt an imprudent and ultimately unconstitutional policy. The breathtaking inanity of the board's decision is evident when considered against the factual backdrop which has now been fully revealed through this trial. The students, parents, and teachers of the Dover Area School District deserved better than to be dragged into this legal maelstrom, with its resulting utter waste of monetary and personal resources.

Just four days after the *Kitzmiller* trial ended, a local election was held in Dover. The verdict of the town's residents was clear: all eight school board members who had voted in favor of presenting intelligent design as an option to evolution were voted out of office.

Of Prayer and Proselytizing

While the debate over what can be taught in public school classrooms (particularly science) is perhaps the longest-running battle between secularists and the Christian Right, the battle over prayer in the public schools is easily the most intense. The rulings by the Supreme Court that declared government-sponsored prayer and moments of silence unconstitutional are routinely cited by Religious Right leaders as the cause of most of the nation's social ills.

In the wake of the tragic 1999 shooting at Columbine High School near Littleton, Colorado, for instance, Jerry Falwell described the Supreme Court's decision to ban state-sponsored prayer as "one of the greatest mistakes in our nation's history," adding that he believed the ruling "was our nation's first step toward our present-day environment of violence and disregard for life." Falwell's comments, however, were mild compared to those of his fellow televangelist and former Republican presidential candidate Pat Robertson, who told his *700 Club* audience the morning after the shootings:

When the Supreme Court of the United States of America insulted Almighty God, and said our Constitution wouldn't permit children to pray in the schools, and when we lifted the religious restraints off of our society in that fashion and suddenly the worship of God became unconstitutional, and the thought that we would have an even hand between atheism and theism in society, it has begun a spiral that hasn't stopped yet.

You say, why are kids killing themselves, and why are they killing each other? Well, you just look back about thirty-some years and you find, in my opinion, the principal reason.

But Robertson did not accurately describe the Supreme Court's ruling. The Supreme Court never declared the worship of God unconstitutional; what the Court said was that the government cannot draft a prayer and require children of all faiths (as well as nonbelievers) to sit and listen to it each morning before the start of school.

The much-despised case to which Robertson was referring, *Engel v. Vitale* (1962), involved a challenge by a group of parents in New Hyde Park, New York, to the daily recitation of the following prayer in the public school: "Almighty God, we acknowledge our dependence upon Thee and we beg Thy blessings upon us, our parents, our teachers, and our country." Twenty-two states filed amicus curiae briefs supporting the State of New York, and the Supreme Court received thousands of letters asking it to uphold prayer in school. But the Court firmly rejected the New York prayer, voting 6–1 that the prayer was "composed by government officials as part of a governmental program to further religious beliefs."

Writing for the majority, Associate Justice Hugo Black said that New York had violated the First Amendment prohibition against the establishment of religion. The establishment clause, Black said, has two main purposes: "Its first and most immediate purpose rest[s] on the belief that a union of government and religion tends to destroy government and to degrade religion." The "inevitable result" of an alliance between government and religion, Black wisely noted, is "the hatred, disrespect, and even contempt of those who [hold] contrary beliefs."

The second purpose of the establishment clause, Black said, is to avoid the tendency of governmentally established religions to result in religious persecution. As he pointed out, England's Act of Uniformity of 1559, which made it a crime for individuals to attend any religious service other than the Church of England and fined those who did not go to church weekly, was passed just a few years after Elizabeth I declared the Book of Common Prayer the only acceptable form of religious service. (The passage of the Act of Uniformity was one of the things that eventually led the Puritans to flee England and, eventually, brave the Atlantic crossing to America.)

The conclusion of Justice Black's opinion rejected the persistent argument that the Court was demonstrating hostility to religion or prayer by declaring the New York statute unconstitutional. "Nothing, of course, could be more wrong," Black said:

It is neither sacrilegious nor antireligious to say that each separate government in this country should stay out of the business of writing or sanctioning official prayers and leave that purely religious function to the people themselves and to those the people choose to look to for religious guidance.

Notwithstanding the clarity and thoughtfulness of Black's opinion, the decision by the Court was greeted with cries of outrage from members of Congress and much of the public. The Court, however, did have some influential backers. At a news conference a few days afterward, the first question posed to President John F. Kennedy asked for his reaction to the school prayer decision. Kennedy, the nation's first Roman Catholic president, said that he hoped people would support the Supreme Court, even if they disagreed with the decision, given the Court's valuable role in preserving the country's constitutional system.

And for those who do disagree, Kennedy said, "We have in this case an easy remedy, and that is to pray ourselves. And I would think it would be a welcome reminder to every American family that we can pray a good deal more at home, we can attend our churches with a good deal more fidelity, and we can make the true meaning of prayer much more important in the lives of all our children."

For one member of Congress, Kennedy's rational suggestion for personal prayer simply did not go far enough. Representative Roy Taylor (D-N.C.) introduced legislation to add a new amendment to the Constitution: "Notwithstanding the first or fourteenth articles of Amendment to the Constitution of the United States, prayers may be offered and the Bible may be read in connection with the program of any public school in the United States."

Taylor neatly anticipated where the Court was headed. The following year, the Court heard a case brought by atheist Madalyn Murray O'Hair and her son William, challenging a Maryland law that required the reading of a Bible chapter and/or the Lord's Prayer each morning. Their appeal was combined with an appeal by Edward Schempp, the father of a public school student, who questioned the constitutionality of a similar Pennsylvania law. The Court, under a ruling listed under the single name of *Abington School District v. Schempp* (1963), overwhelmingly concluded (8–1) that the two state laws were unconstitutional under the establishment clause of the First Amendment, and even the lone dissenter, Associate Justice Potter Stewart, was simply concerned about whether there was sufficient evidence in the trial record for the Supreme Court to make a decision.

Associate Justice Tom Clark wrote the majority opinion, and perhaps sensitive to the enormous criticism received by the Court following the previous year's decision, spent a significant amount of time stressing the importance of religion in American life. After reviewing the Court's interpretation of the establishment clause over the years, however, Justice Clark found that "it has consistently held that the clause withdrew all legislative power respecting religious belief or the expression thereof."

In order for a legislative enactment to survive an establishment clause challenge, Clark added, it must have a "secular legislative purpose" and "a primary effect that neither advances nor inhibits religion." The Court's adoption of the secular purpose/primary effect test for evaluating the practice of Bible readings in the public schools was a preview of the adoption of its more famous three-part *Lemon* test eight years later, which added (at least temporarily) the element of excessive entanglement between government and religion.

In both cases, Justice Clark said, the reading of Bible passages and the mandatory recitation of the Lord's Prayer were religious exercises sponsored by state government, and as such, violated the establishment clause of the First Amendment. Both states argued that there were secular purposes, including "the promotion of moral values, the contradiction to the materialistic trends of our times, the perpetuation of our institutions, and the teaching of literature." But the use of the Bible as the text for those purposes, Clark said, illustrated the religious intent of the law. While individual students did have the right to leave during the readings or prayer, that was insufficient to overcome the establishment clause challenge. "The breach of neutrality that is today a trickling stream," Clark argued, "may all too soon become a raging torrent and, in the words of Madison, 'it is proper to take alarm at the first experiment on our liberties.'"

Clark also dismissed the claim, still frequently heard today, that by holding Bible readings in public schools unconstitutional, the Court would in fact be imposing a "religion of secularism." He agreed that governments may not actively oppose those who are religious, or show hostility to religion in general, since to do so would violate the First Amendment's free expression clause. Nor are governments forbidden from discussing religion generally as part of a public school curriculum, or even teaching the historical and literary significance of the Bible. "But the exercises here . . . are religious exercises," Clark said, "required by the states in violation of the command of the First Amendment that the government maintain strict neutrality, neither aiding nor opposing religion."

The year after the *Schempp* decision, Madalyn Murray O'Hair founded American Atheists, an organization still committed to "the civil liberties of Atheists, and the total, absolute separation of government and religion." Over the years, O'Hair and her organization filed a large number of lawsuits against various governmental expressions of religion, including religious expressions by astronauts on the *Apollo* 8 and *Apollo* 11 space missions, the use of the motto "In God We Trust" by the United States government, and the celebration of Mass by Pope John Paul II on the National Mall in Washington, D.C. None of O'Hair's later suits, however, were successful. In a painful personal irony, O'Hair's son William, her coplaintiff in the Maryland Bible lessons case, discovered God in 1980 and joined the Baptist Church in Dallas, Texas, as a preacher. The two rarely spoke afterward.

Thanks to the decisiveness of the Supreme Court's rulings in both *Engel* and *Schempp*, the issue of prayer in the public schools largely subsided. In the late 1970s and early 1980s, however, after Jerry Falwell and the Moral Majority brought the Christian Right back into the political arena, activists began looking for ways to restore prayer to the schoolhouse. Alabama, for instance, adopted a statute in 1978 that authorized a one-minute moment of silence, which was amended in 1981 to include the purposes of "meditation or silent prayer." The state went further in 1982, authorizing teachers to lead "willing students" in prayer to "Almighty God... the Creator and Supreme Judge of the world."

The Supreme Court previously concluded, unanimously, that the teacher-led, state-written prayer was unconstitutional, and even the plaintiffs in the 1985 case heard by the Court, *Wallace v. Jaffree*, agreed that an unadorned moment of silence was acceptable. The more difficult issue for the Court was whether Alabama's promotion of a moment of silence for specific purposes, i.e., meditation or silent prayer, was "a law respecting the establishment of religion within the meaning of the First Amendment."

Even though the makeup of the Supreme Court had changed substantially over the two decades since *Schempp*, the justices agreed, by an only slightly less-solid margin of 6–3, that the Alabama law was unconstitutional. Writing for the majority, Associate Justice John Paul Stevens said that the applicable standard had been laid out by the Court in *Lemon* and as the district court had recognized at trial, only the first prong was at issue: whether Alabama's purpose in enacting the law was to endorse or promote religion.

To answer that question, Justice Stevens focused on why the Alabama legislature amended its "moment of silence" law in 1981 to include the phrase "or voluntary prayer." The answer was not hard to locate: during the district court's preliminary injunction hearing, the bill's primary sponsor, state senator Donald Holmes, testified that the 1981 amendment was an "effort to return voluntary prayer to our public schools...it is a beginning and a step in the right direction." Holmes also made it clear to the district court that he had no other purpose in proposing the addition of the phrase.

For the majority, at least, Holmes's unabashed testimony left no doubt as to what Alabama was trying to accomplish. "The addition of 'or voluntary prayer' indicates that the state intended to characterize prayer as a favored practice," Stevens said. "Such an endorsement is not consistent with the established principle that the government must pursue a course of complete neutrality toward religion."

Taken together, the Court's decisions in *Schempp, Engel,* and *Wallace* have largely resolved the issue of daily school-sponsored religious exercises. In the twenty years since *Wallace,* the Court has looked at the issue of school prayer in two other contexts: whether a school can include prayer or religious observances in ceremonial events such as school graduations, and whether a school district can outsource the establishment and delivery of prayer to an election by the student body. In both cases, the Court held the challenged practices unconstitutional; however, Associate Justice Sandra Day O'Connor was in the majority each time, and her place on the Court has been taken by the clearly more conservative Samuel Alito. It is not likely that these issues have been put completely to rest.

The first of the significant school prayer cases was *Lee v. Weisman* (1992). Faced with a challenge to a rabbi's prayer at a Providence, Rhode Island, middle school, a 5–4 majority of the Court concluded that the decision of the school principal to include an invocation and benediction was an action attributable to the state, and thus a violation of the establishment clause. Writing for the Court, Justice Kennedy noted that the selection of a particular member of the clergy to deliver those messages has a "potential for divisiveness," a potential that is heightened by the clergy's participation in a secondary school celebration for which no reasonable alternative existed. Moreover, Kennedy said, the principal in question gave the rabbi guidelines for preparing his prayer, thereby further entangling the state in religion.

"It is a cornerstone principle of our establishment clause jurisprudence," Kennedy noted, "that it is no part of the business of government to compose official prayers for any group of the American people to recite as a part of a religious program carried on by government, and that is what the school officials attempted to do."

A significant part of the majority's analysis concerned the "subtle coercive pressure" of including a religious observance in a school event. Kennedy acknowledged that some members of the audience who have no desire to join in the prayer may be willing to simply stand out of respect for the prayer or for the person delivering it. Nonetheless, Kennedy said, "Given our social conventions, a reasonable dissenter in this milieu could believe that the group exercise [of standing] signified her own participation or approval of [the prayer]."

In essence, Kennedy said, what the state was arguing was that the burden was on the individual to take action, i.e., skipping her graduation, to avoid "compromising [her] religious scruples." But "it is a tenet of the First Amendment," he wrote, "that the state cannot require one of its citizens to forfeit his or her rights and benefits as the price of resisting conformance to state-sponsored religious practice."

An even more blatant attempt to impose a school-related religious practice by majority fiat occurred in the case of *Santa Fe Independent School District v. Doe* (2000), in which the plaintiff school district adopted a policy that allowed the student body to vote on whether a prayer should be delivered prior to each varsity football game and if so, to elect a student to deliver the prayer. Writing for a 6–3 majority, Associate Justice John Paul Stevens ruled that the district could not insulate itself from establishment clause problems by delegating the issue of school prayer to the student body.

"This student election does nothing to protect minority views," Stevens said, "but rather places the students who hold such views at the mercy of the majority. Because 'fundamental rights may not be submitted to vote; they depend on the outcome of no elections,' the district's elections are insufficient safeguards of diverse student speech."

Stevens also concluded that the district had failed to demonstrate actual neutrality as to the content of the speech. The policy called for the delivery of a message designed to "solemnize the event," which, Stevens pointed out, most often means a religious message. In fact, the district policy specifically endorsed the delivery of an "invocation," which as a matter of long-standing practice at district games meant "a focused religious message." Stevens also noted that the students themselves were apparently under no illusions as to what was at stake in the election established by the district: "The students understood that the central question before them was whether prayer should be a part of the pregame ceremony." Perhaps most significant for the majority was the fact that the district's election-based policy was a direct outgrowth of its long-standing policy for the selection of a "student chaplain." Given all of that, Stevens said, "It is reasonable to infer that the specific purpose of the policy was to preserve a popular 'state-sponsored religious practice.'"

The district tried to overcome potential constitutional problems by arguing that unlike the graduation ceremony in *Lee*, attendance at a high school football game is truly voluntary, and the pressure to attend is far less than in the case of a graduation ceremony. While conceding that football games are not important to some students, Stevens said that the district still may not require "religious conformity" as the price of attending a high school football game.

Echoing the words of President Kennedy following the Court's ruling in *Engel*, Stevens affirmed: "Nothing in the Constitution as interpreted by this Court prohibits any public school student from voluntarily praying at any time before, during, or after the school day." But the establishment clause of the First Amendment, he added, does prohibit the district from sponsoring "the particular religious practice of prayer."

For the Religious Right, which was heavily involved in briefing the legal issues in the *Santa Fe* case, the Court's decision was particularly galling. Clearly, if the practices discussed in that case are unconstitutional, the Christian Right cannot reasonably hope that the Supreme Court will suddenly decide that its forty-year-old cases removing prayer from the public school classroom should be reversed. Nonetheless, the Religious Right continues to advocate for the appointment of justices willing to allow states to draft and mandate prayers in the public schools.

CHAPTER EIGHT

Cubicle Faith

Religion in the Workplace

IN BEAUMONT, SOUTH CAROLINA, a textile mill operated by Spartan Mills shut down in July 1995, after 105 years in operation. A victim of less-expensive imports, particularly from the Far East, the Beaumont plant was later sold and demolished to make way for the construction of the Spartanburg Regional Medical Center Ambulatory Surgery Center. Lost in the dust and rubble was the fact that the mill had played a small part in one of the Supreme Court's most important cases dealing with religion and the workplace.

In the late 1950s, a woman named Adell H. Sherbert worked at the Beaumont mill, having started there just after World War I. The management of the mill instituted a six-day workweek in 1959, but Sherbert, who was a Seventh-Day Adventist, refused to work on Saturday, which she observed as the Sabbath and as the day the Bible said no work should be done. The mill fired Sherbert and because all the other mills in the area had adopted a similar schedule, she was unable to find another job. She applied for unemployment compensation from South Carolina, but was rejected on the grounds that she did not have "good cause" for turning down suitable work. Sherbert sued the state, alleging infringement of her right to free exercise of her religion, but the South Carolina Supreme Court upheld the denial of benefits.

By a 7–2 vote in *Sherbert v. Verner* (1963), the Supreme Court reversed the state court decision. Writing for the majority, Associate Justice William Brennan said that the first question was whether the state action imposed "any burden" on the free exercise of religion. In this case, he said, it is clear that the state's "ruling forces her to choose between following the precepts of her religion and forfeiting benefits, on the one hand, and abandoning one of the precepts of her religion in order to accept work, on the other hand." That, Brennan concluded, is an unacceptable and substantial infringement on Sherbert's free exercise rights.

The Court then examined whether the state had some compelling interest that would justify the infringement. South Carolina expressed some concern that its unemployment compensation fund would be depleted by spurious claims, and that employers would have trouble finding people to work on Saturday. But Brennan noted that those concerns had not been raised in the state supreme court, and that there was no proof that such abuses either had or would occur. Moreover, even if such concerns were legitimate, he added, the burden would be on South Carolina to show that there were no less-restrictive regulations available to combat fraud without infringing on the First Amendment.

The reversal of the South Carolina Supreme Court, Brennan said, was merely an affirmation of the U.S. Supreme Court's earlier ruling, in *Everson v. Board of Education* (1947), "that no state may 'exclude individual Catholics, Lutherans, Mohammedans, Baptists, Jews, Methodists, Nonbelievers, Presbyterians, or the members of any other faith, *because of their faith, or lack of it,* from receiving the benefits of public welfare legislation.'"

The Court's decision in *Sherbert* predated the resurgence of the Religious Right by nearly two decades, so the movement was not a factor in bringing the case before the Court. Nonetheless, over the years the *Sherbert* case has become an increasingly important part of the Christian Right's legal armament, both in support of religious objections to job requirements and equal access of sectarian organizations to funds from public programs.

Peyote and Sherbert: A Potent Mix

Nearly twenty years after it was decided, the *Sherbert* decision seemed to be on solid ground. In 1981 the Court voted 8–1 in *Thomas v. Review Bd., Ind. Empl. Sec. Div.* that, much like Adell Sherbert, a Jehovah's Witness by the name of Eddie Thomas had been unfairly denied unemployment benefits for exercising his religious beliefs. Thomas worked for the Blaw-Knox Foundry and Machinery Co. in Indiana, and was transferred to a division that made turrets for tanks. He objected to the transfer on the grounds that his religious beliefs precluded him from engaging in the production of armaments, and asked for assignment to a different division of the foundry.

When it turned out that the only job openings in the company were in divisions engaged in the direct manufacture of armaments, Thomas quit and applied for unemployment compensation. His application was denied by the Indiana Employment Security Review Board on the grounds that he left his job without good cause. The board's decision was upheld by the Indiana Supreme Court, and the U.S. Supreme Court granted Thomas's petition for a writ of certiorari.

Writing for the large majority, Chief Justice Warren Burger acknowledged that the Indiana Supreme Court was doubtful about the strength of Thomas's religious conviction, dubbing it a "personal philosophical choice" instead. But, he admonished, "courts should not undertake to dissect religious beliefs because the believer admits that he is 'struggling' with his position or because his beliefs are not articulated with the clarity and precision that a more sophisticated person might employ."

The lone dissent in the case was written by Associate Justice William Rehnquist, who argued that the Court's interpretation of the free exercise clause was overly broad. Ironically, one of his other complaints (given his generally conservative legal views) is that the majority failed to properly apply the three-part *Lemon* test to the facts of the case. "It is unclear from the Court's opinion," Rehnquist wrote, "whether it has temporarily retreated from its expansive view of the establishment clause, or wholly abandoned it. I would welcome the latter."

But even after becoming chief justice, Rehnquist remained an isolated voice on this issue. In *Hobbie v. Unemployment Appeals Comm'n of Florida* (1987), the Court overturned a decision by the Unemployment Appeals Commission of Florida by the same 8–1 margin. The employee in question, a Seventh-Day Adventist named Paula Hobbie, was denied unemployment for refusing to work on Saturday, her Sabbath. The only significant factual difference between *Sherbert* and *Hobbie*, the Court said, was that Paula Hobbie converted to her religion while already employed.

"In effect," Associate Justice William Brennan wrote, "the Appeals Commission asks us to single out the religious convert for different, less favorable treatment than that given an individual whose adherence to his or her faith precedes employment. We decline to do so. The First Amendment protects the free exercise rights of employees who adopt religious beliefs or convert from one faith to another after they are hired."

The *Hobbie* case was one of the first of the religion-workplace cases to attract attention from religious advocacy groups, including the Christian Right. Most notably, an amicus curiae brief, supporting reversal of the Florida commission, was filed by the Rutherford Institute, the Christian Reconstructionist firm founded by John Whitehead.

Just three years later, however, when Oregon residents Alfred Smith and Galen Black appealed a denial of unemployment benefits to the Supreme Court, Religious Right groups were nowhere to be found. Smith and Black worked at a private drug-rehabilitation organization in Oregon, and both were members of the Native American Church. As part of a religious ceremony for their church, Smith and Black ingested peyote, a hallucinogenic drug derived from the peyote cactus that has been used in certain Native American religious ceremonies for thousands of years.

When their employer learned of their peyote use, Smith and Black were fired from their jobs. They applied to the Oregon Employment Division for unemployment benefits, but their claim was denied on the grounds that they were fired for work-related "misconduct." The U.S. Supreme Court agreed to hear the employment division's appeal from the Oregon Supreme Court, which had ruled that the two counselors were unconstitutionally denied their benefits.

In *Employment Div., Ore. Dept. of Human Res. v. Smith* (1990), the Supreme Court overturned the Oregon Supreme Court by a vote of 6–3 and held that the original denial of unemployment benefits was constitutional. Although the state supreme court had based its decision squarely on *Sherbert* and *Thomas*, Associate Justice Antonin Scalia, who wrote the majority opinion, said that those cases were easily distinguished. "The conduct at issue in those cases," Scalia pointed out, "was not prohibited by law." As part of its decision, the Oregon Supreme Court had made it clear that there is no exemption for the religious use of peyote under Oregon law. If Oregon's prohibition of the religious use of peyote is constitutional, Scalia said, then the employment division was not wrong to withhold unemployment compensation.

The critical question before the Court, Scalia said, was whether an individual's religious beliefs entitle him to ignore an otherwise valid state law. Reaching all the way back to *Reynolds v. United States* (1879), in which the Court rejected a religious freedom challenge to Utah's bigamy law, Scalia said that the Court has consistently denied such claims: "We have never held that an individual's religious beliefs excuse him from compliance with an otherwise valid law prohibiting conduct that the state is free to regulate." Since there was no suggestion that Oregon's antidrug statute was designed to regulate religious beliefs, Smith and Black could not use their First Amendment rights to avoid its prohibitions.

The most significant part of Scalia's opinion, however, was his discussion of the *Sherbert* case. Smith and Black argued that since the Oregon law "substantially burdened" the practice of their religion, Oregon was required under the *Sherbert* case to demonstrate that the law was justified by a "compelling governmental interest." The majority, however, disagreed. Scalia pointed out that the rule in *Sherbert* had never been directly applied outside of the context of unemployment benefits, and said that expanding the application of the rule could be disastrous:

> It would open the prospect of constitutionally required religious exemptions from civic obligations of almost every conceivable kind—ranging from compulsory military service to the payment of taxes; to health and safety regulation such as manslaughter and

child neglect laws, compulsory vaccination laws, drug laws, and traffic laws; to social welfare legislation such as minimum wage laws, child labor laws, animal cruelty laws, environmental protection laws, and laws providing for equality of opportunity for the races. The First Amendment's protection of religious liberty does not require this.

The *Sherbert* test, Scalia concluded, is simply inapplicable to the type of challenge raised by Smith and Black; as long as a state's law is not targeted specifically at religion, the state need not show a "compelling governmental interest" for its impact on religious practices.

There is no way to know whether the outcome of the *Smith* case would have been different if Religious Right legal groups had submitted amici briefs to the Supreme Court. Undoubtedly, most mainstream religious groups took a hands-off approach to the case because the religious activity in question involved the use of hallucinogenic drugs (one notable exception was the Council on Academic Freedom, an organization of Seventh-Day Adventists). But certainly, Scalia and the rest of the *Smith* majority adopted much more sweeping language than religious advocates anticipated.

Congress and the Supreme Court Battle over Sherbert
It is difficult to imagine two social policy groups more disparate than People for the American Way (PFAW) and Concerned Women for America (CWA); the former, founded by Hollywood producer Norman Lear, is avowedly liberal, while the latter, founded by Christian Reconstructionist Beverly LaHaye, is devoted to bringing biblical principles into all levels of public policy. The two groups are not often found on the same side of any legal issue, but in the wake of the Court's decision in *Smith*, they found common ground.

Along with a large number of other religious advocacy organizations, PFAW and CWA formed the Coalition for the Free Exercise of Religion and began lobbying for a bill to require the Supreme Court to reinstitute the *Sherbert* test. Michael Farris, who served as cochairman of the coalition's drafting committee and, at the same time, was running for lieutenant governor in Virginia, told the *Washington Post* that when he heard of the *Smith* decision, "I just understood that the Supreme Court had just taken away a very fundamental religious liberty for everyone in America."

The coalition presented to Congress legislation that became known as the Religious Freedom Restoration Act of 1993 (RFRA). The express purpose of the RFRA was to effectively overturn the Court's ruling in *Smith* by legislatively enacting the standard set out in *Sherbert*, which it did in two separate sections:

(a) In general—
Government shall not substantially burden a person's exercise of religion even if the burden results from a rule of general applicability, except as provided in subsection (b) of this section.
(b) Exception
Government may substantially burden a person's exercise of religion only if it demonstrates that application of the burden to the person—
(1) is in furtherance of a compelling governmental interest; and
(2) is the least restrictive means of furthering that compelling governmental interest.

Despite the wide-ranging support the bill enjoyed from many in Washington, including President Bill Clinton, it encountered some significant opposition in Congress. Among other things, law enforcement officers expressed concern that the bill would make it easier for prisoners to disrupt security measures by pleading religious exemptions to incarceration rules. Another significant opponent was the U.S. Catholic Conference, which worried that the RFRA would make it easier for pro-choice advocates to challenge state restrictions on abortion. After extensive discussions with the Coalition for the Free Exercise of Religion, however, the Catholic Conference announced its support for the bill in March 1993, which helped secure the RFRA's passage later that fall. President Bill Clinton signed the measure into law in November 1993.

At about the same time that Congress was considering the RFRA, Saint Peter Catholic Church in Boerne, Texas, applied for a permit to expand the size of its building. At least part of the facility, however, was located within Boerne's recently created historic district, and the city refused to allow any changes to the church structure. After the church's appeal was denied by the city council, the archbishop sued the city on behalf of the church, arguing that the historic district ordinance was unconstitutional and a violation of the RFRA. As the litigation progressed, the city raised a provocative counterargument: that the RFRA was in fact an unconstitutional violation of the separation of powers by Congress, and therefore not available to the church as a basis for challenging the city's ordinance. The district court agreed, but the Fifth Circuit overruled the trial court. Given the importance of the issue, it is not surprising that the Supreme Court granted the church's petition for a writ of certiorari.

In June 1997 a highly unusual alignment of justices voted to reverse the Fifth Circuit in the case of *City of Boerne v. Flores* and in the process, declared the RFRA unconstitutional. Associate Justice Anthony Kennedy wrote the majority opinion for himself and five other members of the Court (Rehnquist, Stevens, Thomas, Ginsburg, and Scalia, although Scalia did not join one section of Kennedy's opinion, in which he recounted the history of the Fourteenth Amendment). All three dissenters (O'Connor, Souter, and Breyer) filed their own individual opinions.

Under Section 5 of the Fourteenth Amendment, Congress has the "power to enforce, by appropriate legislation, the provisions of this article," the most important of which is making sure that no state deprives any person of "life, liberty, or property, without due process of law." The central question, Kennedy said, was whether Congress exceeded the scope of its enforcement power under Section 5 by enacting the RFRA and making its provisions applicable to the states.

There is no question, Kennedy said, that Congress has the ability to pass legislation to protect the free exercise of religion under the Fourteenth Amendment. At the same time, Kennedy argued, "Congress does not enforce a constitutional right by changing what the right is. It has been given the power 'to enforce,' not the power to determine what constitutes a constitutional violation." The Court's task, Kennedy said, is to determine whether the RFRA crosses the line from mere enforcement of a protected right to a substantive change in the right itself.

The archbishop argued that the RFRA was legitimate under the Fourteenth Amendment because it "prevents and remedies laws which are enacted with the unconstitutional object of targeting religious beliefs and practices." But the appropriateness of a law like the RFRA, Kennedy said, depends on the evil it is trying to remedy. Unlike with respect to the Voting Rights Act, which was adopted by Congress to prevent known violations of the constitutional right to vote, supporters of the RFRA could not point to any contemporary instances of laws passed due to religious bigotry. Boerne's historic district ordinance, for instance, was not specifically aimed at religious buildings, but was a general law that happened to affect property owned by the church.

The more significant flaw in the RFRA, Kennedy argued, was the fact that its impact was disproportionate to the harm that it purported to remedy:

> Sweeping coverage ensures its intrusion at every level of government, displacing laws and prohibiting official actions of almost every description and regardless of subject matter. RFRA's restrictions apply to every agency and official of the federal, state, and local governments. RFRA applies to all federal and state law, statutory or otherwise, whether adopted before or after its enactment. RFRA has no termination date or termination mechanism. Any law is subject to challenge at any time by any individual who alleges a substantial burden on his or her free exercise of religion.

Moreover, Kennedy noted, any individual who could successfully claim a "substantial burden" on his or her religious practice would force the governmental agency in question to show both a compelling interest for the law and that the law was the least restrictive means available to accomplish its goals.

"This is a considerable congressional intrusion," Kennedy said, "into the states' traditional prerogatives and general authority to regulate for the health and welfare of their citizens." Since the RFRA "contradicts vital principles necessary to maintain separation of powers and the federal balance," the majority reversed the court of appeals and declared the law unconstitutional.

The concurring opinion of Associate Justice John Paul Stevens was succinct and to the point, consisting of just two paragraphs. "In my opinion," he said, "the Religious Freedom Restoration Act of 1993 (RFRA) is a 'law respecting an establishment of religion' that violates the First Amendment to the Constitution." The RFRA, Stevens pointed out, gives religious individuals or organizations a "legal weapon" that is not available to secular organizations, to atheists, or even to agnostics. "This governmental preference for religion," Stevens argued, "as opposed to irreligion, is forbidden by the First Amendment."

Although the Court's decision in *Boerne* was no doubt disappointing to religious conservatives, the case was not a complete loss for the Coalition for the Free Exercise of Religion. The opinion struck down RFRA as it applied to the Court's analysis of state laws, but the Court did not address the issue of how the law applied to federal laws. That question was answered a few years later, however, when the Court ruled unanimously in *Gonzales v. O Centro Espirita Beneficente União do Vegetal* (2006) that RFRA did govern the Supreme Court's review of a federal law barring importation of hoasca tea, a compound listed by the Drug Enforcement Agency as a Schedule I substance ("high potential for abuse"). In an opinion written by the newly appointed chief justice John Roberts, the Court applied the *Sherbert* standards as instructed and concluded that the federal government had failed to show a compelling state interest for barring the religious use of hoasca tea.

The Civil Rights Act and Religion in the Private Workplace

The Supreme Court's decisions in cases like *Sherbert, Hobbie,* and *Smith* deal with one specific aspect of the interaction between religion and work: whether a state government is required to pay benefits to someone who stops working (or is fired) because of some work-related conflict with their religious beliefs. In each case, resolving that question involves a delicate balance of two constitutional principles, the free exercise clause and the establishment clause.

Balancing the religious rights of employees and the reasonable expectations of private employers is a different exercise altogether. The provisions of the U.S. Constitution are intended to limit or direct state action (i.e., local, state, or federal governments and their agents), and generally do not apply to private individuals, including corporations. As a result, private employers have traditionally had far fewer constraints in how they deal with the religious beliefs of their employees.

Whatever rights employees do enjoy are either derived from common law (relatively few) or are specifically provided by statute. The most significant example of such legislation is the Civil Rights Act of 1964, a sweeping effort by Congress to reduce and ideally eliminate various types of discrimination throughout American society, including the workplace. Among other things, Title VII of the Civil Rights Act states in part that "it shall be an unlawful employment practice for an employer...(1) to fail or refuse to hire or to discharge any individual, or otherwise to discriminate against any individual with respect to his compensation, terms, conditions, or privileges of employment, because of such individual's race, color, religion, sex, or national origin." No doubt unintentionally, Title VII effectively introduced into the private workplace many of the same debates and tensions that governments encounter in their dealings with citizens.

The protection of an individual's religious rights in private employment, while completely understandable and desirable from a social and historical perspective, has raised some particularly complicated enforcement issues. Of all the social categories protected by Title VII, religion is the one that most typically involves conscious choice on the part of the individual, and is also the one most likely to require affirmative acts of adherence that can create conflict in the work environment.

Coincidentally, the United States Supreme Court handed down its decision in *Sherbert* just one year before the adoption of the Civil Rights Act. It is not surprising, then, that one of the first issues to arise under the law was whether an employer would be in violation of Title VII for refusing to hire someone who could not work the employer's normal hours for religious reasons. But in contrast to *Sherbert* and the cases that followed over the years, the Court has provided much less protection for the exercise of religious beliefs in the private workplace.

In 1967 the Equal Employment Opportunity Commission (EEOC) adopted a guideline requiring employers "to make reasonable accommodations to the religious needs of employees and prospective employees where such accommodations can be made without undue hardship on the conduct of the employer's business." Exactly what constitutes a "reasonable accommodation" or "undue hardship," however, was never well defined by Congress. It did expand Title VII's definition of "religion" in 1972 to include "all aspects of religious observance and practice, as well as belief," but offered no further guidance on what steps employers were required to take to avoid religious discrimination.

The issue of what constitutes "reasonable accommodation" by an employer was presented squarely to the Supreme Court by Larry G. Hardison, an employee of the now-defunct Trans World Airlines (TWA) and an adherent of the Worldwide Church of God. Among the tenets Hardison observed was the obligation to refrain from work on the church's Sabbath, defined as extending from sunset on Friday to sunset on Sunday, and to not work on certain church holidays. TWA was initially able to accommodate Hardison's schedule, but when he applied for a transfer to a different location, he was informed that he lacked sufficient seniority to avoid working a Saturday shift. Hardison sued TWA, alleging religious discrimination; he lost at trial, but the verdict was overturned by the Eighth Circuit Court of Appeals.

The Supreme Court in turn reversed the Eighth Circuit. Associate Justice Byron White, writing for a 7–2 majority in *Trans World Airlines, Inc. v. Hardison* (1977), concluded that contrary to the Eighth Circuit's ruling, TWA had acted reasonably in its efforts to accommodate Hardison and that to impose any further requirements on the company would constitute "undue hardship." In addition, White said, there was no intent on the part of Congress to allow the protected categories under Title VII, including religion, to trump a valid and nondiscriminatory seniority system.

"[TWA's] seniority system was not designed with the intention to discriminate against religion," White said, quoting the district court below, "nor did it act to lock members of any religion into a pattern wherein their freedom to exercise their religion was limited. It was co-incidental that in plaintiff's case the seniority system acted to compound his problems in exercising his religion."

The majority also dismissed the suggestions by the court of appeals that TWA should have been willing either to allow Hardison to work a four-day week (which would have necessitated additional hires) or pay "premium wages" to persuade other employees to cover Hardison's Saturday shifts. "To require TWA to bear more than a *de minimis* cost in order to give Hardison Saturdays off is an undue hardship," White wrote. "Like abandonment of the seniority system, to require TWA to bear additional costs when no such costs are incurred to give other employees the days off that they want would involve unequal treatment of employees on the basis of their religion."

The Christian Right Joins the Battle for Religious Freedom in the Workplace

Following the Court's decision in *Trans World Airlines*, the tension between private employers and religious expression lay largely dormant until the early 1990s. The relative calm dissipated quickly, however, when the EEOC inadvertently stepped on the toes of the increasingly powerful Christian Right.

In October 1993 the EEOC proposed new rules designed to clarify the types of behavior forbidden by Title VII in private workplaces. Among other things, "harassment" was defined in the proposed rules as "conduct that 'denigrates or shows hostility or aversion' to someone based on religion, race, color, gender, national origin, age, or disability." However, before a finding of harassment could be made, an offended individual would have to show that the challenged conduct actually created an "intimidating, offensive or hostile work environment or interfered with someone's work or job opportunities."

The proposed regulations attracted little attention when they were first released. But the alarm was sounded on Christmas Eve by the Reverend Lou Sheldon, chairman of the Traditional Values Coalition, a conservative group representing thousands of churches across the country. He read the proposed regulations and began organizing a campaign to protest their adoption. In May 1994 opponents held a press conference in Washington, D.C., to report that they had collected more than eleven thousand letters objecting to the new regulations.

Much of the response was generated by the Christian Coalition, the grassroots political organization that grew out of televangelist Pat Robertson's failed campaign for president in 1988. According to the coalition's executive director, Ralph Reed, the group was working quietly but aggressively to block the regulations. "We used our telephone trees and phone banks to call EEOC and to contact members on the subcommittee," Reed said. "These are draconian measures, daggers aimed at the heart of religious expression, and if they are implemented, we will seek to enjoin them in court."

Rev. John Hagee, pastor of the Cornerstone Church in San Antonio, Texas, described the proposed rules as "a wholesale attack on religious freedom in America against both Christian and Jewish people." He argued that if adopted, the rules would allow the EEOC to prosecute people for wearing the Star of David or keeping a Bible on their desk.

Representatives of the EEOC dismissed those concerns, pointing to the fact that some showing of hostility or denigration is required in order to make a claim of religious harassment. "Obviously, wearing a cross or a yarmulke is not hostile or denigrating to somebody else's religion," Dianna Johnston, assistant legal counsel to the EEOC, said at the time. "It's just not conceivable to us that there could be any valid claim of religious harassment."

The guidelines proposed by the EEOC also drew an angry response from Congress. In the Senate, Hank Brown (R-Colo.) introduced a resolution "expressing the sense of the Senate regarding the issuance under Title VII of the Civil Rights Act of 1964 of administrative guidelines applicable to religious harassment in employment." Among other things, his resolution called for EEOC to withdraw religion from its proposed guidelines and draft new ones that make it clear that "symbols or expressions of religious belief consistent with the First Amendment and the Religious Freedom Restoration Act of 1993 are not to be restricted and do not constitute proof of harassment."

During a floor debate on the issue on June 16, 1994, Senator Brown reiterated many of the wilder claims by Religious Right leaders that the proposed guidelines would strip employees of their right to wear any religious symbol at work:

> Here are some of the things that the guidelines that are being put out will restrict: Wearing a yarmulke could be considered proof of religious harassment. Now, that is absurd. Having a Christmas party could be proof of religious harassment. Having a Hanukkah party could be considered proof of religious harassment. Displaying a picture of Christ on a calendar on a desk or on a wall could be proof of religious harassment. Wearing a T-shirt or hat, clothing which has any religious emblem or even a religious face on it could be considered proof of religious harassment.

Brown's tortured reading of the proposed EEOC guidelines was challenged by Senator Howard Metzenbaum (D-Ohio), who asked Brown to point out the section of the guidelines that would prohibit someone from wearing a yarmulke. Brown responded that his charges were based on the following language: "Verbal or physical conduct that denigrates or shows hostility or aversion toward an individual because of his or her religion or that of his or her relatives, friends, or associates." Metzenbaum responded: "As I understand what you are reading, all that the EEOC is saying is that if you make a snide remark or harass somebody by reason of their dress or conduct, that is religious harassment. But the mere fact that somebody wears the yarmulke, cross, or whatever, that is not a problem, and they are not saying that it is. It just seems to me that you are carrying the reasoning beyond the reality of what is in the proposal."

Brown argued that the real problem with the proposed regulations was not so much what individual employees might do, but instead, that the regulations would inspire corporate lawyers to write very restrictive workplace rules to limit potential corporate liability from religious harassment suits. His colleague Howell Heflin (R-Ala.) agreed, predicting that the average corporate lawyer would instruct his client to prohibit any hint of religious expression in the workplace: "What you are going to have to do is just say, 'Make the workplace religion neutral. You cannot talk about religion on the job. You cannot wear any emblems or do anything like that.'"

The senators apparently found the threat of overly cautious corporate counsel persuasive, voting 94–0 to approve Senator Brown's resolution. A month later, the resolution was added to an appropriations bill for the departments of Commerce, Justice, and State, and the judiciary, and the EEOC was officially ordered to withdraw its guidelines on religious harassment. Over the years, the EEOC continued to propose regulations governing religious harassment, but those efforts were repeatedly rebuffed by Congress. To date, the only guidelines formally adopted by the EEOC are those dealing with sexual harassment.

Given the relatively tame language proposed by the EEOC, it is hard to believe that the Religious Right was really all that concerned about the threat to yarmulkes or Advent calendars. The more likely objective, one the Christian Right successfully achieved, was to preserve the private workplace as an environment for Christian prayer and proselytization (activities that can certainly border on harassment themselves). With the help, ironically, of one of its least favorite presidents, the Christian Right was able to extend the same protection to federal offices as well.

The Clinton Executive Order and the Workplace Religious Freedom Act

President Bill Clinton, to put it mildly, had a fractious relationship with the Religious Right, which after all played a prominent role in the sordid events leading to his 1998 impeachment. But for at least one brief shining moment in the summer of 1997, Clinton basked in the approval of some of his most vehement critics. Less than two months after the Supreme Court invalidated the Religious Freedom Restoration Act in *Boerne*, Clinton signed an executive order laying out "Guidelines on Religious Exercise and Religious Expression in the Federal Workplace."

"Religious freedom is at the heart of what it means to be an American," Clinton said during a White House ceremony announcing the new rules. "These guidelines will ensure that federal employees and employers will respect the rights of those who engage in religious speech, as well as those who do not."

The actual coverage of the new guidelines was limited to federal civilian employees; they did not affect employee rights in state government or private employment. Federal uniformed military personnel also were specifically exempted from the executive order because they have a "different set of concerns and obligations." Nonetheless, religious leaders expressed the hope that Clinton's executive order would serve as a model for state governments and private employers.

According to the Clinton guidelines, which are still in effect today, federal agencies are prohibited from restricting "personal religious expression" by employees unless such expression interferes with the delivery of service to the public, interferes with the rights of other employees, or creates the impression of an endorsement of religion by the government. Subject to reasonable, nondiscriminatory regulation, federal employees are allowed to engage in "personal religious expression" in their private, nonpublic workspaces, engage in religious expression with fellow employees, and even proselytize, so long as none of the activities interfere with workplace efficiency.

The guidelines also incorporate the *Sherbert* test as the standard for agency accommodation of an employee's religious expression. Specifically, the guidelines call for accommodation "unless it would cause an actual cost to the agency or to other employees or an actual disruption of work, or unless it is otherwise barred by law." If an agency's work rule causes a "substantial burden" on an employee's religious expression, then the agency is required to accommodate the expression unless there is a compelling interest in not doing so and no less restrictive means of accomplishing that interest.

One of the few critics of the new guidelines, interestingly, was the Rutherford Institute, the deeply conservative legal organization founded and run by constitutional lawyer John Whitehead. The Rutherford Institute was founded in 1981 with financial assistance from Rushdoony's Chalcedon Institute, and Whitehead himself was a protégé of the reclusive Reconstructionist—although as the media circus surrounding the Paula Jones case intensified in 1997 and 1998, Whitehead took pains to distance himself from Rushdoony's less palatable policy proposals.

Among the institute's early board members were such well-known Religious Right leaders as Francis Schaeffer and financier Howard Ahmanson Jr., and over the years, the institute has been active in many church-state disputes, including the battle over Judge Roy Moore's infamous Ten Commandments monument.

Whitehead claimed that Clinton's 1997 religious-expression guidelines were based on "incorrect legal standards," and said that the "vague and contradictory standards ... will likely generate much confusion in this area of law." Another critic was Crystal Roberts, a legal-policy analyst for the Family Research Council, the public policy wing of James Dobson's Focus on the Family, who stated: "Religious expression is not something that's meant to be compromised."

At about the same time Clinton issued his executive order, senators Dan Coats (R-Ind.) and John Kerry (D.-Mass.) introduced legislation called the Workplace Religious Freedom Act (WRFA). At a 1997 press conference to announce the new proposal, Coats said, "The Workplace Religious Freedom Act is an important step toward restoring the original intent of Title VII of the Civil Rights Act of 1964. Though we know that only a minority of employers refuse to make reasonable accommodations for employees to observe the Sabbath or other holy days, the fact of the matter is that no worker in America should be forced to choose between a job and violating deeply held religious beliefs."

The specific goal of the WRFA is to raise the standard for the accommodation of religious beliefs by private sector employers. Under the test announced by the Supreme Court in *Trans World Airlines, Inc. v. Hardison* in 1977, private employers are required to accommodate religious beliefs and practices only so long as the accommodation results in de minimis expense. Under the terms of the WRFA, employers would be required to show that an accommodation of religious practice or belief would cause "significant difficulty or expense," a more difficult standard for employers to meet. Other provisions of the legislation would impose a requirement on employers of fifteen or more people to make an "affirmative and bona fide effort" to accommodate religious beliefs, and would specify the types of business expenses that can be counted toward the test of "undue hardship," including: "cost of lost productivity, the size of the employer, the number of employees who would require accommodation and the difficulty and cost for employers that have more than one facility or place of business."

Not surprisingly, WRFA was supported by groups across the political and theological spectrum, ranging from the liberal American Jewish Committee to the conservative Southern Baptist Convention. But senators Coats and Kennedy were unable to shepherd the legislation through Congress, and despite being introduced in each succeeding Congress, the bill has remained stalled in committee. Much of the delay stems from the fact that the WRFA is strenuously opposed by the business community, which is concerned that it will significantly increase labor costs and make the workplace environment much more divisive.

Another strong opponent of the bill, interestingly, is the ACLU, which worries that it might be used by employees to defend religious activities that are currently barred. In 2003 the ACLU's legislative counsel, Christopher Anders, told the *Washington Post:* "One of the goals of the religious right is to use Title VII to get extra rights that would harm other people in the workplace. The courts have been telling them no. But if [this bill] passes, the courts may not be telling them no." For instance, Anders argued that WRFA might allow a police officer to refuse to defend an abortion clinic, or a pharmacist to refuse to dispense birth control pills.

The combined opposition of business interests and the ACLU has proven potent. Despite being initially proposed a decade ago and reintroduced every two years or so since, the WRFA is still nowhere near passage. Along the way, the WRFA has picked up some gaudy cosponsors—including 2008 presidential contender Senator Hillary Clinton (D-N.Y.)—but so far, supporters of the bill have been unable to overcome the concerted opposition.

Faith-Based Organizations and Religious Discrimination in Hiring

For the Religious Right, the most significant workplace religion issue over the past decade has been the movement's push to free faith-based organizations (FBOs) from the antidiscrimination provisions of Title VII, while still preserving (and expanding) their access to public funds.

Thanks in large part to the movement's political success in Congress and the White House, billions of taxpayer dollars have been funneled to FBOs; even more importantly, FBOs have been freed of the allegedly onerous obligation of nondiscrimination.

When President Clinton issued his executive order on religious expression in the federal workplace, he tried to strike a delicate balance between the protection of federal employee religious rights on the one hand and the prohibition against government establishment of religion on the other. The order repeatedly warned against the appearance of governmental endorsement, and closed with a flat prohibition against establishment: "Supervisors and employees must not engage in activities or expression that a reasonable observer would interpret as government endorsement or denigration of religion or a particular religion."

But Clinton, unfortunately, was not always able to be so careful about the structural integrity of the Jeffersonian wall between church and state; the current feeding frenzy by FBOs can be traced directly to legislation that Clinton had little choice but to accept. In 1996 Congress passed a fiercely debated welfare reform package called the Personal Responsibility and Work Opportunity Reconciliation Act (PRWORA). The legislation was largely the work of the Republican-controlled Congress that took office in 1994 after the so-called Republican Revolution. Under intense public pressure from the bombastic House Speaker Newt Gingrich, and in the midst of a reelection battle with Senator Bob Dole (R-Kan.), President Bill Clinton signed the legislation on August 22, 1996. Among the numerous provisions included in the legislation was the following language:

> RELIGIOUS ORGANIZATIONS—The purpose of this section is to allow states to contract with religious organizations, or to allow religious organizations to accept certificates, vouchers, or other forms of disbursement under any program described in subsection (a)(2), on the same basis as any other nongovernmental provider without impairing the religious character of such organizations, and without diminishing the religious freedom of beneficiaries of assistance funded under such program.

The PRWORA did acknowledge that the Constitution contains an establishment clause, and declared that any religious organization operating a program to provide social services must do so in a manner consistent with the First Amendment. To reduce charges of undue government entanglement with religion, the law also specifically stated that neither the federal nor state government can require a participating religious organization to change its structure or "remove religious art, icons, scripture, or other symbols."

The "charitable choice" initiative, as it was called, was the work of Senator John Ashcroft (R-Mo.), who received assistance in drafting the new provision from Steve McFarland, who at the time was serving as director of the Christian Legal Society's Center for Law and Religious Freedom (he was later appointed by President George W. Bush to lead the U.S. Justice Department's Task Force for Faith-Based and Community Initiatives). Despite the provision's virtual upending of the traditional relationship between government and religion, media coverage of charitable choice was remarkably limited, and largely lost in the much louder debate about the potential impact of the welfare reform act.

Two years later, as Ashcroft was exploring the possibility of a run for president, he announced that he was planning to expand the charitable choice program "to all federal laws which authorize the government to use nongovernmental entities in providing services to beneficiaries with federal dollars." At a press event at the Bowery Mission Transitional Center in New York City, Ashcroft said that the expansion of his program would allow religious organizations to use "federal funds to provide low-income housing, juvenile crime prevention services, substance abuse prevention and treatment programs, abstinence education, and services for seniors."

A little over a year later, suffering from his own raging case of Potomac fever, Vice President Al Gore threw his support behind Ashcroft's proposal, telling reporters in Atlanta, Georgia, that charitable choice should be expanded to include "other vital services where faith-based organizations (FBOs) can play a role, such as drug treatment, homelessness, and youth violence." Also backing the program at the state level was Texas governor George W. Bush, who signed an executive order shortly after the charitable choice program was first adopted, ordering "all pertinent executive branch agencies to take all necessary steps to implement the 'charitable choice' provision of the federal welfare law."

Less than a month after taking office as president in 2001, Bush issued an executive order that established the first White House Office of Faith-Based and Community Initiatives (OFBCI). The purpose of the order, Bush said, was "to help the federal government coordinate a national effort to expand opportunities for faith-based and other community organizations and to strengthen their capacity to better meet social needs in America's communities." The OFBCI builds on Ashcroft's charitable choice program in several ways, and is authorized to:

- develop, lead, and coordinate the administration's policy agenda affecting faith-based and other community programs and initiatives, expand the role of such efforts in communities, and increase their capacity through executive action, legislation, federal and private funding, and regulatory relief;
- coordinate public education activities designed to mobilize public support for faith-based and community nonprofit initiatives through volunteerism, special projects, demonstration pilots, and public-private partnerships;
- provide policy and legal education to state, local, and community policymakers and public officials seeking ways to empower faith-based and other community organizations and to improve the opportunities, capacity, and expertise of such groups;
- eliminate unnecessary legislative, regulatory, and other bureaucratic barriers that impede effective faith-based and other community efforts to solve social problems.

On the same day that he established the White House OFBCI, President Bush also ordered the creation of similar centers in five federal agencies: the departments of Justice, Education, Labor, Health and Human Services, and Housing and Urban Development. As with the OFBCI, the purpose of the agency centers is to "coordinate department efforts to eliminate regulatory, contracting, and other programmatic obstacles to the participation of faith-based and other community organizations in the provision of social services." Over the course of his administration, President Bush has ordered six other federal departments to create centers for promoting participation by FBOs: the Agency for International Development; the Department of Agriculture; the Department of Commerce; the Department of Homeland Security; the Small Business Administration; and the Department of Veterans Affairs.

Even before he issued his executive order, President Bush proposed legislation that would not only rewrite federal law to make it easier for faith-based organizations to compete for taxpayer funds, but even more remarkably, would allow religious organizations receiving federal funds to discriminate in their hiring on the basis of religion.

Under Title VII of the Civil Rights Act of 1964, religious organizations have always had a limited exemption to discriminate on the basis of religion for religiously oriented positions in their organization (for instance, a Unitarian Church can advertise for and hire only Unitarians to serve as minister). But Title VII's prohibitions against discrimination on other grounds—race, gender, national orientation, etc.—still apply, and when filling purely secular positions, the prohibition against religious discrimination must be observed as well. When Congress passed the Job Training Partnership Act in 1982, it permitted religious organizations to participate in the federally funded program only so long as they agreed not to discriminate on the basis of religion when hiring anyone under the program.

Bush and other members of his administration argued that allowing FBOs to discriminate on the basis of religion when hiring would somehow "level the playing field" and make it easier for them to compete for federal funds. The House of Representatives passed Bush's proposal on faith-based hiring, but the measure got tied up in the Senate. Lawmakers across the political spectrum raised concerns about the administration's apparent indifference to the principle of the separation of church and state, a concern that poll results showed was shared by a large percentage of the public. As Representative Barney Frank (D-Mass.) inimitably put it, "The notion that you need to allow religious groups to discriminate to receive federal funds is a lie. If you dip your fingers in the federal till, you can't complain if a little democracy rubs off on you."

When it was clear that Congress was not going to pass his faith-based proposal, Bush chose to enact the controversial policy through administrative fiat. On December 12, 2002, the president held a signing ceremony in Philadelphia to celebrate the issuance of an executive order titled "Equal Protection of the Laws for Faith-based and Community Organizations." Included in Bush's order was an affirmative statement that "no organization should be discriminated against on the basis of religion or religious belief in the administration or distribution of federal financial assistance under social service programs." Similarly, the executive order provides that "faith-based organizations should be eligible to compete for federal financial assistance used to support social service programs ... without impairing their independence, autonomy, expression, or religious character."

It was a remarkable reversal of decades of federal policy: rather than using federal law to prevent discrimination against individuals, the Bush administration announced that its goal was to prevent discrimination against organizations that discriminate. To help achieve that objective, Bush's executive order amended the provisions of a thirty-seven-year-old executive order issued by President Lyndon Johnson designed to implement the Civil Rights Act of 1964. Johnson's order states that any contractor receiving federal funds "will not discriminate against any employee or applicant for employment because of race, color, religion, sex, or national origin." Bush added a new section to Johnson's order that states that religious groups not only are exempt from the law's nondiscrimination requirements, but in fact, the secretary of labor has the authority, under undefined "special circumstances," to exempt *any* government contractor from antidiscrimination regulations.

The Bush administration's enthusiasm for religious-based hiring has even spilled over to recent battles over reauthorization of one of the government's most successful educational programs, the Head Start program in operation since 1965. During the last two Congresses, Republican leaders proposed similar changes to the Head Start program that would have allowed faith-based providers to discriminate on the basis of religion in their hiring of teachers and other educational staff.

The measures never came up for a vote, however, and when Democrats retook control of Congress in 2006, the House defeated efforts to send a new reauthorization bill back to committee to continue debating the issue.

The Unchallengeable Financial Windfall for Faith-Based Organizations

More than anything else, the OFBCI and the various agency centers have been tremendously successful at awarding funds to faith-based organizations with few if any strings attached. According to a 2006 fact sheet prepared by the White House, a review of more than twenty-three hundred grants awarded by just seven federal agencies showed that FBOs received over $2.1 billion in competitive grants in fiscal year 2005, accounting for nearly 11 percent of the total amount of funding awarded that year. That was a 5 percent increase over the year before, and the White House boasts that federal grants to FBOs in the five leading federal service agencies—the departments of Health and Human Services (HHS), Housing and Urban Development (HUD), Justice (DOJ), Labor (DOL), and Education—are up a startling 38 percent since fiscal year 2003.

As part of his faith-based initiative, Bush also instructed the secretary of Health and Human Services to use his Demonstration and Research Authority, a program within HHS, to establish the Compassion Capital Fund (CCF). According to the CCF's website, the purpose of the fund is to "help faith-based and community organizations increase their effectiveness and enhance their ability to provide social services by building their organizational capacity." The Republican Congress appropriated $30 million for the CCF in FY 2002, and over the next four years, more than doubled the size of the program to $64.4 million in FY 2006.

The CCF's goal of training FBOs to become more effective applicants for the federal funds available under Bush's executive order is disconcerting enough. Even more worrisome is the fact that the CCF does not directly administer its funds itself. Instead, it awards grants to "intermediary organizations" that are charged with providing "technical assistance and capacity-building sub-awards" to smaller FBOs.

The structure of the CCF immediately caused controversy, since one of the first intermediary groups to receive a grant, totaling $1.5 million over three years, was Operation Blessing, a religious charity founded by *The 700 Club* televangelist Pat Robertson. Ironically, Robertson had initially been a fierce critic of Bush's faith-based initiative, but he did not pass up the opportunity to land some federal funding. The grant award to Operation Blessing was criticized by both the Left and the Right: the Reverend Barry Lynn, executive director of Americans United for Separation of Church and State, suggested that "thirty pieces of silver were enough to change [Robertson's] mind." Conservative columnist and former Moral Majority vice president Cal Thomas raised the dangers of entanglement: "Government should not decide who deserves funding and who does not. That is an endorsement of one religion or religions over others. Furthermore, the day will come when religious groups will be required to remain silent about their beliefs if they want to continue receiving government checks."

The $1.5 million award to Operation Blessing was only one of the troubling developments. The CCF also gave nearly $2 million over three years to the National Center for Faith-Based Initiatives, an organization founded by Bishop Harold Calvin Ray, one of President Bush's most vocal allies in the push to create his faith-based initiative. As Steve Benen pointed out in an article for *Church & State*, the lead publication for Americans United, Ray's role as a promoter of federal funds for FBOs has been controversial due to his Christian dominionism views.

"The separation of church and state is a fiction," Ray said in an interview with *Charisma* magazine in February 2001. "The nation is the kingdom of God, period." He expressed similar views in his self-published book, *Creating Wealth, Determining Destiny* in 1996, arguing, "God expects [Christians] to take dominion." Providing federal funds to FBOs, he said, is a strong step in that direction.

One of the significant problems with the Bush faith-based initiative is that no one really knows where the money is going. In January 2006, Josephine Robinson, director of the Office of Community Services within the Health and Human Services Department, conceded to the *Chicago Tribune* that given the number of staff in her office, there was definitely a limit to how much monitoring of grant recipients could take place. FBOs are not supposed to use federal money for "inherently religious" activities, but the combination of vague guidelines and inadequate oversight makes it virtually impossible to know if the boundaries of the Constitution are being observed.

According to a report prepared in September 2006 by the General Accounting Office, which conducts investigations on behalf of Congress, faith-based and community organizations have received over $500 million in new money from federal agencies since 2001, when Bush first launched his initiative. But the GAO found that the Bush administration was not doing enough to prevent religious discrimination and had not instituted standards for measuring the performance of the groups receiving money.

The more significant story was contained in David Kuo's 2007 book, *Tempting Faith: An Inside Story of Political Seduction.* Kuo, the number two official in OFBCI from 2001 to 2003, wrote a classic ex-administration-insider, where-the-bodies-are-buried book, the chief purpose of which was to complain that Bush and his political advisers had in fact not done *enough* to channel funds to FBOs—by Kuo's calculation, just 1 percent of what Bush had publicly promised.

A portion of his book is devoted to a discussion of the political uses of the Compassion Capital Fund, in which a handpicked-panel of Religious Right activists graded the grant applications. Many groups, Kuo said, received high scores (and thus grants) more on the strength of their support for the Bush administration than their ability to provide assistance to the poor and downtrodden. A review panel member reportedly told Kuo some time later that when she saw an application from a non-Christian group, she simply gave the application a zero and moved on. According to the panelist, many of her peers did the same thing.

Not surprisingly, a wide variety of groups have begun to file lawsuits challenging specific programs and their use of federal money. In Massachusetts, for instance, the ACLU filed suit against the Department of Health and Human Services in 2005 to stop funding for the Silver Ring Thing program, which put on multimedia shows for teens at which they are encouraged to purchase a silver ring to show their intent to remain a virgin until marriage. At the same time, however, Silver Ring Thing also used the shows to urge children to commit their lives to Jesus Christ, and inscribed each ring with a verse from the New Testament. The department agreed to put a hold on the group's grant of $1 million in federal funds while it looked into concerns about the program.

While specific programs can be challenged when they cross the fading line separating church and state, what about the White House's operation of the Office of Faith-Based and Community Initiatives itself? Among other things, the OFBCI organizes conferences around the country that are designed to provide FBOs with "an understanding of the president's Faith-Based and Community Initiative, information about the federal grants process and funding opportunities, and the basic legal responsibilities that come with federal funding." The specific objective of the conferences is to educate FBOs on how to most effectively apply for public funds offered by the various federal faith-based agency centers.

In 2004 a Wisconsin-based group called Freedom from Religion Foundation (FFRF) filed a lawsuit against the OFBCI, alleging that both the OFBCI and its conferences constitute the establishment of religion by the Bush administration. Three years later, the newly constituted Roberts Court heard oral arguments in the case of *Hein v. Freedom from Religion Foundation* (2007) and rejected the challenge, ruling 5–4 that the FFRF did not have standing to challenge President Bush's faith-based initiative. Both of President Bush's nominees, Chief Justice John Roberts and Associate Justice Samuel Alito, joined the majority in dismissing the lawsuit against the OFBCI. Along with the 5–4 ruling that upheld the partial-birth abortion ban, the *Hein* decision helped make the end of the Court's term very satisfying for the Religious Right.

Supporters of the concept of separation of church and state were disappointed, but relieved that the damage wasn't worse. Typically, taxpayers are not allowed to sue the federal government to protest any specific appropriations. However, in *Flast v. Cohen* (1968), the Supreme Court created an exception for taxpayer lawsuits that allege violations of the establishment clause. The Roberts Court granted certiorari to determine whether *Flast* applies to a program that is not funded by a

specific act of Congress, but instead is paid out of general appropriations to the executive branch.

The lead opinion was written by Alito and joined by just two other
justices: Chief Justice Roberts and Justice Kennedy. Alito said that the
expenditures at issue in *Flast* "were made pursuant to an express congressional mandate and a specific congressional appropriation." But in
Hein, the monies in question were provided to the executive branch by
Congress "to fund its day-to-day activities." The fact that the money
expended by the OFBCI cannot be traced to a *specific* congressional enactment is sufficient, Alito said, to take the FFRF lawsuit outside of
Flast's narrow exception. Without saying so explicitly, the three justices
used the same logic that the majority applied in *Zelman*, the 2002 Ohio
school-selection case: choice, either on the part of parents or the president, apparently is sufficient to rid a program of constitutional infir-
mity.

The six other justices openly scoffed at the plurality's conclusion,
with two separate groups of justices agreeing that there is no logical
distinction between the type of congressional act contemplated by *Flast*
and the general grant of money by Congress to the executive branch.
But while Associate Justices Scalia and Thomas argued that *Flast* should
simply be overruled, they still concurred that the FFRF lawsuit should
be dismissed. Had just one of the other three justices in the majority
agreed with Scalia and Thomas, then, arguably, taxpayers would be
barred from ever arguing that a federal expenditure violates the establishment clause of the First Amendment.

Justices Stevens, Ginsburg, Souter, and Breyer agreed with Scalia
and Thomas that the distinction drawn by Alito was illogical, but concluded that under the holding of *Flast*, the FFRF should have been allowed to proceed with its lawsuit. Writing for the four dissenters, Justice
Souter opined:

> Here, there is no dispute that taxpayer money in identifiable
> amounts is funding conferences, and these are alleged to have the
> purpose of promoting religion. The taxpayers therefore seek not
> to "extend" *Flast*, but merely to apply it. When executive agencies
> spend identifiable sums of tax money for religious purposes, no less

than when Congress authorizes the same thing, taxpayers suffer injury.

FFRF argued to the Court that if the *Flast* case does not apply to discretionary expenditures, then the OFCBI-sponsored conferences will be merely the first misstep on a very slippery slope. What would prevent the executive branch from building a house of worship, for instance, or hiring clergy of one denomination to proselytize? Would an executive branch agency be able to purchase religious symbols and distribute them?

Alito dismissed those concerns as a mere "parade of horribles," and pointed out that despite the limited application of *Flast* over the years, "none of these things has happened." But Alito was too quick to dismiss FFRF's concerns. There have been two born-again presidents in the nearly forty years since *Flast* was handed down (Jimmy Carter and George W. Bush), but only one issued an executive order making it easier for FBOs to obtain government funding and disregard antidiscrimination laws.

While the White House (so far) has not hired a clergyman, there is little doubt that the Compassion Capital Fund is overwhelmingly weighted toward evangelical Christians, to the near exclusion of other religions. And although the OFBCI has not embarked on a church-building program, the Bush administration did announce in 2003 that it would start making direct grants to religious organizations for building maintenance under a program called Save America's Treasures. The Justice Department (well-stocked with former Christian Right staff attorneys) has advised the Bush administration that similar direct grants to religious organizations may be legal under other federal programs as well.

What is particularly disturbing is that with the help of the Court's decision in *Hein*, the Bush White House and OFCBI have not only managed to crush the wall of separation, but are actively chipping away at the concept of checks and balances as well. Despite Bush's inability to persuade Congress that religiously discriminatory hiring is appropriate, his executive orders have accomplished nearly all that the Religious Right could have hoped. The passage of a federal law would be preferable, of course, since another president could rescind Bush's executive orders with the stroke of a pen. But the much more significant and potentially far-reaching victory for the Christian Right occurred at the Supreme Court. Thanks to the movement's decades of work in support of a more conservative Supreme Court, the blatant blending of church and state by the Bush administration is apparently beyond legal challenge, and could be replicated or perpetuated by future presidents. It is a compelling, albeit painful lesson, in how a particularly powerful and surprisingly efficient special-interest group can weave the three branches of government into a lucrative and protective trellis.

CHAPTER NINE

The Last Freedom

The Right to Privacy

WITHOUT QUESTION, it is the Supreme Court's acknowledgment of a fundamental right to privacy that has driven much of the Religious Right's political activism. The movement's steadfast objective has been to push for the nomination and confirmation of constitutional scholars like Judge Robert Bork and Justice Antonin Scalia, who view the right to privacy as a vague and ill-defined doctrine constructed out of whole cloth to satisfy the liberal social agendas of the justices who endorse it. In Bork's 1990 book, *The Tempting of America*, which he wrote three years after being rejected for a seat on the Supreme Court, he accused the Court of adopting a prong of liberal ideology— "moral relativism or the privatization of morality." Bork wrote, "This may be seen very dramatically in the Court's creation of the 'right to privacy,' which has little to do with privacy but a great deal to do with the freedom of the individual from moral regulation."

Adding to the disgruntlement of conservative legal theorists is the fact that the case most often credited with introducing the right to privacy, *Griswold v. Connecticut* (1965), was written by Justice William O. Douglas, undoubtedly one of the most liberal justices in the Court's history. The only way to avoid such arbitrary and unpredictable pronouncements, conservative theorists argue, is to ground constitutional interpretations in one of the two main strands of originalism: a strict adherence to the intent of the people who drafted the Constitution, or application of the common meaning of the Constitution's words at the time the document was adopted (so that, for instance, "freedom of the press" would be interpreted according to how people understood that phrase in 1791).

There is considerable overlap between judicial originalists and the Religious Right, at least insofar as the doctrine of originalism rejects the validity of a "right to privacy." For most members of the Christian Right, originalism is less a guiding philosophy than a means to a specific end, the overturning of *Roe v. Wade.* If there is no right to privacy under the U.S. Constitution, the Christian Right reasons, then the *Roe* decision—which relied heavily on a woman's right to privacy in overturning the Texas abortion ban—must be invalid.

For the much smaller but far more virulent Reconstructionist wing of the Religious Right, even the laudable goal of overturning *Roe* is itself merely a temporary objective. They advocate their own version of originalism: that the judiciary should be guided by the intent of God and the language of the Old Testament in governing society. Unquestionably, one of the more pernicious effects of the Christian Reconstructionists is that when Republican presidents and their advisers consider potential judicial nominees, mere judicial originalists end up looking like moderates compared to nominees who would bring a biblical worldview to the bench.

But as the debate over the right to privacy illustrates, originalism is not in fact a moderate approach to judicature. It is a deeply conservative approach, one that hews to a procrustean view that society should be chopped or stretched to conform to a fixed and rigid constitution. The framers, in fact, envisioned a different scenario, one in which the language of the Constitution would adapt, albeit slowly, to the changing sensibilities and exigencies of the times. They did, after all, draft a constitution, rather than a lengthy library of statutes on specific topics. And it was no accident that Thomas Jefferson, one of the most enlightened of the framers, created his own more rational version of the

Bible by cutting out the New Testament's description of miracles, leaving a book that consisted primarily of Jesus's moral teachings and some Middle Eastern history.

Technology and the "Right to Be Let Alone"

The brilliance of the framers in drafting a flexible constitution designed for interpretation can be seen in the U.S. Constitution's remarkable ability to remain relevant over the last two centuries. As technological advances have shaped society, the courts—and in particular the Supreme Court—have been able to respond by adapting the governing legal principles of the United States to new circumstances. In light of massive population increases and increasingly invasive technology, no constitutional adaptation is more important than the identification and development of a right to privacy.

In the mid-nineteenth century, two separate technological inventions together served as midwives to the birth of the right to privacy. In 1839 Louis-Jacques-Mandé Daguerre appeared before the French Academy of Sciences and announced the perfection of his new photography technique, called the daguerreotype. The French government acquired the patent on the process from Daguerre, and on August 18 of that year donated the details of the process to the world, thus making photography one of the first open-source technologies. The news of Daguerre's invention set off a photography craze around the world; within two years, more than one hundred photography studios opened in New York City alone.

Just four years after Daguerre's announcement, a New York resident named Richard Hoe invented the rotary printing press, which was dramatically faster than the venerable flat-bed press, a technology first invented by Johannes Gutenberg circa 1450 and largely unchanged over the succeeding four centuries. In 1870 Hoe improved on his invention by developing a model that could print an image on both sides of a sheet of paper at the same time.

Hoe's inventions helped spur a phenomenal growth in the newspaper industry. In 1850 the U.S. Census listed 2,526 separate newspaper titles. By 1880, the powerful combination of the faster presses, greater demand for news (largely spurred by the telegraph and dramatic reports from the Civil War), and population increases helped drive the number of newspaper titles to a staggering 11,314 (by contrast, in 2007 there were just 1,450 paid dailies in circulation). With all that agate to fill, it is not terribly surprising that society gossip, celebrity sightings, and fashion news quickly became staples of the daily newspaper (similar epidemics have occurred on television and the Web). The final linkage between newspapers, photography, and privacy fell into place in 1880, when Stephen H. Horgan first used a halftone screen to print a photograph in the March 4 edition of the *New York Daily Graphic*. The era of photojournalism had begun.

While some celebrities reveled in the attention from what some newspaper editors sniffingly described as "unscrupulous snapshotters" and "Kodak fiends," others, not surprisingly, were less enthusiastic. Novelist Frances Hodgson Burnett, for instance, whose works include *A Little Princess* and *The Secret Garden*, complained to the *New York Times* that her notoriety as a playwright and novelist denied her "the ordinary immunities of private life." In an editorial on March 15, 1889, the *Times* gently scoffed at Burnett's assertion that the threat of lost privacy might cause an artist to forgo creating a masterpiece.

> Nevertheless the right of privacy with respect to what are properly private affairs is a real right, while curiosity about other people's ways of living is an emotion of which well-bred people are rather ashamed, and which they try to suppress. Such a curiosity, when it goes the length of attempting to satisfy itself without the consent of the object, is equally impertinent and vulgar whether it is entertained by one person or by a million.

The *Times* editorial concluded by noting that virtually alone of all countries, France protected personal privacy with legislation (Article 9 of its Civil Code), and suggested that "an effective prohibition against the publication of unauthorized gossip about the private life, even of public characters, would be an excellent thing if such a prohibition could be devised."

Later that same summer, Marion Manola, a well-known actress of the time who was appearing on Broadway in the comic opera *Castles in the Air*, sought an injunction against the company's manager and a photographer to prevent them from making any use of a flash photograph they surreptitiously took of her while she was on stage in tights. The perils of the photographic age were quickly made apparent: according to the *Evening Journal* in Waukesha, Wisconsin, following Manola's publicity spat, "photographs amply displaying her nether limbs have been exhibited in almost every music shop window along [Broadway]. They are all taken in 'Boccacio' costumes." The reference to *Boccaccio, or the Prince of Palermo*, was intended to be somewhat scandalous: it is a risqué comic opera, first produced in 1879, that recounts the exploits of Giovanni Boccaccio, a fourteenth-century Italian poet and author of the famously bawdy *Il Decameron*. Ms. Manola first played the role of Fiametta and then the title role in the McCaull Opera Company's 1888 production of *Boccaccio*, and it is presumably during those performances that the revealing photographs of her "nether limbs" were taken.

Those incidents and others like them provided the cultural context for one of the nineteenth century's most influential law review articles: "The Right to Privacy," written by Boston attorneys Louis Brandeis and Samuel Warren for the December 1890 edition of the *Harvard Law Review*. The two friends had finished first and second respectively at Harvard Law School in 1877, and two years later founded the now well-known firm of Nutter, McClennen and Fish; Brandeis later would be nominated by President Woodrow Wilson to serve as an associate justice on the U.S. Supreme Court, which he did from 1916 to 1939. Warren and Brandeis opened their article with one simple but profound observation: "That the individual shall have full protection in person and in property is a principle as old as the common law; but it has been found necessary from time to time to define anew the exact nature and extent of such protection."

They began their argument by tracing the history of personal legal protection, which was originally limited to remedies for physical injuries and damage to property. Over time, however, the scope of protection expanded to include freedom from the mere threat of battery (i.e., assault), freedom from emotional harm, and later, protection of not merely physical property but intangible or intellectual property as well. But "recent inventions," Warren and Brandeis warned with eerie prescience, make it necessary for the scope of protection to expand again to include "the right to be let alone":

> Instantaneous photographs and newspaper enterprise have invaded the sacred precincts of private and domestic life; and numerous mechanical devices threaten to make good the prediction that "what is whispered in the closet shall be proclaimed from the house-tops." ... The press is overstepping in every direction the obvious bounds of propriety and of decency. Gossip is no longer the resource of the idle and of the vicious, but has become a trade, which is pursued with industry as well as effrontery. To satisfy a prurient taste, the details of sexual relations are spread broadcast in the columns of the daily papers. To occupy the indolent, column upon column is filled with idle gossip, which can only be procured by intrusion upon the domestic circle. The intensity and complexity of life, attendant upon advancing civilization, have rendered necessary some retreat from the world, and man, under the refining influence of culture, has become more sensitive to publicity, so that solitude and privacy have become more essential to the individual; but modern enterprise and invention have, through invasions upon his privacy, subjected him to mental pain and distress, far greater than could be inflicted by mere bodily injury.

The young solons argued that a "right to privacy" was a reasonable extension of existing common law (particularly with respect to violation of contract or breach of trust). "But since the latest advances in photographic art have rendered it possible to take pictures surreptitiously," they wrote, "the doctrines of contract and of trust are inadequate to support the required protection, and the law of tort must be resorted to." They concluded their article by offering some suggestions as to the element of the new tort, as well as the appropriate remedies.

Both Brandeis and Warren were no doubt familiar with the glacial pace with which the law typically changes, and so it probably came as no surprise to them that their suggestions initially fell on deaf ears. It would be fifteen years before the right to privacy was recognized by a state court judge, and even longer before state legislatures began passing privacy statutes. But the vindication of Brandeis and Warren is complete: nearly a hundred and twenty years after their article was published, the right to privacy has become one of the most widely debated and highly valued concepts in modern society.

The Slow Judicial Recognition of a Right to Privacy

In general, Warren Court bashers among the ranks of judicial originalists and the Religious Right seem to suggest that when Associate Justice William O. Douglas wrote the 7–2 majority opinion in *Griswold,* he plucked the idea of a right to privacy clean out of the rarified and liberal air blowing through the justice's chambers. Judge Bork, for instance, himself refers to the "invention of the right of privacy" when he talks about the Supreme Court's alleged misadventures in *Griswold.* But his characterization is simply not accurate as a matter of legal history: the passage of more than a century since Brandeis and Warren's law review article certainly belies the novelty of the doctrine. Far more importantly, long before the U.S. Supreme Court first incorporated the concept of personal privacy into the Fourteenth Amendment (in cases that themselves predated *Griswold*), the right to privacy had earned the overwhelming approval of state supreme courts and lower federal courts around the country.

For one young woman, unfortunately, recognition did not come quickly enough. In 1899 the Rochester Folding Box Company somehow obtained a photograph of an attractive eighteen-year-old woman named Abigail Roberson and reproduced it on an advertisement for Franklin Mills Flour, the "flour of the family." Twenty-five thousand such posters were printed and distributed throughout the area, which the modest Roberson said caused her "great distress and suffering both in body and mind." She filed a lawsuit against Rochester Folding Box Co. seeking $15,000 in damages—roughly the equivalent of $370,000 in 2007.

The trial court sided with Roberson and rejected the box company's efforts to dismiss the case. "It seems to me that the sale and circulation of the lithographic copies of plaintiff's likeness, without her consent, is an invasion of her private rights," Judge John M. Davy concluded.

"Every woman has a right to keep her face concealed from the observation of the public. Her face is her own private property, and no photographer would have a right to take advantage of the privilege of taking her photograph for his own private use to make copies from the negative and sell them to the public."

The case eventually wound its way up to New York's highest court, the court of appeals, which ruled in *Roberson v. Rochester Folding Box Co.* (1902) that Judge Davy had too eagerly anticipated an expansion in the common law. "An examination of the authorities leads us to the conclusion that the so-called 'right of privacy' has not as yet found an abiding place in our jurisprudence," chief judge Alton B. Parker said, "and, as we view it, the doctrine cannot now be incorporated without doing violence to settled principles of law by which the profession and the public have long been guided." The court of appeals reversed the trial court's award of damages to Roberson, and left the recognition of a right to privacy for another day.

The *Roberson* decision sparked considerable criticism of the court of appeals in general and Judge Parker in particular. Even President Theodore Roosevelt, the *New York Times* said at the time, was restrained only by the dignity of his office from inflicting "personal chastisement" upon impertinent photographers. "If there be, as Judge Parker says there is, no law to cover these savage and horrible practices, practices incompatible with the claims of the community in which they are allowed to be committed with impunity to be called a civilized community," the *Times* editors wrote somewhat long-windedly, "then the decent people will say that it is high time that there were such a law."

Just three years later, the Georgia Supreme Court reached precisely the opposite conclusion from the New York court of appeals in the case of *Pavesich v. New England Life Ins. Co.* (1905), making it the first American court to explicitly recognize a right to privacy. The case was similar to *Roberson*: it involved a claim by an artist, Paolo Pavesich, that New England Mutual Life Insurance obtained a photograph taken of him, and used it in an advertisement published in the *Atlanta Constitution.* In addition to using his likeness without permission, the insurance company also attributed statements to him about the quality of his life following his "decision" to purchase a whole life policy.

Writing for the court's majority, Judge Andrew J. Cobb conceded that the "right to privacy" had not yet been recognized as an independent right, but had always been joined with some other wrong, such as breach of contract or injury to property. However, he clearly believed—as judicial originalists do not—that the law is capable of evolution and growth:

> The entire absence for a long period of time, even for centuries, of a precedent for an asserted right should have the effect to cause the courts to proceed with caution before recognizing the right, for fear that they may thereby invade the province of the lawmaking power; but such absence, even for all time, is not conclusive of the question as to the existence of the right. The novelty of the complaint is no objection when an injury cognizable by law is shown to have been inflicted on the plaintiff. In such a case "although there be no precedent, the common law will judge according to the law of nature and the public good."

The right of privacy, Judge Cobb asserted, is one of those rights that "has its foundation in the instincts of nature."

Judge Cobb's carefully reasoned opinion not only laid out a compelling case for the recognition of a right to privacy, but also offered a remarkable foreshadowing of future debates over its legitimacy. For instance, he argued that the right to privacy comes within the meaning of the word "liberty" as used in the Fourteenth Amendment. "Each [person]," he wrote, "is entitled to a liberty of choice as to his manner of life, and neither an individual nor the public has a right to arbitrarily take away from his liberty." He also dismissed concerns that establishing the boundary between one individual's right to privacy and liberties enjoyed by other persons would prove too difficult for the courts to handle: "In regard to cases that may arise under the right of privacy," Judge Cobb said, "as in cases that arise under other rights where the line of demarkation [sic] is to be determined, the safeguard of the individual on the one hand and of the public on the other is the wisdom and integrity of the judiciary."

In subsequent decades, far more state courts followed the reasoning in *Pavesich* than followed *Roberson*. Indeed, a century after *Pavesich* was handed down, it was still being cited approvingly, for example, in the Utah case of *Jensen v. Sawyers* (2005) for the proposition that "American jurisprudence has long recognized the tort of invasion of privacy."

The federal courts were somewhat slower to follow suit, in large part because they generally do not deal with lawsuits involving personal torts. But as early as 1909, lawyers were arguing over the applicability of a right to privacy in a libel case before the Supreme Court. A woman named Peck sued the *Chicago Tribune* for publishing a photo of her in an advertisement with the following caption: "After years of constant use of your Pure Malt Whiskey, both by myself and as given to patients in my capacity as nurse, I have no hesitation in recommending it as the very best tonic and stimulant for all weak and rundown conditions, &c., &c.," all under the name "Mrs. A. Shuman." Writing for a unanimous Court, in *Peck v. Tribune Co.* (1909), Associate Justice Oliver Wendell Holmes said that the whiskey advertisement was sufficiently embarrassing to the teetotalist plaintiff that she was entitled to bring an action in libel against the *Tribune*. The Court did not discuss, however, whether the use of Peck's image in the advertisement also violated her right to privacy.

The question of how much protection the U.S. Constitution provides for the "privacy of citizens" was squarely presented to the Court just five years later. In Kansas City, a seller of illegal lottery tickets named Weeks was arrested and his house was searched by a U.S. Marshal. Neither the arrest nor the search occurred pursuant to a warrant; nonetheless, the district court allowed various papers seized by the marshal to be introduced as evidence. Weeks argued to the Supreme Court that the seizure of his private papers without a warrant was a violation of his Fourth and Fifth Amendment rights.

In *Weeks v. United States* (1914), the Supreme Court unanimously agreed, and said that the illegally seized evidence should have been excluded. "If letters and private documents can thus be seized and held and used in evidence against a citizen accused of an offense," Associate Justice William Day wrote, "the protection of the Fourth Amendment declaring his right to be secure against such searches and seizures is of no value, and, so far as those thus placed are concerned, might as well be stricken from the Constitution."

But to paraphrase Shakespeare, the true course of privacy never did run smooth. When confronted with a challenge to a warrantless wiretap conducted by the government, a 5–4 majority of the Court concluded in *Olmstead v. United States* (1928) that it was not a violation of the Fourth Amendment. After reviewing the Court's search-and-seizure cases and the language of the Fourth Amendment, Chief Justice William Howard Taft concluded, "The amendment does not forbid what was done here. There was no searching. There was no seizure. The evidence was secured by the use of the sense of hearing and that only. There was no entry of the houses or offices of the defendants." The language of Taft's opinion makes it clear that he would have found common ground with later originalists like Judge Bork or Justice Scalia: "The language of the amendment," Taft wrote, "can not be extended and expanded to include telephone wires reaching to the whole world from the defendant's house or office."

In one of the most eloquent and frequently cited dissents ever written, Associate Justice Louis Brandeis painstakingly rebutted Taft's pinched and formulaic reading of the Fourth Amendment. Writing nearly forty years after his groundbreaking article on privacy as a private attorney, Justice Brandeis made it clear that he still understood the implications of technology, both for his own time and the future:

> Whenever a telephone line is tapped, the privacy of the persons at both ends of the line is invaded and all conversations between them upon any subject, and although proper, confidential, and privileged, may be overheard. Moreover, the tapping of one man's telephone line involves the tapping of the telephone of every other person whom he may call or who may call him. As a means of espionage, writs of assistance and general warrants are but puny instruments of tyranny and oppression when compared with wire-tapping.

Brandeis rejected Taft's "unduly literal construction" of the Fourth Amendment and argued that when the framers drafted the Bill of

Rights, "they conferred, as against the government, the right to be let alone—the most comprehensive of rights and the right most valued by civilized men." And in words that are painfully applicable today, Brandeis argued that the good intentions behind the government's many months of wiretapping were insufficient to justify the warrantless intrusion into private conversations:

> Experience should teach us to be most on our guard to protect liberty when the government's purposes are beneficent. Men born to freedom are naturally alert to repel invasion of their liberty by evil-minded rulers. The greatest dangers to liberty lurk in insidious encroachment by men of zeal, well-meaning but without understanding.

Technology has changed dramatically in the six decades that have passed since Brandeis penned his *Olmstead* dissent, but his articulation of the fundamental principles at stake is timeless. Although Brandeis's remarks were directed at the surveillance of individuals by federal agents, much the same can be said about the efforts of the Religious Right to steadily and irrevocably chip away at the fundamental principle of a separation between church and state.

Griswold v. Connecticut:
Exploring the Penumbras of the Constitution

Although the concept of a right to privacy entered federal jurisprudence four decades before Chief Justice Earl Warren took office—and long before the Christian Right became a political force—there is no disputing the fact that the Court under Warren's leadership gave privacy its fullest expression. The expansion of personal privacy rights under the Constitution began with the Warren Court's reexamination of some earlier Fourth Amendment decisions in the criminal context, and was then extended to other personal decisions that society over the decades had come to view as private and not properly the subject of government interference. Neither development pleased the nation's conservatives, Christian or otherwise.

In *Mapp v. Ohio* (1961), the Court examined the question of whether the Fourth Amendment rule excluding illegally obtained evidence from trial should be extended to the states under the Fourteenth Amendment. Twelve years earlier, in *Wolf v. Colorado* (1949), the Court had reaffirmed the importance of the exclusionary rule to the right of privacy, but for various factual reasons, had declined to impose the rule upon the states. In the intervening years, Associate Justice Tom Clark said, it had become clear that the constitutional right to privacy could only be adequately protected from illegal search and seizures by barring the use of such evidence in both federal and state trials.

The Court also revisited the issue of federal wiretaps in *Katz v. California* (1967). The appeal was brought by a gambler named Charles Katz, who used a public pay phone in Los Angeles to place bets. The pay phone, however, had been tapped by the Federal Bureau of Investigation (FBI), which recorded Katz's conversations and used them to convict him of illegal gambling. Both the district court and the Ninth Circuit, relying on *Olmstead*, denied Katz's motion to exclude the tape recordings, reasoning that there was no physical intrusion by the FBI into the phone booth where Katz was talking.

Seven members of the Court voted to overturn Katz's conviction, but none of the four opinions in the majority was able to command more than three votes. The lead opinion was written by Associate Justice Potter Stewart, who acknowledged that over the preceding forty years, the intellectual underpinning of *Olmstead* had been substantially eroded. "The government's activities in electronically listening to and recording the petitioner's words," Stewart said, "violated the privacy upon which he justifiably relied while using the telephone booth and thus constituted a 'search and seizure' within the meaning of the Fourth Amendment."

Although it was undoubtedly cold comfort to the FBI, Stewart pointed out that a U.S. magistrate probably would have issued a search warrant for the wiretap based on the circumstances of the *Katz* case. Nonetheless, because the recordings were made without a warrant, it was necessary under the Fourth Amendment to suppress them. "Wherever a man may be," Stewart wrote, "he is entitled to know that he will remain free from unreasonable searches and seizures. The government agents here ignored 'the procedure of antecedent justification...that is central to the Fourth Amendment,' a procedure that we hold to be a constitutional precondition of the kind of electronic surveillance involved in this case."

Not surprisingly, there were foreshadowings of later surveillance debates in the various opinions by the justices. Associate Justice Byron White, appointed by President John F. Kennedy in 1962, argued that no warrant at all should be required for wiretaps "if the president of the United States or his chief legal officer, the attorney general, has considered the requirements of national security and authorized electronic surveillance as reasonable." In response, Associate Justice William O. Douglas said that he viewed White's suggestion as "a wholly unwarranted green light for the executive branch to resort to electronic eavesdropping without a warrant in cases which the executive branch itself labels 'national security' matters."

For conservatives, the willingness of the Supreme Court to identify and apply a right to privacy in the context of police searches and seizures was bad enough. But for many, particularly on the Religious Right, the Court went seriously astray when it began considering whether the right to privacy was violated by state laws designed to set social policy.

The issue was first squarely presented to the Court in the spring of 1965 when Estelle Griswold, executive director of the Planned Parenthood League of Connecticut, and Dr. C. Lee Buxton, a professor at the Yale School of Medicine, asked the Supreme Court to overturn their convictions under a Connecticut law (admittedly rarely enforced) that prohibited the use of contraceptive devices and barred doctors from providing medical advice about their use. Griswold and Buxton had opened a birth control clinic in New Haven, Connecticut, with the express purpose of challenging the Connecticut law; not long after they did so, they were arrested, convicted, and each was fined one hundred dollars. The convictions were affirmed by the Connecticut state courts.

Writing for a large (7–2) majority in *Griswold v. Connecticut* (1965), Justice Douglas made it clear that the Court "does not sit as a superlegislature to determine the wisdom, need, and propriety of laws that touch economic problems, business affairs, or social conditions." Nonetheless, Douglas said, the *Griswold* case "concerns a relationship lying within the zone of privacy created by several fundamental constitutional guarantees." He noted that the earlier Courts had frequently applied liberty guarantees in the Bill of Rights to situations not expressly named in the amendments themselves, such as the right to choose the school which one's children attends, or the right to study German in a private school.

"[These cases] suggest that specific guarantees in the Bill of Rights have penumbras," Douglas said, "formed by emanations from those guarantees that help give them life and substance. Various guarantees create zones of privacy." In the majority's view, such emanations could be detected from the First, Third, Fourth, Fifth, and Ninth Amendments. Noting that the Court had frequently discussed the concepts of "privacy and repose," Douglas concluded that "the right of privacy which presses for recognition here is a legitimate one."

By simply outlawing the use of contraceptive devices rather than attempting to achieve its goals through regulation of manufacture or sale, the Court said, the Connecticut law had "a maximum destructive impact" on a constitutionally protected relationship between husband and wife, and doctor and patient. "We deal with a right of privacy older than the Bill of Rights—older than our political parties, older than our school system," wrote Douglas, himself a veteran of four weddings. "Marriage is a coming together for better or for worse, hopefully enduring, and intimate to the degree of being sacred."

The Court's invalidation of Connecticut's 1879 "Little Comstock" law, modeled after the federal law that New York censor Anthony Comstock championed in 1873, drew relatively little attention, in large part because the end of the Court's term in 1965 was overshadowed by the growing war in Vietnam, increased U.S. involvement in Latin America, and a brewing battle over the reapportionment of congressional districts. There was some kvetching from the right—conservative columnist James J. Kilpatrick wrote that "a majority of the Supreme Court last week tossed precedent to the winds"—but most seemed to agree with the editorial board of the *North Adams Transcript* in Massachusetts, which wrote: "The Connecticut birth control decision did not shake the foundation of the Republic or of Constitutional government. It did interpret the Constitution in favor of the individual as against the state. The decision was a wise one." Even a longtime opponent of contraception agreed: the Most Reverend Henry J. O'Brien, archbishop of the Roman Catholic Church in Hartford, praised the legal reasoning used by the Court in reaching its decision, although he also made it clear that the Church's moral ban on contraceptives would remain unchanged.

Seven years later, even fewer people seemed surprised when the Court extended its holding in Griswold to unmarried couples, in Eisenstadt v. Baird (1972). Writing for a plurality of just four justices (two others concurred in the result, but on different grounds), Associate Justice William Brennan said that a Massachusetts law banning the provision of contraceptives to single persons was unconstitutional. But unlike in Griswold, the Court did not base its decision exclusively on the right to privacy. Instead, Brennan said, the central constitutional provision was the equal protection clause of the Fourteenth Amendment: "Whatever the rights of the individual to access to contraceptives may be, the rights must be the same for the unmarried and the married alike." Since the Massachusetts law treated those two classes of individuals differently— and there was no compelling reason to do so— it violated the Fourteenth Amendment.

The right to privacy made a limited appearance in the Eisenstadt opinion, but Brennan's treatment of the issue set off alarm bells for some Court watchers. The oral arguments for Eisenstadt were held in mid-November 1971; just one month later, the Court heard arguments in the even more difficult case of Roe v. Wade, a lawsuit filed by a then-anonymous plaintiff (now known to be Norma McCorvey) against the Texas law banning abortions. Some saw Brennan's expansive description of the right to privacy in the Eisenstadt decision as a preview of how the Court might rule on the abortion issue:

It is true that in Griswold the right of privacy in question inhered in the marital relationship. Yet the marital couple is not an independent entity with a mind and heart of its own, but an association of two individuals each with a separate intellectual and emotional makeup. If the right of privacy means anything, it is the right of the *individual*, married or single, to be free from unwarranted governmental intrusion into matters so fundamentally affecting a person as the decision whether to bear or beget a child.

Among those who were dismayed with Brennan's language was Chief Justice Warren Burger, who dissented from the decision in *Eisenstadt*. "By relying on *Griswold* in the present context," Burger said, "the Court has passed beyond the penumbras of the specific guarantees into the uncircumscribed area of personal predilections."

Roe v. Wade: *Touching Off a Cultural and Political Revolution*

According to some investigative reporting by the *Washington Post*, Burger was reportedly sufficiently concerned about the potential outcome of the *Roe* case that he broke with long-standing tradition to delay the Court's decision. When the *Roe* case was argued in December 1971, the Court was missing two members: Hugo Black, who had died in September, and John Marshall Harlan, who died a few days after Christmas that year. Their replacements, Lewis Powell and William Rehnquist, respectively, were not sworn in until January 7, 1972, making them ineligible to participate in the Court's deliberations and decision in *Roe*.

The chief justice is responsible for assigning the drafting of decisions to the various justices, including himself. If the chief justice is in the minority, he will typically permit the senior associate justice in the majority to assign the opinion. Based on conversations with "reliable sources," the *Washington Post* said that following the justices' initial conference on *Roe* and a companion case out of Georgia, *Doe v. Bolton*, Burger assigned the opinion-drafting to Associate Justice Harry Blackmun, despite Burger's having voted with the minority. The senior associate justice, William Douglas, drafted a memorandum arguing that he should be allowed to assign the opinion, but Burger simply overrode his objection.

Blackmun's draft was ready by late spring, but before a formal vote could be taken on it, Blackmun withdrew it and suggested that the two cases should be reargued in the fall. "Court observers," the *Washington Post* said, "speculated that Burger convinced Blackmun that his opinion was too broad, and that the case ought to be reargued before all nine justices." New arguments were heard in the second week of the Court's October 1972 term, and largely because so much work had already been done in drafting an opinion, a decision was issued just three months later, in mid-January 1973. Seven justices signed on to the majority opinion written by Associate Justice Blackmun, including three of the four justices appointed by Richard Nixon: Chief Justice Burger and Associate Justices Blackmun and Powell. Justices White (appointed by Kennedy) and Rehnquist (Nixon) each dissented.

As with *Griswold,* the right to privacy was at the core of the decision in *Roe.* Blackmun noted that the Constitution does not specifically mention a right to privacy, but pointed out that the Court had recognized "zones" of privacy arising out of various enumerated guarantees in the Bill of Rights. "This right of privacy," Blackmun wrote, "whether it be founded in the Fourteenth Amendment's concept of personal liberty and restrictions upon state action, as we feel it is, or, as the district court determined, in the Ninth Amendment's reservation of rights to the people, is broad enough to encompass a woman's decision whether or not to terminate her pregnancy."

But Blackmun rejected the argument that the right of privacy gave a pregnant woman the absolute right to terminate her pregnancy "at whatever time, in whatever way, and for whatever reason she alone chooses." The Court's privacy decisions, Blackmun said, have consistently recognized that some state regulation may be appropriate. In the case of pregnancy, the Court concluded that the state does have a number of interests, including safeguarding the health of the mother, the monitoring and enforcement of proper medical procedures, and the protection of potential life.

"At some point in pregnancy," Blackmun wrote, "these respective interests become sufficiently compelling to sustain regulation of the factors that govern the abortion decision. The privacy right involved, therefore, cannot be said to be absolute."

The remainder of the majority's opinion in *Roe* was spent discussing the competing concerns and drawing the appropriate lines for balancing personal privacy and state regulation. The Court has frequently been criticized for engaging in that exercise, on the grounds that it was effectively legislating from the bench. But the Court, of course, is constantly asked to strike a balance between competing fundamental interests; one example, for instance, are the cases in which the Court is called upon to balance the competing interests of the establishment clause and the free expression clause of the First Amendment.

Thanks to the efforts of Francis Schaeffer and others like him in the Religious Right, the *Roe* decision quickly became a rallying cry in the battle against legalized abortion, and has remained a controversial issue in political races and judicial nominations for the last thirty-five years. But the Christian Right has had far less success demonizing the intellectual underpinning of *Roe*—the fundamental right to privacy—and as each year passes, the growing importance of that right makes it less likely that even the Roberts Court will flatly overrule *Roe*.

Judge Bork Educates America on the "Right to Privacy"
In 1986 President Reagan rewarded the Religious Right for its enthusiastic and effective support by nominating Judge Robert Bork to the U.S. Supreme Court. Across the conservative spectrum, Bork was seen as someone who could lead the Court back from the apostasy of the Warren Court. But ironically, at least some of the credit for the continuing durability of the right to privacy can be given to Bork. Rather than persuading the Senate that he would rescue the Court and the Constitution, his confirmation hearings served as a classic "teachable moment" for Americans on both the existence of a right to privacy and the potential consequences of its reversal. Much of that had to do with Judge Bork's staunch defense of his long-standing belief that *Griswold* was an erroneous and "unprincipled" decision.

"Courts must accept any value choice the legislature makes," Bork once wrote, "unless it clearly runs contrary to a choice made in the framing of the Constitution." In his originalist view, since the framers of the Constitution did not choose to create a right to privacy when they drafted the document, Justice Douglas and the other members of the Warren Court had no business locating one in the shadows of more clearly enumerated rights. On largely the same reasoning, Bork dismissed the Burger Court's decision in *Roe v. Wade* as a "wholly un-justifiable judicial usurpation of state legislative authority."

As *New York Times* reporter Linda Greenhouse perceptively noted at the time, over the course of the months leading up to Bork's nomination hearings and, in particular, during the fifteen days of the hearings themselves, the "right to privacy" was transformed from a code word for abortion to political shorthand for "the whole theme of fundamental rights." And as senators listened to their constituents during that summer, they realized that most voters found it hard to fathom that the Constitution would not protect the decisions that they and their spouses made in the privacy of their bedrooms. No doubt, many constituents were also legitimately worried about what other rights might wither away under Bork's hostile gaze.

The Bork hearings also educated Americans about the right to privacy in one other significant way: the startling amount of personal information that is routinely collected during the course of the day, and the increasing ease with which that information can be accessed and distributed. In September 1987 a reporter illicitly obtained a copy of Bork's video rental records from a Washington, D.C., video store and sold it to the *Washington City Paper*, which happily published it. There was nothing particularly remarkable about the contents of the list, but both supporters and opponents of his nomination were outraged at the invasion of Bork's privacy.

The incident led to the passage of numerous "Bork bills" in states around the country, making it a crime for video rental stores to disclose customer information; Congress passed a similar federal statute, called the Video Privacy Protection Act, in 1988. For many people, the disclosure of Bork's video records was the first time that they were ineluctably confronted with the impact of technology on their own personal privacy—and forced to consider the role that the Supreme Court should play in protecting that fundamental right.

It is no great surprise, then, that in the confirmation hearings that have taken place in the twenty years since Bork was rejected, senators have focused their questions more on the general concept of privacy than on the specific issue of abortion. Some suggested, for instance, that Justice Kennedy's unanimous confirmation to the Supreme Court was greatly aided by his clear ratification of the central concept in *Griswold*, the existence of a right to privacy.

"It is central to our American tradition," Kennedy said. "It is central to the idea of the rule of law. That is there is a zone of liberty, a zone of protection, a line that is drawn where the individual can tell the government: 'Beyond this line you may not go.'" As many of his later decisions would demonstrate, that was not a philosophy likely to be particularly comforting to the Religious Right.

Virtually every nominee sent to the Senate by a Republican president since has said the same thing, although the precise phrasing has varied somewhat over the years.

- David Souter: "I believe that the due process clause of the Fourteenth Amendment does recognize and does protect an unenumerated right of privacy."
- Clarence Thomas: "My view is that there is a right to privacy in the Fourteenth Amendment."
- John Roberts: "The right to privacy is protected under the Constitution in various ways. It's protected by the Fourth Amendment, which provides that the right of people to be secure in their persons, houses, effects, and papers is protected. It's protected under the First Amendment, dealing with prohibition on establishment of a religion and guarantee of free exercise, protects privacy in matters of conscience. It was protected by the framers in areas that were of particular concern to them that may not seem so significant today, the Third Amendment, protecting their homes against the quartering of troops."
- Samuel Alito: "The Constitution protects a right to privacy, and it protects the right to privacy in a number of ways. The Fourth Amendment certainly speaks to the right of privacy. People have a right to privacy in their homes and in their papers, and in their persons. And the standard for whether something is a search is whether there's an invasion of a right to privacy, a legitimate expectation of privacy."

Whether the Roberts Court and its members will honor their statements before the Senate Judiciary Committee remains to be seen. At the end of its first term, the Court handed down its decision in *Gonzales v. Carhart* (2007), a case challenging the constitutionality of the Partial-Birth Abortion Ban Act of 2003 (PBAB). The concept of a right to privacy was largely tangential to the Court's analysis, but the language used by the majority (Justice Kennedy, writing for Chief Justice Roberts and Justices Scalia, Thomas, and Alito) was not comforting to the supporters of the privacy right.

"We assume the following principles for the purposes of this opinion," Justice Kennedy wrote. "Before viability, a state 'may not prohibit any woman from making the ultimate decision to terminate her pregnancy.'" Kennedy's use of the phrase "for the purposes of this opinion" does not bespeak a commitment to bedrock principles, nor does the fact that the majority went on to uphold the PBAB despite the fact that on its face, the act applies to procedures that might be used before a fetus is viable, i.e., able to survive on its own outside of the womb. Among other things, the *Roe* decision states that previability decisions are within a woman's zone of privacy.

"The question," Kennedy said, "is whether the act, measured by its text in this facial attack, imposes a substantial obstacle to late-term, but previability, abortions. The act does not on its face impose a substantial obstacle, and we reject this further facial challenge to its validity." *Gonzales* is the first case post-*Roe* to authorize any restriction at all on previability abortions.

The Bork hearings and the growing concern over the impact of technology on privacy has made it clear to Supreme Court nominees that it is politically expedient to endorse publicly the existence of a right to privacy. And in truth, there may be few members of the Court who would go as far as Bork and openly reverse *Griswold, Eisenstadt,* or perhaps even *Roe.* The *Carhart* decision, however, raises the disturbing possibility that a majority of the Roberts Court is willing to nibble away at the right to privacy without appearing to abandon it.

While the Religious Right, even with the appointment of Chief Justice Roberts and Associate Justice Alito, still does not have the Court it would like, its efforts to reshape the Supreme Court clearly have not been fruitless. If *Gonzales* proves to be merely the first salvo in a Court retrenchment not merely on abortion but on privacy as well, the Christian Right itself may come to rue its push for originalist justices: the right to privacy is a profoundly ecumenical concept.

CHAPTER TEN

The Culture of Life

Three Pyrrhic Victories for the Religious Right

M UCH IF NOT MOST of the Religious Right's crusade to reshape the Supreme Court is driven by its belief that the Court is hostile to the movement's "culture of life." What constitutes the culture of life is occasionally difficult to pin down, but at the very least, it includes protection of embryos and fetuses, and an opposition to anything the movement considers to be euthanasia. A key component of the Christian Right's judicial advocacy has been the identification and promotion of nominees who endorse the culture of life.

Although the Christian Right enjoyed considerable success with and influence on the judicial nomination process during the first six years of George W. Bush's presidency, the 2006 midterm election proved unusually costly. First, a number of important incumbents actively supported by the Right were thrown out of office, including Senator Rick Santorum (R.-Pa.), Senator Mike DeWine (R-Ohio), Senator Jim Talent (R-Mo.), Representative J. D. Hayworth (R-Ariz.), Representative Jim Ryun (R-Kans.), Representative Anne Northup (R-Ky.), and, through retirement, Representatives Tom DeLay (R-Tex.) and Mark Foley (R-Fla.). Second, the overall election results were bad enough to give Democrats control not merely of the House of Representatives, which many had anticipated would happen, but also of the Senate, which almost no one had predicted. Overnight, the Religious Right's prospects for reshaping the federal judiciary dimmed considerably, and the impact was felt immediately.

On November 15, 2006, in a show of bravado following the disappointing election results two weeks earlier, President Bush renominated six individuals to the federal bench who had previously been denied votes on the Senate floor due to Democratic opposition. The nominees included Michael Wallace for a position on the Fifth Circuit Court of Appeals; William Haynes and Terrence Boyle for the Fourth U.S. Circuit Court of Appeals; William G. Myers and Norman Randy Smith for the Ninth Circuit; and Peter Keisler for the D.C. Circuit Court.

Senator Patrick Leahy (D-Vt.), the incoming chairman of the Senate Judiciary Committee, said that he was frustrated by the president's nominations. "Barely a week after the president promised to change course by working in a bipartisan and cooperative way with Congress," Leahy said, "it is disappointing that he has decided to 'stay the course' on judicial nominees by renominating a slate of his most controversial past choices." Outgoing chair Arlen Specter (R-Pa.) made it clear that he had no intention of trying to force hearings or votes on the president's nominees during the Senate's lame-duck session between Thanksgiving and the New Year.

Of the six judicial nominees, four either withdrew their nomination or had it withdrawn by the White House after the new Democratic-controlled Congress convened in January 2007: Wallace, Haynes, Boyle, and Myers. Norman Randy Smith was unanimously confirmed for a seat on the Ninth Circuit on February 15, 2007, and the nomination of Peter Keisler to the D.C. Circuit was still pending at the end of 2007 while Congress argued over whether the D.C. Circuit actually needs any new additional judges.

It is not entirely certain that all of the nominees that President Bush sent to the Senate in November 2006 would have been confirmed even if the Republicans had retained control of the Senate. While the Gang of 14 agreement the year before prevented the use of the so-called nuclear option to destroy the filibuster, it still allowed the use of the controversial procedure in "extraordinary circumstances." The opposition to Boyle, Haynes, and Myers in particular was strong enough that the Democratic members of the Gang of 14 might have invoked the extraordinary-circumstances clause of their agreement and filibustered their nomination anyway. Myers had, in fact, been specifically exempted from the Gang of 14 agreement in the first place.

In any case, the 2006 midterm election debacle for the Republicans rendered the filibuster battle moot. In an era in which incumbents have an enormous inherent advantage (roughly 95 percent of congressional officeholders are reelected), the Democrats defeated six Republican senators and thirty-one Republican representatives. It was a remarkable turnaround from the 2004 election, and as the following vignettes demonstrate, much of the responsibility lies with the Religious Right and the uncompromising demands it made on Republican leadership.

Between the end of March 2005 and April 2007, three discrete but not unrelated events took place that compellingly demonstrated the extent to which the Christian Right had co-opted the Republican Party. Collectively, these events also demonstrated the lengths to which George W. Bush, Karl Rove, and various presidential aspirants were willing to go to cater to this faction's increasingly strident demands. The first was the reaction of Congress and President Bush to the tragic state court battle over the efforts of Michael Schiavo to discontinue life-prolonging measures for his wife, Terri, who had been in a persistent vegetative state since 1990. The second was Bush's veto in July 2006 of the Stem Cell Research Enhancement Act, a bill that had been passed by a large margin. And the third was the controversial 5–4 decision by the new Roberts Court, as mentioned earlier, in the case of *Gonzales v. Carhart* (2007), in which the Court upheld the constitutionality of the Partial-Birth Abortion Ban Act of 2003.

On the surface, certainly, each of these events appeared to be a victory for the Religious Right. But the victories proved to be classically Pyrrhic. Individually, each event was politically and socially outrageous enough to alienate broad swaths of the electorate. But collectively, they forced voters to consider the Christian Right's frightening control of the social agenda of the Republican Party. Although voters had many reasons to choose Democratic candidates in the 2006 midterm elections, there is no question that the so-called values voters who allegedly provided President George W. Bush with a "mandate" in 2004 (consisting of about 3 percent) were overwhelmed by voters who chose to enforce a separation of church and state one ballot at a time.

The Palm Sunday Compromise

For fifteen years, Theresa Marie Schiavo lay in various Florida institutions in a persistent vegetative state, following an unexplained collapse in February 1990. Eight years after she was first taken ill, her husband, Michael, petitioned the Florida state courts for permission to remove the feeding tube that was keeping his wife alive. Michael's request was bitterly opposed by Terri's parents, Robert and Mary Schindler, but after seven years of complicated and exhaustive litigation, Florida County Circuit Court Judge George Greer granted Michael's request and on March 18, 2005, issued an order instructing that Terri's feeding tube be removed.

In the months preceding Judge Greer's final order, the Schiavo case had become a cause célèbre for the Religious Right. Her plight was viewed as part and parcel of the Right's ongoing battle to promote a "culture of life." As the litigation over her fate slowly ground toward a final conclusion in the Florida state courts, the Christian Right put enormous pressure on Governor Jeb Bush and legislators in both Tallahassee and Washington to intervene. Lawmakers received thousands of calls and e-mails, and former Operation Rescue leader Randall Terry—president of the now-defunct Society for Truth and Justice—said, "Legal experts from around the country agree that Governor Bush has the authority to save Terri Schindler-Schiavo's life. We know he has the power, the question is, does he have the political will?" Governor Bush certainly tried, repeatedly, to intervene in the case, but Terry's legal analysis was completely incorrect; both state and federal courts said that the governor did not have the authority to block a legitimate court order, and that the efforts by the Florida legislature to give him that authority were unconstitutional.

Led by House majority whip Tom DeLay (R-Tex.) and Senate majority leader Bill Frist (R-Tenn.), Congress explored a variety of options to slow or stop the Florida court process. Regardless of their personal feelings on the matter, both had powerful reasons for intervening in the Schiavo controversy. In late February and early March 2005, DeLay had been hammered by a series of headlines linking him to political lobbyist Jack Abramoff, who was indicted in August of that year on a variety of criminal charges connected with lobbying he performed on behalf of Native American gambling interests. DeLay was undoubtedly grateful to have something to talk about besides his fondness for illegal Cuban cigars and Abramoff-hosted golf junkets to Scotland.

For Frist, the Tennessee physician who had rapidly risen to Senate majority leader, the stakes were even higher. Frist had well-publicized presidential aspirations and, with the opening skirmishes of the 2008 presidential campaign just two years away, he was eager to demonstrate his fidelity and effectiveness to one of the Republican Party's most important constituencies. The Schiavo case seemed to play into two key strengths for Frist: his leadership of the Republican-controlled Senate, and his medical background. During a largely self-congratulatory telephone conference with the Family Research Council (FRC), a Religious Right think tank and lobbying group founded by James Dobson in 1981, Senator Frist made it clear that among his top priorities were dealing with "activist judges" and the Schiavo matter.

"This is at the top of the challenges that we must overcome in this Congress," Frist said to applause from the FRC. "We all know that activist judges in the past have recently cited international law written by U.N. bureaucrats. They directly undermine marriage being between a man and a woman. They struck down our partial-birth abortion bans. And these activist judges are not interpreting the Constitution. They're rewriting it, and that's wrong. And it's something that I know you're committed to, and I'm committed to."

At the same time, Frist told the FRC Washington briefing that in between budget votes, he was working to bring the Terri Schiavo case into federal court. "Florida is dealing with the case now but it's unclear whether they will be able to," Frist said. "And so I can promise you that I will not leave tonight or tomorrow until we do everything we can and ultimately save life by preventing the starvation of Terri Schiavo.... And I think hopefully that speaks directly to the fact that this Congress, under this leadership, focuses on the dignity of life and the sanctity of life in a very direct way."

Just how far Frist, DeLay, and much of the rest of Congress were willing to go was simply breathtaking. It's worth noting that, in deference to the so-called values voters credited with tipping the balance in the 2004 election just four months earlier, all too few Democrats joined Representative Henry Waxman (D-Calif.) and Senator Ted Kennedy (D-Mass.) in opposing the Christian Right–inspired excesses. At the urging of the Republican leadership, committees in both the House and the Senate issued subpoenas for Michael and Terri Schiavo to appear before congressional hearings at the end of March. Legislators conceded that Terri was in no condition to testify, but argued that since federal law makes it a crime to injure or tamper with someone under a congressional subpoena, the subpoenas would make it illegal to remove Schiavo's feeding tube.

Judge Greer frostily rejected that argument: "I see no cogent reason why the committee should be able to intervene into a case involving the decision of whether or not to remain on life support," Greer said. "I don't think that legislative agencies or bodies have business in court proceedings." The House Committee on Government Reform asked the U.S. Supreme Court to enter an injunction against Judge Greer to permit service and execution of its subpoena, but Associate Justice Anthony Kennedy, sitting in his capacity as circuit justice for the D.C. Circuit, denied the request, as did the rest of the Court.

When the subpoena ploy failed, Congress rushed to pass "An Act for the Relief of the Parents of Theresa Marie Schiavo" over Easter weekend, a narrow piece of private legislation that threw open the doors of the federal courts to the Schindlers. The passage of the bill, which was colloquially referred to as the Palm Sunday Compromise, was notable for a number of things, but one particularly remarkable development was the eagerness President Bush showed for signing the bill. Despite his infamous devotion to his "downtime," Bush cut short Easter vacation at his Crawford, Texas, ranch and flew to Washington, D.C., on Air Force One to sign the legislation at an hour equally atypical for the early-retiring president: his wake-up call came at 1:10 a.m., about a half hour after the legislation cleared Congress.

From a legal perspective, one of the most significant aspects of what was designated Public Law 109–003 (just the third law passed by the

109th Congress) is that it created special jurisdiction for the U.S. District Court for the Middle District of Florida "to hear, determine, and render judgment on a suit or claim by or on behalf of Theresa Marie Schiavo" that her constitutional rights had been violated by Judge Greer's order to disconnect her life support. Even more remarkably, the legislation dictated how the district court should evaluate the merits of the proceeding:

> In such a suit, the district court shall determine de novo any claim of a violation of any right of Theresa Marie Schiavo within the scope of this act, notwithstanding any prior state court determination and regardless of whether such a claim has previously been raised, considered, or decided in state court proceedings. The district court shall entertain and determine the suit without any delay or abstention in favor of state court proceedings, and regardless of whether remedies available in the state courts have been exhausted.

The Schindlers filed suit in federal court the morning after President Bush signed the legislation, but on March 22, U.S. District Court Judge James Whittemore denied their request for a temporary injunction. Applying traditional injunctive relief analysis, Judge Whittemore weighed the Schindler's likelihood of success on the merits of their case—chiefly an assertion that Judge Greer had denied Terri due process of law—and concluded that they were not likely to prevail. His decision was upheld by the Eleventh Circuit Court of Appeals the following day, and a week later, the United States Supreme Court denied their petition for a writ of certiorari. The most compelling summation of the week's events was written by Eleventh Circuit Judge Stanley F. Birch Jr.:

> A popular epithet directed by some members of society, including some members of Congress, toward the judiciary involves the denunciation of "activist judges." Generally, the definition of an "activist judge" is one who decides the outcome of a controversy before him or her according to personal conviction, even one sincerely held, as opposed to the dictates of the law as constrained by legal prece-

dent and, ultimately, our Constitution. In resolving the Schiavo controversy it is my judgment that, despite sincere and altruistic motivation, the legislative and executive branches of our government
have acted in a manner demonstrably at odds with our founding
fathers' blueprint for the governance of a free people—our Constitution.

Judge Birch's wise admonition fell on deaf ears, at least on Capitol
Hill. Following the federal court rejection of the Schiavo case, Representative Tom DeLay said that the courts had "thumbed their nose at
Congress and the president." He also made what could only be interpreted as a not-so-veiled and intemperate threat: "The time will come
for the men responsible for this to answer for their behavior, but not
today."

DeLay was not the only strident voice. In the Senate, John Cornyn
(R-Tex.) took to the floor a week after Schiavo's death on March 31
and suggested that the Supreme Court was lowering respect for the judiciary in general by taking on the role of policymaker.

I don't know if there is a cause-and-effect connection, but we have
seen some recent episodes of courthouse violence in this country—
certainly nothing new; we seem to have run through a spate of
courthouse violence recently that has been on the news. I wonder
whether there may be some connection between the perception in
some quarters on some occasions where judges are making political decisions yet are unaccountable to the public, that it builds and
builds to the point where some people engage in violence, certainly
without any justification, but that is a concern I have that I wanted
to share.

His remarks followed on the heels of similarly inflammatory comments
by Pat Robertson. "[Federal judges are] destroying the fabric that holds
our nation together," Robertson said during an interview with ABC's
This Week in April. "Over one hundred years, I think the gradual erosion
of the consensus that's held our country together is probably more serious than a few bearded terrorists who fly into buildings."

These comments, particularly those by DeLay and Cornyn, were roundly condemned. An editorial not long afterward in the *Miami Herald* did not mince words: "This is reprehensible, irresponsible conduct by people who should know better. Rep. DeLay and his cohorts are sworn to uphold the Constitution, not undermine its most basic tenets. Yet they don't seem remotely familiar with the Constitution's demand for co-equal branches of government and a distinct separation of powers." The *New York Times* offered a similar assessment: "It was appalling when the House majority leader [DeLay] threatened political retribution against judges who did not toe his extremist political line. But when a second important Republican [Cornyn] stands up and excuses murderous violence against judges as an understandable reaction to their decisions, then it is time to get really scared."

Frist tried to distance himself from the controversy by saying that Terri Schiavo received "a fair and independent look" from the federal judges involved in her case. Nonetheless, Frist still agreed to participate in "Justice Sunday," the April 24, 2005, antijudiciary meeting organized by James Dobson's Focus on the Family and its lobbying wing, the Family Research Council. The primary purpose of the meeting was to put pressure on Senate Democrats to end the filibuster against some of President Bush's judicial nominees. But many of the speakers also took the opportunity to criticize the judges who had refused to halt the disconnection of Terri Schiavo's life support. Addressing the crowd of seventeen hundred at the Highview Baptist Church, a megachurch in Louisville, Kentucky, James Dobson described the Supreme Court as "unelected and unaccountable, arrogant and imperious, determined to redesign the culture according to their biases."

In an effort to minimize criticism of his participation but still avoid snubbing the meeting's Religious Right organizers, Frist appeared by videotape. In his four-minute-long comments, he focused purely on the politics of the Senate filibuster and avoided any mention of religion. He also implicitly rebuked DeLay: "When we think judicial decisions are outside mainstream American values, we will say so," Frist said. "But we must also be clear that the balance of power among all three branches requires respect—not retaliation. I won't go along with that."

Frist's decision to cast half a loaf on the Justice Sunday waters, not surprisingly, pleased no one. He was widely criticized for appearing to support religious-based attacks on the judiciary, but his unwillingness to attend the event in person reinforced questions about his commitment to Christian Right issues. When Dobson organized the even more aggressively hostile "Justice Sunday II" in August 2005, Frist—probably to his considerable relief—was not invited to speak. Among those who did address the crowd in Nashville, Tennessee, were Tom DeLay, Robert Bork, Phyllis Schlafly, and Zell Miller.

The Bush Stem Cell Veto

Frist's omission from the Justice Sunday II lineup was the direct result of a startling speech that the Senate majority leader gave on July 29, 2005. After years of aiding the Bush White House in opposing any efforts to loosen restrictions on the federal funding of stem cell research, Frist announced that he was changing his position. "The limitations put in place in 2001 will, over time, slow our ability to bring potential new treatments for certain diseases," Frist said, "Therefore, I believe the president's policy should be modified." It was, Senator Arlen Specter said, one of the most important speeches given on the floor of the Senate in all of 2005.

"In all forms of stem cell research," Frist said that morning, "I see today, just as in 2001, great, great promise to heal. Whether it is diabetes or Parkinson's disease, or my own field of heart disease, Lou Gehrig's disease or spinal cord injuries, stem cells offer hope for treatment that other lines of research simply cannot offer."

The significance of Frist's speech was at least twofold: First, President Bush had previously put a policy in place that strictly limited federal funding for stem cell research, and had already repeatedly said that he would veto any legislation changing that policy. Frist's decision to support a bill to expand federal research, the Stem Cell Research Enhancement Act, undoubtedly angered the president, a fellow Republican who always valued loyalty above most other qualities.

Second, the stem cell research bill was strenuously opposed by the Religious Right, a key supporter of Bush, and Frist's change of position on the issue was likely to damage his nascent bid for the 2008 Republican presidential nomination, at least in the generally partisan primaries. In fact, that same day, Focus on the Family's Dobson said in a statement, "It is an understatement to say that the pro-life community is disappointed by Senator Frist's decision to join efforts to void President Bush's policy limiting the funding of embryonic stem-cell research. Most distressing is that, in making his announcement, Senator Frist calls himself a defender of the sanctity of human life—even though the research he now advocates results, without exception, in the destruction of human life." Less than a month after Frist's speech, a Christian Right group called the Center for Reclaiming America launched a series of TV ads in Iowa, an important early campaign stop, that harshly criticized Frist's decision.

The battle over stem cell research was the latest skirmish in the ongoing battle over federal funding of human embryo research stretching back for the last few decades. In the wake of the Supreme Court's decision in *Roe v. Wade*, liberal activists celebrated the legalization of abortion and the securing of a woman's right to choose; social conservatives in Congress, in the meantime, set about proposing and passing measures to block virtually all federal funding of abortion, which effectively limited the right to choose to those who had the financial resources to do so. The first and most successful of those measures was the Hyde Amendment, a bill proposed by Representative Henry Hyde (R-Ill.) to prohibit the federal Medicare program from paying for abortions except when the life of the mother was in danger. Although the restrictions have been eased slightly, the Hyde Amendment is still in effect today. Additional limitations on federal abortion funding were adopted during the so-called Republican Revolution in 1994 and again following the election of President George W. Bush in 2000.

Equally disconcerting is the impact that the Religious Right has had on the funding of basic scientific research by the federal government. In the mid-1970s, exciting and innovative work was being done on human fertility, leading to the successful in vitro fertilization of a human egg that culminated in the July 25, 1978, birth of Louise Brown, the world's first "test-tube baby"—now married and the mother of her own naturally conceived son. Due to concerns over the safety and ethics of the fertilization research, the Department of Health, Education, and Welfare (HEW) had put a hold on all federal funding for the work pending a comprehensive ethics review. As the news of Brown's birth spread, HEW was petitioned to relax its prohibition and start funding in vitro research in the United States, which it did a year later (although its guidelines forbade, among other things, "extramarital" conceptions).

On January 9, 1980, the state of Virginia announced plans to open the first in vitro clinic in the United States at the Eastern Virginia Medical School. A local antiabortion group, the Virginia Society for Human Life (VSHL), promised both state and federal lawsuits to halt the project. "This is the first serious crack in the wall of a public health policy that has been clearly against experimentation with human embryos," Charles D. Dean Jr., the group's leader, told the *New York Times.* "We hope to have the ability to prevent their putting up the first 2-by-4 for the clinic." The VSHL was unsuccessful in stopping the Virginia clinic, and in vitro technology has proven enormously popular: in the seventeen years since the first in vitro clinic opened, more than one hundred thousand children in the United States have been born as a result of advances in artificial fertilization techniques.

The advances in human fertility opened up a brave new world of scientific research into human genetics, and at the same time raised profound ethical questions: Is it ethical to conduct research on the tissue of aborted fetuses? Should embryos be created purely for research purposes alone? Just when does life begin anyway? And for every answer derived from the combination of research and improved technology, a host of new questions arose.

For the Religious Right, the answer to the questions raised by embryo research was essentially the same as the ones raised by sex and drugs: "Just Say No." In 1995 Representatives Jay Dickey (R-Ark.) and Roger Wicker (R-Miss.) proposed legislation to bar federal researchers from conducting experiments on embryos obtained from private in vitro fertilization labs. The bill passed as an amendment to a large appropriations bill that year, along with a prohibition on the funding of abortion through the federal employees' health insurance program and the elimination of the U.S. government's primary family planning program.

Dickey, an attorney and successful Taco Bell franchisee from Pine

Bluffs, Arkansas, first won election to Congress in 1992 with the active support of the Christian Coalition. He defended his ban on federal embryo research in a 1995 op-ed in the *Washington Post* titled "Lethal Experiments."

"Opening a whole new field for controversial experiments of questionable benefit—experiments that set aside the usual norms on respect for human subjects in order to destroy and discard developing human life—is not my idea of a responsible use of taxpayers' money," Dickey wrote. "There is plenty of research in need of funding that does not require such forays into the ethical wilderness."

But however unwilling Congress was to enter the ethical wilderness, there was little they could do about the fact that the wilderness would come to them. Although the Dickey Amendment undoubtedly slowed the pace of research into embryonic cells, the scientific and economic potential was sufficiently great to attract the research efforts of private companies around the country. One of the more promising developments in that research occurred in 1998, when two research teams independently announced that they had succeeded in isolating a special type of cell known as a human embryonic stem cell.

The specifics, needless to say, are complicated, but the general concept is that stem cells are the basic building blocks of larger organisms, the first cells that develop after fertilization of an egg by a sperm. As the embryo develops in the womb, the original stem cells differentiate into a wide variety of more specialized cells, each with a particular function (brain, nerves, skin, liver, etc.). Medical researchers believe that such stem cells can be coaxed into specializing in the laboratory, and then used to treat a potentially staggering array of human illnesses, including Lou Gehrig's disease (ALS, or amyotrophic lateral sclerosis), heart disease, macular degeneration, liver and kidney damage, Alzheimer's, Down syndrome, and so on.

In January 1999 the National Institutes of Health made a determination that stem cell research did not violate the terms of the Dickey Amendment, which is limited to situations in which human embryos are "destroyed, discarded, or knowingly subjected to risk of injury or death...." Specifically, NIH lawyers concluded that since stem cells cannot grow to viability on their own if implanted in the uterus, they are not the equivalent of embryos. Moreover, since federal researchers could obtain stem cells from private laboratories, they would not be engaged in the destruction of any embryos. Opponents, including Dickey, disagreed with the NIH's analysis and argued that federal researchers would nonetheless be "complicit" in the destruction of embryos, since at the time, stem cells could not be extracted from an embryo without destroying it.

Despite the objections, the NIH went ahead and issued regulations eighteen months later authorizing federally funded scientists to conduct stem cell research, but only on stem cells extracted from embryos that would have been discarded anyway by an in vitro fertilization clinic. President Bill Clinton praised the new guidelines and suggested that the controversy over the research would soon die down. "I think that if the public will look at, first of all, the potentially staggering benefits of this research," Clinton said, "everything from birth defects to Parkinson's, certain kinds of cancer, diabetes, spinal cord injuries.... It's a potential change for the future."

But following the election of President George W. Bush in the fall of 2000, the Christian Right pressured the White House and congressional Republicans to reverse the NIH's decision. The issue eventually became important enough that on August 9, 2001, Bush devoted his entire first televised prime-time address to the topic. He announced that he was allowing federal financing of embryonic stem cell research, but only on approximately sixty stem cell lines already in existence. That would enable researchers, Bush said, to determine the potential of the new research without destroying any additional embryos.

But less than a month later, the Bush administration was already conceding that only a third of the stem cell lines described by the president were actually ready for research by scientists. Secretary of Health and Human Services Tommy Thompson promised a Senate panel that additional colonies of stem cells would be available at the same time as federal funding. In his dramatic speech on the floor of the Senate in 2005, however, Frist pointed out that the number of stem cell colonies available for federally financed research never exceeded twenty-four, and scientists had grave concerns that the stem cells in question were contaminated, having been maintained in culture dishes containing genetic material from rodents. Frist said that both of those factors helped change his mind on the need for more expansive rules on federally financed stem cell research.

The House passed an expanded stem cell research bill in 2005 by a solid but not veto-proof margin (238–194). On July 18, 2006, the Senate followed suit: the bill passed 63–37, four votes short of the total necessary to override President Bush's threatened veto. Five and a half years into his presidency, Bush had not yet vetoed a single bill, but the day after the Senate vote, he rejected the stem cell research legislation, saying, "This bill would support the taking of innocent human life." He announced his decision at a White House event attended by two dozen or so "snowflake" babies—boys and girls born through in vitro fertilization from frozen embryos "adopted" by childless couples; the infants were invited to the ceremony by the White House and the Embryo Adoption Awareness Campaign. But as Senator Specter pointed out, the supply of frozen embryos vastly exceeds the demand for adoption: at the time of Bush's veto, just 128 frozen embryos had been adopted out of the 400,000 or so available. Virtually all unused embryos are simply discarded.

Senate supporters of stem cell research promised to continue pushing for an increased federal role. "We will not give in," Senator Ted Kennedy said. "We are going to continue this battle, and we have every intention of success in winning this battle for families in our country and for people all over the world." Even Senator Orrin Hatch (R-Utah), a staunch abortion opponent, regretfully admitted that the president's veto "sets back embryonic stem cell research another year or so."

If, as Senator Richard Durbin (D-Ill.) suggested, the Republican leadership hoped that a quick veto would prevent stem cell research from becoming a 2006 campaign issue, they were sorely mistaken. There is no better example of the strength and importance of the issue for average Americans—the vast majority of whom would welcome the possibility of better treatments for themselves and their families—than the success of a proposal that fall in Missouri to amend the state constitution to authorize stem cell research. The Religious Right has long been a powerful force in the state; in 2002 it helped conservative Republican Jim Talent narrowly defeat Jean Carnahan in a special election to fill the remainder of her deceased husband Mel Carnahan's term. But in 2006, despite calls from Christian Right leaders to oppose the stem cell amendment, Talent dithered (the amendment had strong support from the Missouri business community), and he ended up losing his reelection bid to Democrat Claire McCaskill. And the stem cell research amendment? It passed by a margin of 51–49 percent.

The Religious Right lost on a variety of other initiatives around the country on election night 2006, including proposals in California and Oregon to require women under the age of eighteen to notify their parents before getting an abortion; a proposal in South Dakota to ban all abortions except to save a pregnant woman's life (rejected by a surprisingly large 56–44 margin); and, for the first time, a same-sex marriage ban that went down to defeat in Arizona. When combined with the conservative candidates who also lost, it was a bad election for the Christian Right. There is little doubt that much of the credit (or blame) for those results can be traced to the Palm Sunday Compromise and the president's veto of federally funded stem cell research.

The Partial-Birth Abortion Ban Act

The Roberts Court's decision in *Gonzales v. Carhart* was not handed down until the end of June 2007, long after the midterm election booths had closed. But in much the same way that the Bork confirmation hearings educated Americans about the growing threat to the right to privacy and other fundamental constitutional rights, the *Carhart* decision helped illustrate just how far the Christian Right has come in its efforts to overturn the Supreme Court's rulings on abortion.

The origins of the *Carhart* decision reach back to Wednesday, November 5, 2003, when President George W. Bush traveled to the Ronald Reagan Building and International Trade Center to hold a signing ceremony for a particularly significant piece of legislation. Fittingly, on the ground floor of the same building is a large piece of the old Berlin Wall, its gray Cold War concrete resplendent in vivid multicolor graffiti. The wall segment was donated to the United States by the citizens of Berlin and employees of Daimler-Benz in recognition of Reagan's famous challenge to Mikhail Gorbachev, then general secretary of the Communist Party of the Soviet Union: "Mr. Gorbachev, open this gate! Mr. Gorbachev, tear down this wall!"

The legislation that Bush signed in the Reagan building that day, the Partial-Birth Abortion Ban Act of 2003 (PBABA), knocked one more chunk out of the wall separating church and state in this country, although just how large a chunk would not be known until the inevitable appeal to the United States Supreme Court. And there was no question that the law would be challenged: Not only was the PBABA the first federal abortion restriction signed into law since the Supreme Court's 1973 decision in *Roe v. Wade*, but far more significantly, Congress in its legislative findings specifically rejected the idea that the procedure could ever be necessary to protect the health of the mother:

> There exists substantial record evidence upon which Congress has reached its conclusion that a ban on partial-birth abortion is not required to contain a "health" exception, because the facts indicate that a partial-birth abortion is never necessary to preserve the health of a woman, poses serious risks to a woman's health, and lies outside the standard of medical care. Congress was informed by extensive hearings held during the 104th, 105th, 107th, and 108th Congresses and passed a ban on partial-birth abortion in the 104th, 105th, and 106th Congresses. These findings reflect the very informed judgment of the Congress that a partial-birth abortion is never necessary to preserve the health of a woman, poses serious risks to a woman's health, and lies outside the standard of medical care, and should, therefore, be banned.

That finding and others like it in the PBABA were a gauntlet thrown directly at the feet of the Supreme Court, which just three years earlier had rejected a similar Nebraska law in *Stenberg, Attorney General of Nebraska, et al. v. Carhart* (2000), in large part because it failed to make any exception for the health of the mother. For precisely that reason, President Bill Clinton had twice successfully vetoed versions of the PBABA.

Three abortion rights groups, led by the National Abortion Federation, challenged the constitutionality of the law literally within minutes of its being signed by President Bush, and U.S. District Court judges in Nebraska and California quickly issued injunctions against enforcement of the law. After lengthy and detailed trials, both district courts ruled that the PBABA was unconstitutional, in large part because Congress did not include any exception for the health of the mother when it adopted the law. Both the Eighth Circuit (which covers Nebraska) and the Ninth Circuit (which covers California) affirmed the decisions of the federal trial courts. The cases were argued before the Supreme Court on November 8, 2006 (coincidentally, one day after the 2006 election), and the Court issued its decision five months later.

In the years since the Court issued its decision in *Roe v. Wade* in 1973, the issue of abortion has appeared on the Court's docket numerous times, as various conservative states passed restrictions on abortion that they hoped would pass constitutional muster. With the appointment of a number of more conservative justices, the Court showed an increasing willingness to uphold state restrictions, and some justices—most notably Chief Justice William Rehnquist and Associate Justices Antonin Scalia and Clarence Thomas—have urged the Court to abandon *Roe* altogether.

The most direct assault on *Roe* occurred in *Planned Parenthood v. Casey* (1992), when the Court considered the constitutionality of a variety of abortion restrictions contained in the Pennsylvania Abortion Control Act of 1982. As with so many abortion cases, the decision of the Court was badly fragmented, but the bottom line was that five of the justices (a plurality of O'Connor, Kennedy, and Souter, with Stevens and Blackmun concurring) reaffirmed the central tenets of *Roe* while at the same time upholding most of the Pennsylvania law's restrictions. Significantly, however, the plurality opinion, written by O'Connor, modified the *Roe* decision by lowering the standard for evaluating abortion restrictions from "heightened scrutiny" to "undue burden." The Court also abandoned *Roe's* trimester formula and said that a state's interest in potential life can outweigh a woman's right to obtain an abortion in the second trimester at the point of viability of the fetus, which advances in medical technology had reduced to as little as twenty-two weeks.

Although most of the Pennsylvania law was upheld (only a spousal-notification requirement was struck down), the *Casey* decision was a major disappointment for the Religious Right. Eight of the nine members of the Court at that point had been appointed by Republican presidents, after all, and five of them had voted to uphold *Roe*. Particular venom was directed at Associate Justice Kennedy, who had been confirmed just three years earlier and who had appeared to give antiabortion assurances to Senator Jesse Helms (R-N.C.). It was unfathomable to many on the Right that Kennedy could sign an opinion that stated, as O'Connor's did, that:

> Our cases recognize the right of the *individual*, married or single, to be free from unwarranted governmental intrusion into matters so fundamentally affecting a person as the decision whether to bear or beget a child. Our precedents "have respected the private realm of family life which the state cannot enter." These matters, involving the most intimate and personal choices a person may make in a lifetime, choices central to personal dignity and autonomy, are central to the liberty protected by the Fourteenth Amendment. At the heart of liberty is the right to define one's own concept of existence, of meaning, of the universe, and of the mystery of human life. Beliefs about these matters could not define the attributes of personhood were they formed under compulsion of the state.

In an interview with the *New York Times* some years later, Robert Bork offered a characteristically blunt assessment: "What the hell does that [language] mean?" Bork asked. "Obviously it doesn't mean the individual is unbounded by any law. So it must mean that the individual is unbounded by laws the justices don't like. It's simply an assertion of power, in a way that's particularly empty of intellectual content. It sums up what's wrong with the court."

Conservative anger at Kennedy intensified after his vote and opinion in *Lawrence v. Texas* (2003), in which the Court ruled that a Texas law making homosexual sodomy a crime was unconstitutional. Writing for the 6–3 majority, Kennedy said that intimate consensual sexual conduct is within the liberty interest protected by the substantive due process provision of the Fourteenth Amendment. The outcome of the case was bad enough for religious conservatives, but what truly outraged many in the Christian Right (and conservative legal circles in general) was Justice Kennedy's citation of European legal authority in support of the Court's decision.

When National Public Radio's Nina Totenberg later revealed in March 2004 that the private papers of the deceased Harry Blackmun showed that Kennedy had initially voted to overrule *Roe* in the *Casey* decision but changed his mind, some Religious Right leaders were so incensed with Kennedy that they actually called for his impeachment.

At a conference of religious conservatives called "Confronting the Judicial War on Faith," held in Washington, D.C., on April 7–8, 2005, Michael Farris described Kennedy as "the poster boy for impeachment." "If our congressmen and senators do not have the courage to impeach and remove from office Justice Kennedy," Farris charged, "they ought to be impeached as well."

Speaking at the same gathering, Eagle Forum leader Phyllis Schlafly urged Congress to pass legislation stripping the federal courts of their ability to hear cases involving religious displays, the Pledge of Allegiance, same-sex marriage, and the Boy Scouts. She also called for Justice Kennedy's impeachment, on the grounds that his decisions upholding sodomy and barring capital punishment for juveniles (which also relied in part on international legal norms) were a violation of the Constitution's "good behavior" standard for federal judges.

Given all that, it is somewhat ironic that Justice Kennedy authored the Roberts Court's first abortion opinion—and that his opinion was at least as upsetting to the Left as his earlier opinions had been to the Christian Right. Kennedy began his opinion with a lengthy and explicit description of the abortion procedure banned under the PBABA. Known medically as "intact dilation and extraction" but dubbed "partial-birth abortion" by its opponents, the procedure is used in a relatively small number of second-trimester abortions, so the practical impact of PBABA was likely to be limited. But the critical questions, from a legal perspective, are: first, whether PBABA furthers a "legitimate government interest," and second, whether it does so without imposing an "undue burden" on a woman's fundamental right to privacy, particularly given the fact that it makes no exception for the health of the woman (unless the woman's life is actually in danger).

The Court concluded that PBABA does further a legitimate gov-

THE CULTURE OF LIFE | 249

ernment interest. "The act," Kennedy said, "expresses respect for the dignity of human life. Congress was concerned, furthermore, with the effects on the medical community and on its reputation caused by the practices of partial-birth abortion." The majority also put considerable emphasis on the efforts of Congress to protect women from the consequences of agreeing to the intact dilation and extraction procedure or to even having an abortion in the first place (something not at issue, obviously, in the case before the Court):

> While we find no reliable data to measure the phenomenon, it seems unexceptionable to conclude some women come to regret their choice to abort the infant life they once created and sustained. Severe depression and loss of esteem can follow....
>
> The state has an interest in ensuring so grave a choice is well informed. It is self-evident that a mother who comes to regret her choice to abort must struggle with grief more anguished and sorrow more profound when she learns, only after the event, what she once did not know: that she allowed a doctor to pierce the skull and vacuum the fast-developing brain of her unborn child, a child assuming the human form.

The Court also ruled that the restrictions contained in the PBABA do not impose an "undue burden" on the rights of women. "The act is not invalid on its face where there is uncertainty over whether the barred procedure is ever necessary to preserve a woman's health," Kennedy wrote, "given the availability of other abortion procedures that are considered to be safe alternatives."

In a one-paragraph concurrence, Associate Justices Clarence Thomas and Antonin Scalia stated flatly that "the Court's abortion jurisprudence, including *Casey* and *Roe v. Wade*, has no basis in the Constitution" and concluded that Roe should be overturned.

Associate Justice Ruth Bader Ginsburg, on behalf of her colleagues Stevens, Souter, and Breyer, wrote a powerful and emphatic dissent. "Today's decision is alarming," Ginsburg said. "It refuses to take *Casey* and *Stenberg* seriously. It tolerates, indeed applauds, federal intervention to ban nationwide a procedure found necessary and proper in certain cases by the American College of Obstetricians and Gynecologists (ACOG). It blurs the line, firmly drawn in *Casey*, between previability and postviability abortions. And, for the first time since *Roe*, the Court blesses a prohibition with no exception safeguarding a woman's health."

The bulk of Ginsburg's dissent was spent dissecting the factual underpinnings of both the act and the majority's opinion. Among other things, Ginsburg pointed to the congressional finding that a medical consensus existed that the banned procedure was never necessary to protect a woman's health. Both district courts, Ginsburg noted, had heard extensive evidence that no such consensus in fact existed. Moreover, she noted, several medical organizations presented uncontradicted testimony that the partial-birth abortion ban would jeopardize the health of some pregnant women. "Based on thoroughgoing review of the trial evidence and the congressional record," Ginsburg said, "each of the district courts to consider the issue rejected Congress's findings as unreasonable and not supported by the evidence." She described the majority's willingness to disregard the findings of both district courts as "bewildering."

Ginsburg reserved particular scorn for Kennedy's efforts to ground the constitutionality of the law, at least in part, in Congress's desire to protect the emotional well-being of women. "Ultimately," she said, "the Court admits that 'moral concerns' are at work, concerns that could yield prohibitions on any abortion.... Notably, the concerns expressed are untethered to any ground genuinely serving the government's interest in preserving life.... Revealing in this regard, the Court invokes an antiabortion shibboleth for which it concededly has no reliable evidence: Women who have abortions come to regret their choices, and consequently suffer from 'severe depression and loss of esteem.' This way of thinking reflects ancient notions about women's place in the family and under the Constitution—ideas that have long since been discredited."

Although the majority's opinion did not do what Justice Thomas or Justice Scalia (or for that matter, the Christian Right) hoped, Ginsburg and her fellow dissenters correctly noted that it was not a decision that showed much respect for the concept of precedent. It also raised the possibility that future factual pronouncements by Congress, however divorced from reality or theologically motivated, could serve as the basis of otherwise unconstitutional laws. Ginsburg's conclusion is particularly powerful:

> In sum, the notion that the Partial-Birth Abortion Ban Act furthers any legitimate governmental interest is, quite simply, irrational. The Court's defense of the statute provides no saving explanation. In candor, the act, and the Court's defense of it, cannot be understood as anything other than an effort to chip away at a right declared again and again by this Court—and with increasing comprehension of its centrality to women's lives.

In light of the fact that Justices Kennedy, Roberts, and Alito were willing to "assume" the constitutionality of *Roe*'s main holdings for the purposes of *Carhart*, it is clear that the Religious Right still has not achieved one of its primary goals. But then, the constitutionality of *Roe* itself was not squarely presented in *Carhart*, and Justice Kennedy framed the decision in relatively narrow terms. Undoubtedly, the hope in the Christian Right is that if presented with the right case, the majority in *Carhart* would stop assuming that *Roe* is constitutional and simply declare that it is not. Although the Religious Right may still be short of its goal of radically reversing *Roe* and the other Warren Court decisions that it despises, it is nonetheless absolutely clear that after thirty years of activism, the Right has succeeded in changing the conversation at the Court. Increasingly, the question is just how much of the right to abortion will survive the Roberts Court. If Christian Right advocates like Jay Sekulow and Michael Farris continue to play a prominent role in the selection of Supreme Court nominees, other fundamental concepts such as the right to privacy and the separation of church and state itself could be among the movement's next victims.

Requiem for a Court?

CONTEMPLATING POSSIBLE CHANGES to the Court's membership can make an analyst feel somewhat ghoulish. But insurance companies compile actuarial tables for a reason, and as durable and long-lived as the members of the Supreme Court have been recently, it is inevitable that the lineup of justices on the Court will change. As the minor seizure suffered in July 2007 by the relatively young Chief Justice Roberts demonstrates, even Supreme Court justices are hostages to fate. Nonetheless, there are some reasonable assumptions that can be made about how the Court is likely to change in the relatively near future and how those changes might affect the Court's handling of religious issues.

For those who believe strongly in the concept of a strong separation of church and state, it is sobering to realize that for the foreseeable future, the current Roberts Court may be as good as it gets. The two oldest members of the current Court, as this book goes to press in the fall of 2007, are the eighty-seven-year-old John Paul Stevens and the seventy-four-year-old Ruth Bader Ginsburg. Although both have had health issues—Stevens had open-heart surgery more than thirty years ago, and Ginsburg had successful cancer surgery about eight years ago —neither has given any indication that they intend to retire from the

Court, particularly during a Republican administration. Stevens, in fact, has already hired his law clerks for the 2008–9 term of the Court, a generally optimistic sign that he intends to keep serving.

Not far behind Ginsburg are Antonin Scalia, well known as one of the Court's most conservative members, and Anthony Kennedy, a more moderate justice and the likely replacement for Sandra Day O'Connor (who retired at age seventy-six) as the Court's swing vote between the liberal and conservative blocs. The two next oldest justices, Stephen Breyer and David Souter, typically align themselves with the Court's liberal wing, although Souter does so more consistently and emphatically than Breyer. The stark reality, then, is that over the next fifteen to twenty years, future presidents and senators will be selecting nominees to replace the *entire* liberal wing of the current Court, as opposed to just one member (albeit an influential one) of the Court's conservative bloc.

Even with a Democrat in the White House, the Court may continue its long, slow drift to the right. Any nominee to the Supreme Court requires fifty-one votes in order to be confirmed, of course, and possibly sixty if the minority party filibusters the nomination. If the Senate remains as evenly divided as it was in 2007, it is highly unlikely that a former lawyer for the National Organization for Women and the American Civil Liberties Union (key elements of Ginsburg's résumé) would be confirmed. After all, when President Clinton nominated Ginsburg in 1993, Democrats held a solid 57–43 plurality, effectively eliminating the possibility of a successful filibuster against her nomination.

Religion and the Roberts Court

While keeping in mind that there are no guarantees as to how the members of the Court will vote on a particular issue (as the Religious Right is painfully aware), there are some predictions that can be made about how the relatively new Roberts Court might decide various religious issues, and what might happen in the future.

The *Lemon* Test. It is difficult to hold out much hope for the continued viability of the *Lemon* test, the current standard for evaluating whether a particular government program or action violates the principle of separation of church and state. With increasing frequency, conservative members of the Court have shown a willingness to simply ignore the *Lemon* test, or have narrowly construed it to the point of insignificance. The Roberts Court may formally abandon it altogether.

The replacement of William Rehnquist with John Roberts is not likely to make much difference in the Court's actual voting pattern, but it is worth remembering that Roberts worked on the solicitor general's brief in *Lee v. Weisman*, in which the elder Bush administration asked the Court to abandon the test altogether. Of much greater potential significance is the replacement of Sandra Day O'Connor with the presumably more consistent Samuel Alito. On issue after issue, Alito may tip the Court in a more conservative direction.

In *Lee*, for instance, O'Connor joined the majority opinion drafted by Anthony Kennedy. If Alito had been serving instead, it seems likely that the majority opinion would have been written by Justice Scalia, thereby abandoning *Lemon* and upholding prayer during school graduation ceremonies. Far more importantly, it is likely that Scalia would have used the case to announce a much narrower church-state test, one that would find "establishment of religion" by a government program only when there was financial support for religion *and* the threat of penalty for noncompliance or nonadherence (such as jail time for not attending church). To put it mildly, Scalia's approach would eviscerate contemporary boundaries between church and state.

The Ten Commandments. The church and state issue on which the Court seems the most divided is the publicly supported display of the Ten Commandments, as discussed in Chapter 6. In 2005 the Supreme Court simultaneously issued two contradictory 5–4 decisions involving different types of Decalogue displays: in *Van Orden v. Perry* the Court voted to uphold the constitutionality of a stone monument on the state capitol in Texas, but in *McCreary County v. ACLU of Kentucky* it struck down a Kentucky law requiring the courthouse display of the Ten Commandments.

Given the narrow margins and the struggles by the lower courts to interpret and apply the Court's decisions, it seems likely that the Court will take up the issue again in the near future. One entertaining possibility is the *Summum v. Pleasant Grove City* case, in which a relatively new religion is suing to have its pyramid-shaped monument, inscribed with its Seven Aphorisms, displayed next to the city's Ten Commandments monument. The American Center for Law and Justice, the legal foundation established by *700 Club* televangelist Pat Robertson, is actively soliciting funds to help take the case to the Supreme Court on behalf of the city.

If a new Ten Commandments case reaches the Supreme Court, it is likely to get a sympathetic hearing. Justice O'Connor voted against the constitutionality of the Ten Commandments display in both *Van Orden* and *McCreary*. If both Chief Justice Roberts and Justice Alito align themselves with the existing conservative bloc of the Court, they could arguably legalize the publicly supported display of the Ten Commandments in every public building in the country.

Public-Supported Holiday Displays. The issues surrounding holiday displays, also discussed in Chapter 6, seem more settled. Admittedly, the decision in *Allegheny County v. Greater Pittsburgh ACLU* is hardly an example of doctrinal clarity, given the number of separate opinions written by the Court, but the justices have not shown any interest in revisiting the issue in nearly twenty years. However, it is important to remember that four members of the *Allegheny County* Court (Chief Justice Rehnquist and Justices White, Scalia, and Kennedy) voted to uphold the constitutionality of Pittsburgh's Nativity display, notwithstanding its prominent placement in a government building, its lack of secular elements, and its overtly sectarian message.

Prayer in the Public Schools. As noted in Chapter 7, the Court decided *Wallace v. Jaffree,* the case that struck down the Alabama law providing for a moment of silence "for meditation or silent prayer," more than twenty years ago. It seems unlikely, even given the personnel changes that have occurred since then, that the Court will revisit the issue of prayer in the classroom.

A more likely candidate for reconsideration is the issue of prayer at school graduations or other events, such as football games. The *Lee v. Weisman* case, which invalidated the practice of prayer in graduation ceremonies, was a 5–4 decision made narrower by the fact that Justice Kennedy switched sides during the deliberations. The margin on the football-game prayer decision, *Santa Fe Independent School District v. Doe,* was slightly larger (6–3), but hardly unassailable. In both cases, Justice

O'Connor joined the majority in invalidating the challenged governmental practices. Should the Court reverse one or both of those decisions, then not only will the practice of prayer become far more prevalent at school functions, but the Court would inevitably be entangled in doctrinal battles over how such prayers may be phrased and delivered. The Court has enough of a challenge conducting the constitutional parsing for which it is trained; it would be particularly ill-suited to the task of splitting theological hairs. More importantly, such debates by their very nature will shatter the concept of separation of church and state.

Evolution. As for the Christian Right's repeated efforts to water down the teaching of evolution, the chances seem low that the Roberts Court will take up the issue in the near future. The Court's ruling twenty years ago in *Edwards v. Aguillard,* also discussed in Chapter 7, firmly (7–2) rejected the parallel teaching of "creation science," and the 2005 U.S. District Court decision in *Kitzmiller v. Dover Area School District* appears to have substantially slowed the push to get public schools to incorporate "intelligent design" into their curricula.

Religion in the Workplace. The Court's position regarding the role of religion in the workplace, discussed in Chapter 8, is somewhat less ideologically consistent than other church-state issues. When the Court ruled in *Employment Div., Ore. Dept. of Human Resources v. Smith* that employees could not claim a "free exercise" exception to a generally applicable criminal law, the 6–3 majority consisted of justices from the Court's left, right, and center voting blocs. Only the Court's most liberal justices (William Brennan, Harry Blackmun, and Thurgood Marshall) dissented.

When Congress tried to reverse the *Smith* decision legislatively, by passing the Religious Freedom Restoration Act, a similar 6–3 majority (equally mixed ideologically) struck down the law as it applied to state legislation in *City of Boerne v. Flores.* Justice O'Connor (along with Justices Souter and Breyer) dissented in *Boerne,* arguing that the Court had erred in *Smith* by making it easier for a government to justify a "substantial burden" on a religious practice.

The Religious Right usually does not have much positive to say about Justice O'Connor, but in this one area, at least, the movement may see her departure as a loss. In balancing the religious rights of the individual versus the police power of the state, O'Connor made it clear that the state should be required to show both a compelling state interest and a narrowly tailored approach. That is not a view likely to be endorsed by her replacement, Justice Alito.

The Right to Privacy. Forty years after the Supreme Court first recognized a "right to privacy," the legal doctrine seems firmly and securely established. As noted in Chapter 9, every member of the current Supreme Court (aside from Justice Stevens) has publicly stated that he or she believes that the Constitution contains such a right, even though neither the phrase nor even the word "privacy" appears in the Constitution. Absent the unlikely appointment of a justice with views as legally rigid as Robert Bork, there is little likelihood that the Court will flatly overturn the right to privacy that evolved from the *Griswold* and *Eisenstadt* cases. Only in the Christian Right's most salacious dreams would state government regain the ability to dictate a couple's birth control choices, for instance, or once again jail someone for fornication (the crime of sex between unmarried individuals).

But in 2007, as discussed in Chapter 10, in *Gonzales v. Carhart*, five justices (Scalia, Kennedy, Thomas, Roberts, and Alito) for the first time since *Roe v. Wade*, upheld a law that places limitations on a woman's decision to have a previability abortion, a period of time which the Court had previously said was exclusively within a woman's zone of privacy. It is worth noting that the only opinion that even mentioned the term "privacy" was Justice Ginsburg's impassioned dissent, which was joined by Justices Stevens, Souter, and Breyer. And as Ginsburg pointed out, the challenge to the "undue restriction" imposed by the Partial-Birth Abortion Ban was not an attempt "to vindicate some generalized notion of privacy; rather, [it centers] on a woman's autonomy to determine her life's course, and thus to enjoy equal citizenship stature."

The fact that a majority of the Court was willing to endorse an infringement on a woman's right to privacy without even discussing the concept or using the word does not bode well for the full preservation of the citizenship stature of women in the future. Equally disturbing is the Court's willingness to defer to congressional findings that were repeatedly and conclusively shown to be false or at best misleading.

And as Justice Ginsburg noted, the language used by the Court's majority opinion reveals a "hostility to the right *Roe* and *Casey* secured." There is good reason to worry that even while the Roberts Court in this or future iterations will not go so far as to abandon the right to privacy altogether, the Court will be increasingly receptive to greater and greater intrusions on a woman's right of privacy and self-determination.

A Forgotten and Threatened Court

Since the 1970s, in the wake of Francis Schaeffer's call to arms, the Religious Right has viewed the composition of the Supreme Court as a political problem, and Christian conservatives have aggressively used the tools of politics to try to solve that problem. If Americans who value such fundamental principles as separation of church and state and personal privacy do not do the same, they may be stunned by the rapidity with which those values are severely diminished or eliminated altogether.

More than anything else, the relative success of the Religious Right in reshaping the Supreme Court—and there is no question that it has done so—has stemmed from the fact that all too many people take the decisions of the Warren Court for granted. More than any other single interest group, the Christian Right has educated its supporters on the connection between political success and judicial change, and it has consistently and aggressively worked for the appointment of federal judges and Supreme Court justices who share its philosophical opposition to the Warren Court's rulings. The time has come for the nation's political left to remind voters that so many of the rights and privileges that people enjoy today were established more than a generation ago by a Supreme Court that viewed the Constitution as a tool for expanding and defending human dignity and independence.

If that education does not take place, much of what the remarkable Warren Court accomplished will be weakened or wiped out by a social and political movement that more than anything else wants to baptize the United States as a Christian nation and use the Bible as its primary source of legal authority. In the end, the goal of the Religious Right is nothing less than to bring this country to its knees.

Acknowledgments

Throughout the months required to research and write this book, I have had the assistance and encouragement of a wide range of people, all of whom have contributed to the final shape of this project. Like innumerable writers before me, I am grateful for the endless patience and support shown to me by my friends and family.

It is difficult, if not impossible, to acknowledge everyone who has played a role in the process of writing this book, but a number of individuals deserve particular recognition. First and foremost, my thanks and appreciation to Linda Greenspan Regan, the editor of my previous project, *The Decency Wars*, for suggesting the topic that eventually evolved into *The Court and the Cross*.

My agent, Jessica Faust, of BookEnds, LLC, did a terrific job of honing the book proposal and placing it with Beacon Press. Her suggestions on how to better frame and present this project were invaluable. It is in working with an agent that a broad idea first hits the cold wall of market reality, and I am fortunate that Jessica is both encouraging and practical.

At Beacon, I have had the pleasure of working closely with editor Brian Halley. His careful reading of my manuscript and thoughtful suggestions were a tremendous help in balancing clarity and detail in the discussion of often-complicated legal and political issues. Cutbacks in both the quantity and quality of editorial services is a frequent complaint among writers, but it is clear that Beacon is bucking the trend.

As is the case with many (if not most) writers, environment plays an important role in the writing of a book. Much of this book was written in tea shops and coffee houses, both in Burlington, Vermont, and on the road. I'd like to extend my particular thanks to the great staffs at Dobra Tea and Speeder and Earl's for their friendship and their enthusiastic interest.

I was fortunate to have the assistance of several different libraries while researching this book. My thanks to the many librarians who helped locate various resources at the Durick Library at St. Michael's College; the Library at the Yale Club of New York City; the East Hampton Public Library; and the Neilson Library at Smith College. And increasingly, the online library that Google is building, one scanned book at a time, is profoundly useful. It is a remarkable thing to be sitting in a tea shop and reading a nineteenth-century book stored in a library several hundred miles away.

Among my family and friends, I'd like to thank the following for their support and encouragement: my parents, Warren and Anne Lane, and my siblings—Jon and Alison Lane, Jeremy and Elizabeth Murdock, Kate Lane and Matt Van Sleet—Harvey and Glenda Werbel; Jonathan Werbel; Jeanné Collins; Chris Donnelly and Nina Chill; Josh Brown and Zoe Richards; Kristen Smoragiewicz; Adam Ernst; Fred Person.

Three people deserve my warmest and most heartfelt thanks. Over the last six months, my sons, Ben, fourteen, and Peter, twelve, have shown remarkable patience and a growing interest in American history and politics. It has been fascinating to watch their growth and their increasingly sophisticated understanding of the institutions and issues that will affect their lives. I hope that they will continue to appreciate the remarkable freedoms that they enjoy, and that they will work to preserve and pass them on.

Above all, I am grateful to my partner, Amy Werbel, for her patience, support, and love. It is a huge help to live with another writer, someone who appreciates the often odd and demanding rhythms of the writer's life. Amy's advice, comments, and editorial suggestions have been a critical part of this project from start to finish, and her encouragement is woven into every page. My heartfelt thanks to her for the myriad ways in which she has made this book—and my life—better.